The bird and her Father

Wrestlings, Nestlings, Testings,
Rejoicings, and Confessings—with
a few extra twigs twisted in.
Like the weaving of a nest.

Robin Powell

Written over a lifetime
For such a time as this.

Parson's Porch Books

The bird and her Father
ISBN: Softcover 978-1-960326-77-5
Copyright © 2024 by Robin Powell

Parson's Porch Books is an imprint of Parson's Porch *&* Company (PP*&*C) in Cleveland, Tennessee. PP*&*C is a self-funded charity which earns money by publishing books of noted authors, representing all genres. Its face and voice is **David Russell Tullock** (dtullock@parsonsporch.com).

Parson's Porch *&* Company *turns books into bread & milk* by sharing its profits with the poor.

www.parsonsporch.com

The bird and her Father

Contents

PEACE

PASSION

POINTERS, SISTERS

PRAYERS

PARABLES

POEMS

PRECIOUS

PEAK

Preface

This gathering of words is not for hours of reading at a time.

It's a paragraph by paragraph, poem by poem, story by story kind of reading,
With ample time for thought in between.

Some of the writings are keyhole glimpses into my very private life. What you
will read are excerpts of my journaling about specific situations. Full
explanations have been completely left out, and that is not by accident. You
don't need to know specifics, my goodness, you have your own to deal with –
why listen to mine? It's not the severity of the crisis that is the focus. It's the
work of The Christ in me (and in you) as He sees us through the crisis. I want
to make sure that you see my Savior who buoyed me through each storm, Who
aloed me through each fire, Who calmed me through each calamity. Who spoke
to me in ways that I could understand. I have done nothing to earn it and
there's no way to repay it. But He has graciously lavished His Presence into
this waif of a girl child.

Both then and now.

This life of dust has been writing now for 50 years.

Thank you for reading my mud.

Introduction

So, how does one start?

By starting.

For years (years, years and more years), my hubs has encouraged (requested, directed, came really close to badgered) me to collect my writings and pool them into one place. He would use the phrase, "You should write a book." "*Yeah, yeah, yeah*" was always my immediate knee jerk response (just to make him hush). "There's plenty of time," I'd think. "*I'll do that. Someday.*" He loves me so. And so, I would continue to write with my "Someday" target date, sticking everything written into any nook and cranny that wasn't already stuffed with notes.

Let's be honest, does the proverbial Someday ever come? Sadly, the answer for the majority of us is no. Too many times our excuse of Someday becomes the reality of None Day. The regret of Yesterday.

This morning became my Someday. Today the pool begins. Somebody, go turn on the hose. Steven, *this pool's for you.*

I've written all my life. I have pieces of paper shoved in many nooks and crannies, dropped like breadcrumbs as a trail to me. I'm not saying that what I write is good. I'm not saying that the words I pen have weight. But I will say that there are times I must and therefore I do. I write because I hear the words, the phrases, the pros … I hear the rhythm and the rhyme, and I cannot not. I've never written to compile. I've written because, well, that's what I do. Writers gonna' *write*. Poets gonna' *poe*. And so, here I go. It's an overwhelming thought and even more fearful task, but today is the day to prayerfully begin. Scared lion of Oz, I'm begging for courage too. I thank God that the Lion of Judah will lead me through.

I shall proceed if you first hear my full disclosure. This collection that's been retrieved from boxes and binders has only one purpose, one desire, one destination, one hope, one assignment, one goal, and that is to point me (and you) to (or back to) Christ. I have no other agenda. No other desire. The Lord Jesus is the Giver of all gifts. All talents. Each of us has those assigned to us and we each are responsible for using that given gift for His glory. It is my duty and my honor to offer this gift, as meek and weak as it is, back to Him. An old Southern gospel quartet used to sing, "Little is much when God is in it." Lord, here's my little.

Father, words on a page mean nothing unless the Word of the Ages is known. Let all who read the notes now exposed inside these covers know You. Receive this offering placed at Your feet. Use it for Your Glory. Multiply it like bread. Bask in the praise You are due. Let the Redeemed of the Lord say *poe*.

Not to us, LORD, not to us, but to YOUR NAME be the glory
Because of Your faithful love, because of Your truth. Psalm 115

Poetry aka Poe

I know the LORD has purpose for each of His creation. I believe He reveals that purpose throughout that person's life in ways that person can understand. One of the first revelations for me was in elementary school with the assignment of writing "creative sentences." I still have the construction paper stapled at the side "Creative Sentences" booklet where I wrote a story of my daddy taking us kids hunting. Inside the story I wrote the phrase, *"in the forest the birds sounded like an overwound jewelry box,"* and the teacher wrote in pen beside the phrase. She wrote the word *"Good."* I don't remember the teacher or what grade I was in. Nor did I understand this first marker in my life. My first published work in a way complete with my first review. I do still have that booklet with her written word in ink – an arrow of sorts – pointing me toward my purpose. A stick pin stuck in the map of my life. Neither of us knew then. Many, many days later, I came to know. One day too that teacher will know, whoever she was. That day when all things come together, that day when all things are known.

That happened in the late 60's, early 70's, the beginning of my public-school adventure. Fast forward to 2022. I wrote a letter to the teacher who taught me English Literature in the 12th grade, the end of that same adventure, yet some 40 years after graduation. She introduced me to Wuthering Heights, the Ancient Mariner, and Canterbury Tales. She impressed on me words that made impression. In that letter, I thanked her for her passion of teaching and tried to relay to her how her passion had imprinted me. I included a couple of my writings. She wrote me back and said, "You should publish."

Two teachers, the front and back covers perhaps, push pins in my map, decades apart, who instructed me to do the thing He'd gifted me to do. Jesus often said to his gatherings, "(She) who has an ear, let (her) hear." I finally heard.

Hearing is one thing. Doing is another.

Here I am, Lord. Let's do this.

Praise

He Reigns, He Reins, He Rains

BLESSED BE THE GOD OF THE REIGN, THE REIN, THE RAIN. THE NAME ABOVE ALL NAMES.

Psalm 100 instructs, "Enter into His gates with thanksgiving, and into His courts with praise. Be thankful to Him and bless His Name. For the LORD is good, His mercy is everlasting, and His truth endures to all generations."

So that is how I shall enter in. I am thankful He has given me courage to enter this gate, I praise Him for walking with me through it. I bless the Name of Jesus, for He is very good. I think we all have learned that sometimes life isn't so much (good, that is) … but the Word of Life is enduringly, eternally so. And it is there I stake my peg. I drive it hard into the ground.

Praise (2003)

Father, there is no life unless first there is death. That is my only word that can adequately describe my heart. Father, I succumb to this life, I lay it down, I give it up. I die to self. I wave the white flag of surrender over my desires, my flesh, my will. I ask you Father God to hear my cry, hear my pleas, hear my groans. Oh Lord, deep within me, be. Lord, I search for You. I run after You in this. I ask for the Joy of the Lord to be my strength. I ask for the Hope of the Lord to be eternal in my life. I stand up and set my face like flint, knowing full well that Your Will and Your Way will be accomplished. That is what I wait for. The accomplishment by You, for You, through You. Let all else fail. Let what You deem prosper. Lest a seed fall to the ground and die … Lord, I die to myself today. I ask for resurrection power through your Holy Spirit. I give this clod of dirt to you today. Mine it for gold, Lord God. Mine it for gold.

There is power in praise, especially when it is a sacrifice to praise Him. When it's hard to do yet you do it anyway. Somewhere deep down within you, in that secret place between you and God, speak words of praise to Him. Praise Him when you don't feel you have reason. Praise Him for the heat of the fire that's molding and refining. Purifying. Praise Him for that white flag of surrender that you wave when you can't take another step. Praise Him for His Presence, even when you can't seem to sense it. When emptiness tries to swallow you, Praise Him for His Fullness. There is power in your praise. There is strength in your praise.

Let that praise well up from deep within, even if it's through gritted teeth and clinched fists, praise Him. Even if it's from a spiritual fetal position and all you can do is whimper like a feverish child, Praise. Him. Sing a song of praise to Him. Sit with Job in the ashes, when all the world is tumbling around you and say with Brother J, "Though He slay me, yet will I trust Him."

Praise Him. There is power in your praise. Sacrifice the gift of praise to Him. 24/7, 365. Then let's watch what happens.

Thanking Through

Through hardness, sadness, pain
Through joy and love and gain
Through waiting for the rain
I thank You.

Through light that's quick and fast
Through dark that seems to last
Through shadows that are cast
I thank You.

Through clothes and shoes on feet
Through daily bread and meat
Through wins and through defeat
I thank You.

Through life that makes no sense
Through struggles, oh so dense
Through past and present tense
I thank You.

Through all my numbered days
Through all my splintered ways
Through all this heart displays
I thank You.

A Meditation of Thanks (2010)

Thankful today for Bethlehem
And thankful too for Calvary
Thankful for the Manger low
Thankful too for the Dying tree

Thankful for the Great Light Star
Thankful too for the Crown of Thorns
Thankful for the angel's song
Thankful too for Flesh, so torn

Thankful for the Breath of Life
Thankful for His last breath drawn
Thankful for the shepherd's flight
Thankful for that Sabbath dawn

Thankful for the wise men's gold
Thankful too for the borrowed tomb
Thankful for the Rock that rolled
Thankful too for the virgin's womb

Thankful for the Baby's Plan
Thankful too for Joseph's dream
Thankful for the Nail Scarred Hand
Thankful for my Risen King

"Jesus, Jesus, Jesus, There's Just Something About That Name." – The Gaithers

John 1:29: "Behold, the Lamb of God who takes away the sin of the world!"

"That's my King. Do you know Him?" – Pastor S. M. Lockridge

My Life Poem

Thankful for the good
Thankful for the bad
Thankful for the happy
Thankful for the sad

Thankful for the easy
Thankful for the hard
Thankful for the smooth
Thankful for the charred

Thankful for the level
Thankful for the steep
Thankful for the shallow
Thankful for the deep

Thankful for the dark
Thankful for the bright
Thankful for the dawn
Thankful for the night

Thankful for the chaos
Thankful for the calm
Thankful for the pain
Thankful for the Balm

Thankful for the moments
Thankful for the years
Thankful for the laughter
Thankful for the tears

Thankful for the was
Thankful for the when
Thankful for the here and now
Thankful to the end

I will offer you a sacrifice of thanksgiving and
call on the NAME of the LORD. Psalm 116:17

James 1:2-4 Consider it a great joy my brothers and sisters, whenever you experience various trials. The testing of your faith produces endurance. Let endurance have its full effect, so that you may be mature and complete, lacking nothing.

Blessed Beyond Measure, Loved Beyond My Understanding (2006)

I watch the birds swoop and sway and I hear Him say, "I see, and I know them, but you are so much more." I see the sun rise and the moon glow and I hear Him say, "I hold them all in perfect place, in perfect order, but walking life with you is so much more." I get caught up in the awesomeness of God, the overwhelming bigness of Him, and then, just as quickly I get way too absorbed in my own little speck of life. Not too long ago, I was driving down the parkway, bemoaning some little something that wasn't happening for me the way it was happening for someone else. I asked the LORD, "Why does it always happen for them and not me?" (Do you hear a little selfie-self in that? Eek) and I clearly heard the Lord speak into my spirit so calmly yet assuredly, "Robin, I have something better."

He has something better. Well, glory. He has creation in perfect order, yet He has something better for me. He feeds the birds and clothes the lilies, yet He has something better for me. He calls the stars by name, not one of them is missing, yet He has something better for me. He sees the end from the beginning and all things in between yet He has something better for me. I never know when, I never know how, and I surely can't fathom why … but He has something better. I thank Him in advance for the better that is to come. I will seek the treasure of His Presence, Look for Him in all things viewed. I will get out the compass of His Word and find Him there, waiting and smiling. And then I'll know. I will have solved the mystery. Turn to Him. It's Him. HE IS THE BETTER. I will let Him have first place. I will get lost in His bigness, get caught by His goodness, get held under His wonder, and then say to myself, "HE IS something better for me." Wherever you are in life, whatever you're facing, whatever the situation, I know this to be true: the Lord is good. Correction: The Lord is better. His mercy never ends. He knows you. He planned you. He loves you. And He is the better. Let go of the bitter. Grab hold of The Better.

For the LORD God is a sun and shield. The LORD grants favor and honor;
He does not withhold the good from those who live with integrity.
Happy is the one who trusts in You, Lord of Armies!
Psalm 84

20

Thank You, LORD

Thanks You, LORD
For saving
Who I was
Where I was
Why I was
How I was

> **Thank you, LORD**
> For making
> Who I am
> Where I am
> Why I am
> How I am

> **Thank you, LORD**
> For planning
> Who I'll be
> Where I'll be
> Why I'll be
> How I'll be

> I owe ALL of
> who I am
>
> To The ALL TIME GREAT
> ***IAM***

"For I know the plans I have for you"
This is the LORD's declaration
"Plans for your well-being – not for disaster
Plans to give you a future and a hope."
Jeremiah 29:11

Piano Playing PK (2005)

I love music. I always have. Always will. It's a calming, soothing, quieting, powerful thing. Certain chords bring peace, certain melodies bring power, certain refrains usher in hope. You can experience every emotion in the scale of a song. Things can be mended in music.

Growing up a piano-playing PK, at some point in most every day I'd find myself alone in the church conveniently located next to my house or just a short bike ride away. This was a benefit not many people had, but when your daddy is the preacher and your mom is the preacher's wife, and you and your brothers are the preacher's kids, you get easy access to the Lord's House, pretty much 24/7. Whether it be through an unlocked door or an open window, it was fairly easy to get in. (I clearly remember on Wednesday nights in the winter, being sent to the dark church with matches, so I could light all the room gas floor space heaters. You remember the ones – they sat along a wall and had waffly looking vertical beige bricks with a thin metal front (a safety feature to keep you from catching fire – ha) and you would light it like a gas stove. The knob on the side and the toothpick holes lined along the rim, and in a sudden sulphury poof – FIRE. Now, as a child, being trusted to do that – well, that was scary. Let's just be honest. (#firesafety #childwithmatches #I'mstillhereandsoarethechurches #GraceofGod) At some point in every day, without asking permission, I'd amble or scramble my way into the church house, into the sanctuary, and head to the piano. Either my foot through a found unlocked door or my belly over a found open window. One way or another, I was *"gittin in."* The silent, hollow, dark would scare me so I'd turn on a few lights and talk to myself so the thick blanket of quiet would be held at bay. Playing the piano was something I had to do. Had to play. It wasn't a past-time to while away the daytime, it was a magnet drawing steel to the black and white keys, the green hymnal, the oak cabinet. I had to have access to a piano and a hymn book in front of me and no one around so I could sit and play and sing for hours on end. I can't explain what that did for me other than to say it calmed me, soothed me, fulfilled me, empowered me. Built me. Music is a powerful muscle. It was like taking an empty glass and filling it right up to the rim. I'd go into the sanctuary empty; I'd walk out (or crawl out) hours later filled up. I could solve all my problems with a piano and a hymn.

I'd flip through the green book with red edged pages and play melodies like,

"Jesus, Jesus, Jesus, Sweetest Name I know; Fills my every longing; keeps me singing as I go."

Or

"Holy, Holy, Holy, Lord God Almighty, Early in the morning, my song shall rise to Thee."

I'd be a good Baptist and sing every verse (even the third). I'd sing fast ones like "When the Roll is Called Up Yonder" and slow ones like "Amazing Grace." I'd sing songs of hope like "He lives!" songs of repentance like, "Lord, I'm coming home" and songs of the future like "When we all get to Heaven." I'd flip the pages through "Unclouded Day, Love Lifted Me, Let the Lower Lights be Burning, Bringing in the Sheaves." The empty hollow sanctuary, with Sunday's flowers wilted on the offertory table, leftover bulletins underneath pews, and angled rays of light shooting through the stained-glass windows like beams to fill with song. Even the sunlight would hit the wooden pews in such a way where I could see the dust dancing as I played. I'd sit there on that bench behind that half knotted-pine wall and - unbeknownst to me – worship the LORD with song. With voice. Perhaps that is why I love music so … the LORD knitted my soul to His using melody, verse and rhyme without me even knowing it. He took me by surprise as a young girl and continues to do so even today.

Sometimes my dad would wander through and join me in a song. His office was always somewhere behind the swinging door that led out of the sanctuary to the classrooms, and he would come and go as preachers do. I now think he wandered through on purpose. You see, music was a magnet for him as well and he was pure steel. He knew the power of praise.

I'm grown now, no longer a PK, and those easy access, empty church days are over. No longer can I just crawl through an open window to slide myself into the sanctuary and consider it "my time." Rarely do you even find a piano in a sanctuary these days. Those beautiful, wooden instruments have been replaced by silver sheen skinny legged keyboards without even a bench, surrounded by a praise band. Everything that once was has been, over time, removed, replaced. Rolled out. Renovated. Upgraded? (The jury's still out on that one.) Everything now has a plug. The hymn books replaced by a screen from the ceiling. The songs of faith written generations ago replaced by contemporary praise choruses that seem to change every week written by Christian artists who have (ahem) "taken church music to the next level." (I beg to differ) This is all well and good and the LORD is pleased with our praise in every generation and I'm the first to join in with the new songs. I applaud the newness and the freshness of worship. The anointing of songs of the One and Only Jesus, fresh and new. But I'm beginning to realize that there is a part of me that longs for the songs of the past. When things get hard and life gets tough, it's the great hymns that rise up in my spirit and sing me back to faith. There is great power in the words that were written centuries before by the

Redeemed who had their own anguish in life but had their eyes forever on Him. When we sing "Great Is Thy Faithfulness" we join our voices with the uncountable myriads of saints who have sung it before us, and the power of the words multiplies. When we lower our heads to sing "The Old Rugged Cross" we remember the One who died silently to give us melody, we somehow join hands with the trillions of believers before us and unite with their voices and connect with one faith. Past, Present, Future. We join hands and join voices with those mighty forces of faith. The body of Christ, past and present, singing together of their future together with Christ on His Throne in our midst.

Perhaps the dancing dust I saw in the Light beam was them? That cloud of witnesses? Who knows?

The book of Psalms is actually a book of Songs. Must have been important to an important Someone to remember the old songs if the original praise choruses are recorded for eternity in Holy Writ. Just something to think on.

When my daddy was the preacher, we started every service with The Doxology. This chorus written in 1695 by someone who understood the awesomeness of God. An Anglican Bishop Thomas Ken, perhaps after a study of Psalm 103, was overwhelmed with the need to praise our Lord so much so that he wrote down 4 lines of verse, set them to music, which even now some 328 years later are alive and ever new and oh so very needed to start every day of our life:

Praise God from Whom all blessings flow
Praise Him all creatures here below
Praise Him above ye heavenly hosts
Praise Father, Son and Holy Ghost
Amen

Don't get me wrong. I love the songs of the Now as long as the focus is on Him and His Glory. (and that is a whole different conversation, by the way.) When that is the case, I'll learn a new chorus and sing along with my fellow believers. But my soul yearns to sing the songs of the Then. I wish we could go back and rescue the songs of the saints and introduce them anew and afresh to our kids. This in my eyes is a great loss.

But those days seem to be over. And that makes me very sad. At some point in every day I wish I could once again make my way to the empty sanctuary, sit down at the piano and play. I would sit in the stillness, watch the sun hit the pew, put my hands in position, press down the first chord and begin to sing,

My Jesus, I love Thee
I know Thou art mine
For Thee all the folly of sin I resign
My blessed Redeemer
My Savior art Thou
If ever I loved Thee
My Jesus, tis now.

Then I'd look up to see the dance of the dust in the Beam.

Two times I know the angels sang – When HE was born, and when I was born again.

Praise Him, Praise Him
All ye little children
God is love, God is love.

There (2011)

My father was a songwriter, a lyricist, and a musician. I have no idea where his acoustic guitar ended up with the leather strap that read "Bro. Bob," although I wish it was hanging on one of my home's walls. He wrote his first song after my brother Butch passed away. It was entitled "Look Beyond." Funny to think now how the LORD brought melody from the death of my father's first born. From that one song, he wrote many others, recorded two albums, traveled with the band, "The Delta Singers," wearing matching checkered blazers and chunky black velvet bow ties. My brother Randy, the drummer for a time, can testify this to be true. Randy, Roger and I all three began to write, it's in our blood. I hope to share some of their writings in this journey. Time will tell.

l never thought I'd write a song, but seems I've now written two. A song is just basically poetry set to music. Sitting at the piano tinkering out melodies with lyrics can begin as a tangled mass of blankness and lead to a rhythmic, patterned, poetic bliss, depending on how long you sit. The following song was written in 2011, and I play it most every week for my own personal worship.

It's taken from Isaiah 43.

I The LORD am always by your side
I The LORD will always be your guide
Through the storm, through the fire and through the flood
I will be there
you just look up

I The LORD will guide you with My hand
I the LORD will give you strength to stand
Call My Name, Seek My Face and you will see
I the Lord will fight for thee

Through the storm, I will be there
Through the fire, I will be there
Through the dark of the night
I will be there

Don't let go, I will be there
Don't lose hope, I will be there
I the LORD JEHOVAH will be
Forever there

On the day when wars on earth shall cease
On the day when the Prince brings final peace
We will rise to meet Him in the air
And we will say, "LORD, You were there

Through the storm, LORD, you were there
Through the fire, LORD, you were there
Through the dark of the night, LORD, you were there

I held on because You were there
I pressed on because You were there
I am Yours forever
Because
You're
forever
there

I have called you by name. You are Mine.
When you pass through the waters, and when you pass through the rivers
They will not overwhelm you.
You will not be scorched

When you walk through the fire,
and the flame will not burn you.
For I AM the Lord your God
The Holy One of Israel
And I AM your Savior. Isaiah 43

Rely

The second song is entitled Rely. Not sure when it was written but the page I found is filled with the following words.

First, a prayer. Lord God, Jehovah, through the Name and the Blood of our Lord Jesus Christ, I come. Father I am without. Nothing. Empty. Father, I want to enter communion with You right now. How can I do that? Where are You? Lead me in the way of Your Presence. Draw me close to Your side. Hide me in the secret place. There is no good within me. No words I could speak that would attract anyone or anything. There are no flattering words that I could convey that would change anything or anyone. There is no power within me, save You, Oh Lord. I rely on the Love of my Lord. I rely on the Love of my Lord. I rely on the Love of my Lord.

Then a melody came.

I rely on the Love of my Lord
I rely on the Love of my Lord
He loved us so much
He blew breath into dust
I rely on the Love of my LORD

I rely on the Love of my LORD
I rely on the Love of my LORD
Then He laid down on wood
His Love poured out Blood
I'm adored by the Love of my LORD

I rely on the pow'r of His Name
I rely on the pow'r of His Name
He is Jireh, Jehovah, my Compass, my King
I will sing of the Pow'r of His Name

I rely on the Pow'r of His Name
I rely on the Pow'r of His Name

He is Rapha, my Refuge, Shalom, Adonai
I will hide in the Pow'r of His Name

I rest in the Grace of my God
I rest in the Grace of my God
For His Grace is sufficient, I'm weak He is strong
I will long for the Grace of my God

I will thrive in the Truth of His Word
I will thrive in the Truth of His Word
He is seated in heaven, the Word is Alive
I will thrive in the Truth of His Word

Let this earth fall away
I am safe in His Hand
I will stand in the Love of my Lord

I rely on the Love

I rely on the Pow'r

I rest in the Grace

I thrive in the Truth

Do you know the Love of my Lord?

He is (2004)

He is.
All I need.
More than enough for me.

He is the Protector of the weak and the Healer for the sick.
The Shelter for the fearful and the Calm for the anxious.
He is the Balm for my soul and the Food for my spirit.
He is Grace and Goodness and Mercy all the days of my life.
He is the Path on which I walk, and my feet stand on a level place.
He is the Peace for the troubled and the Blessed Assurance for the perplexed.
He is the Anchor in the tempest and the Sail of the Spirit.
He is Rest for the weary and the Horn of the mighty.
He is the Salve for the broken and the One who holds all things together.

He is.
All I need.
More than enough for me.

He's the Blood on the doorposts protecting all that's within.
He is the Shepherd for the sheep and the Light for the darkness.
He is the Passover for His family and the Defender of His own.
He is the Friend to the lonely and the Gatherer of the remnant.
Closer than a brother, the Desire of my heart.
He is the Salvation for the lost and the Power for the saved.
He is the Help for the hurting and the Compassion for those who grieve.
He is the Joy that comes in the morning,
He is Endurance in times of mourning.
He is the Tenderness in tough places.
He is the Treasure of my soul,
the Pearl of great price
He is the Torn Veil, beckoning my entrance
He is the Weaver of the tapestry
The Bridegroom, the Carpenter
The One Who Was, Who Is, Who Is To Come.
The Great IAM
I am His and He is mine
Oh what a delightful God.

He is.
All I need.
More than enough for me.

Now to Him Who is able to do exceedingly, abundantly more than we could ever think or imagine, according to the Power that works in us – to HIM be glory in the church and in Christ Jesus to all generations, forever and ever. Amen. Ephesians 3:20

Let Me Tell You

Glory to our Lord and Savior Jesus Christ, the Father God Jehovah Who Reigns, the Holy Spirit Who is our Constant Traveling Companion, giving whispers of counsel and strength and hope as we walk this Way. Praise His Holy Name, for He is great and has done great things.

Can I just tell you that my life is a testimony of how our Lord can take a tangled mass of mess and calmly and consistently untie every tangle and lay it out straight? How He can take a crumpled wad of paper and compassionately yet firmly with the palm of His hand smooth out all the scarred indents? He has removed every mountain; we have passed thru every watery grave on dry ground. I've stood in the fire, and I've seen the flame, but I have not been burned. I see my husband's life being put back together, I see my Lazarus being loosed, I see the favor of the LORD working out all things for our good and for His Glory.

I am convinced that neither death nor life, nor principalities or powers, or situations or circumstances, or bondages or strongholds, or bad decisions or fears or anxieties, can separate us from our Father's Love. His Love Holds Strong. And in that strength, I dance with JOY!

I can't wait to circle up with those three Hebrew boys and tell them the story of the fire we endured. I can't wait to talk to Paul and tell him about when the scales fell off my own eyes. I can't wait to laugh with Sarah over the miracle power of Jehovah. You're never too old to see a NEW BIRTH!

That's my story. And I'm sticking to it.

The 19th Psalm (2022)

The Psalm is broken into four categories: The view of constant GLORY, the perfection of the WORD. Once we read through that, we are reminded of how UNHOLY we are, and we REPENT and ask FORGIVENESS. We then PRAY to have the words and meditations in our hearts that are acceptable. Words that match creation's song and the Word's Truth.

How is it that we can start with a word like HEAVEN – where there's no width, depth, measurement? And end reflecting on our own life, our own soul? Isn't that just like the Way, the Truth, the Life?

The very first verse (let's be visual now) – "The heavens declare the glory of GOD."

Heavens refer to HEIGHT.

Well, let's all look out the window right now. We see creation declaring GLORY. Do we truly have the eyes of a child to see?

If we were to elevator up to a hotel penthouse, we would look out the window, and see creation declaring GLORY from a different, higher vantage point … and it would seem somehow more beautiful, hmm?

Then we go even higher, flying in an airplane, and we watch the sun setting down into the clouds that we are now above, and we see creation declaring GLORY. And somehow it seems even more beautiful.

Then we are even higher, watching reflections from the Hubble space camera and we are AWESTRUCK DUMBSTRUCK MUTE at how the heavens are truly without hesitation continuously declaring HIS GLORY ... and there are no words to describe these images.

It seems the higher we go, the thicker the GLORY.

Well, sisters, we will go even higher one day ... and Hubble ain't got nothing on the GLORY that we will see at the feet of Jesus. The Word tells us that there is no sun there because THE LAMB LIGHTS THE WHOLE HEAVEN ... HIS GLORY ...

Whatever plain you stand on today, His Glory is visible. Find it. See it. Declare it. Because just 10 Psalms over we are told that "Everything in His temple cries, **"Glory!"** (Psalm 29) You might as well start now.

Mute (2008)

Dear Friends,

Before I get completely "sucked back into reality," I wanted to share a few moments from my recent vacation with you. Being a word person, it's almost as if I can't keep it to myself ... I **MUST** share it; I **MUST** tell it. (and poor ya'll have to listen!) I'll try not to be lengthy (now, that's funny and most likely a fib), using just enough words that will definitely **inadequately** describe my experience out West.

As most of you know, the weeks before my vacation were a Tasmanian blur. My job stress was at an all-time high, planning three events back-to-back. There were many moments of the complete realization and panic that I had more work than one middle-aged woman could accomplish. By the end of the third meeting, I was "spent" in every way – physically, mentally, spiritually. Completely empty and drained. I headed home from that trip and had just a couple of days to prepare for Wyoming. And to be honest, at that point, I could not have CARED LESS! But my name was on the ticket, so I had no choice but to go. Again. I pulled out the smallest suitcase we own, threw in some shorts and t-shirts, my journal and my MESSAGE New Testament (which is a story in itself) and headed toward the car ... then I thought, *'I need a book!'* So, I headed back to the bookshelf and immediately – without thought – chose DESIRING GOD by John Piper. This book was a gift from friend Janet last year and for whatever reason, I chose it. And off I went – Wyoming-bound with my two brothers, my niece, my nephew, and my mama. To be honest, at that point, I was exhausted and frustrated and would've rather just stayed home.

Thank God I didn't.

Fast forward to my first day there, staring up at the Grand Teton mountains for the first time. I was not prepared for the majesty, the beauty, the grandeur, the peace. I was literally wordless (and ya'll know that doesn't happen often - ha) We drove on to the geyser area where I looked down at the most peculiar, freakishly wonderful sight I have ever seen ... water of all different brilliant colors, crystal clear, coming from deep within the core of the earth, and steam rising above it. Again, I found myself without words but overflowing with emotion. We made our way up to Yellowstone to the North Rim where I stood at the precipice, staring at the most beautiful sight I have ever seen ... the Painted Pots Canyon with the waterfall in the distance. I stared in disbelief at the beauty, I listened to the roar of the waters, I watched the stillness of nature and was overcome. We stood at the roped-off edge of Old Faithful, and watched it gush and spew (and I screamed with joy like a little girl much to the chagrin of my bookend brothers), we drove within a few feet of bison and elk, we saw fields of flowers hidden in wide open spaces ...my goodness, I saw massive, uprooted trees with their mangled mass of roots straight up in the air, and it was a masterpiece to behold, just sculpted there in a field. I watched it all without words immersed in complete wonder ... amazed at the handiwork of our Father. We drove from beauty to beauty to beauty ... almost to the point that I could not take it in. I was completely silent and still, soaking in the beauty of Big Sky that is now hidden deep within me.

On the plane ride over, I began reading DESIRING GOD (and let me just say, it is one of my top five books that I've ever read.) Somewhere around the third or fourth day I really looked at the cover. And it stopped me in my tracks.

ARE THOSE THE GRAND TETONS ON THE FRONT OF THE COVER OF THE BOOK I GRABBED ON MY WAY OUT THE DOOR? AAHHMMM!!!! SURE LOOKS LIKE IT! Needless to say, I was rendered mute. I didn't even look at the cover when I pulled it off the shelf nor did I even know what a Grand Teton was before I saw it for the first time myself. But the two things cataclysmically collided at just the most perfect precious moment in my life. **The LORD is SO FUNNY!**

HE reminded me right then, right there, that as I saw HIM in His Creation, HE saw me, His creation, right in the middle of it! And to Him, according to Genesis 1, I am much more beautiful and precious. HE knew exactly where I was, exactly what I'd been thru to get there, and most importantly, HE knew exactly what I needed in order to be restored and renewed, rejuvenated and resurrected!

And here's the lesson I learned that I pass on to you. When you get completely to the end of your chain in this life, and don't have the energy to do one more thing, drive yourself out into His handiwork, take a blanket and sit down. Watch. Wait. Allow your senses to purify. Gaze into the beauty of His Holiness. Cry Glory with the wind, sing with the waters, clap with the trees. Join with Creation and give Glory to His Name. **Because EVERYTHING in HIS TEMPLE TRULY CRIES "GLORY!"** *(Psalm 29)*

I wish I were still there! As I sit here in this office, staring at this computer, doing things that really don't matter; somewhere out there right now, is a waterfall roaring to the floor, a mountain raising to the heavens, a field of flowers hidden in the hills. That, to me, is a slice of Heaven. And I'm so thankful that one day that's where I'm going to live. **Forever**.

Bird Ballet (2005)

It's a beautiful March day. There's a feeling that winter is over, the cold, hard, barren ground is being disrupted by tiny, frail, curled shoots steadily pushing their way courageously upward to the sun. Life is coming up and out of this hard clod of darkness. Beauty is on its way. The robins are hopping in groups, hoping to be the first to find that delicacy that will fill them. And the Word says that the birds are fed straight from the Father's hand. He knows when one tiny, feathered friend falls. He provides for His creation. He pushes winter on past so that spring, waiting in the wings, waited on by the wings, can come. Let it be so in our lives. Let this cold, hard clod be disrupted by Life!

I was driving the other day when I saw this flock of tiny birds (one of my favorite things to watch) as they were flying in one direction and then quickly turned to fly back and up and over and swoop and back. It was a beautiful bird ballet. A sight to behold. I was stunned at how awesome it looked against the blue sky and so thankful I took the time to see it. Then it hit me – they are dancing in the presence of their Creator God. El Elohim.

Oh, how I wish I could dance.

One Christmas

"Tell me the story of Jesus …." Is the first line of an old hymn we used to sing in my growing up days. It told an old, old story. Words that meant nothing as a child, mainly because life was too new and too fast to stop and focus on something called OLD. But now as a mama who is realizing how many years have actually flown past, and seeing the new schemes this materialistic world wants me to believe, I long to hear it. The Real old, old story … perhaps in a new way, but the old story just the same. This Christmas Eve morn, with the dishwasher running and the pies cooling, and the sausages burnt to a Christmasy crisp, I want to hear the story. Here today, in this hustle and bustle of stressed-out folks who obviously have set up camp in the Walmart parking lots, right now as I prepare to wade my way through a very busy, noisy day where at the end will bestow a trunkload of unneeded, most unwanted trinkets … right now I want to find a quiet place and hear it. The old story. The story where the Greatest Gift gave Himself for me. I want to hear solid Truth in the midst of slippery counterfeit worldly tales.

I've been thinking this morning of the Babe. The precious Child that had been promised, lying in the manger in the dark. I like to see Him in my mind's eye, surrounded by sheep warming Him with their fur. Sheep that somehow felt connection, perhaps compassion for the Lamb of God. He came into this world as a whisper, silently entering the darkness in secret. The Son of God, the Promised One, the Holy One, the Only One handed down from Heaven, wrapped in hand me downs on earth, Who came to exchange robes with man.

Did they really know who He was? Mary and Joseph had been given specific instructions and they had obeyed. But did they really know? The Bible tells us that when Mary, a young Jewish girl dwelling in darkness, was told of her bright future, she sang a song to the Lord for the Light that was to come. She worshipped Jehovah for the Promise of the Child. The Jewish shepherds, dwelling in darkness, were awestruck with angels, spangled in the heavenlies, interrupting the darkness with Light, and they were told of the Peace that had come down from heaven to men, they were told of the Hope that had been born in the night, and their first response was, "We have to find Him!" When they did, they began to praise Him. They didn't know that He would save them from their sins, they didn't know that He would die their death so that they could have His life, they didn't know that they knelt before the Greatest Shepherd of Heaven and Earth, a Shepherd that knew His sheep. The Shepherd that seeks the lost then carries him home on His shoulders. They didn't know that this Baby was the Lamb of God, slain before the foundation of the world. They didn't know the healings, the wonders, the miracles, the prophecies … all they knew was what the angels had sung … Peace and Joy and Good News would be found in Him … and that was all they needed to know. That was all they craved. They ran to the place where Peace and Joy and Good News lay, for those are the things they longed for. Those are the things they hungered for. Hundreds of miles away, the Wise Men, Gentile astrologers dwelling in darkness in a far country, saw His Great Light and would not, could not remain still. They packed their bags and loaded their camels and wrapped their gifts. Then with joyful anticipation, set out toward the Light … for that is what they needed. They didn't know the Light of the World had come down from heaven to open the eyes and ears of man. They didn't know this King of Kings, this Wonderful Counselor, this Prince of Peace … but they saw the Light. And it drew them out of darkness. They didn't know that this Baby under the Star was the One Who flung the stars into space and knows each one by name. They only saw Light and chose to move toward it. For Light is what they needed. The Bible says they traveled toward Him with the Light as their guide, and when they found Him, they worshipped Him. And Light invaded their souls. They knew in a strange way that they had found Home. They had found the Light of the World. And they would never be the same.

I ask you today, are you dwelling in darkness? Are you living a peaceless, joyless lightless life? Do you have any hope? Do you not know your future because your past and present have blinded your eyes and bound your hands and feet? I bring good news to you today, my friend. There is a Light that conquered darkness. A Light that will not be moved. Never extinguished. There is a Peace that untangles every distorted complex vortex of life. There is a Hope that can see clearly beyond today. A Hope that is anchored to the Hem of His Garment. There is a Great Shepherd Who knows His sheep. There is a King, crowned with many crowns, who was born in a stable but now sits on a throne. There is a Joy that will set numb feet to dancing. There is a Light that will propel you on a journey toward Him, toward Life, toward Light, toward Peace, toward Joy, toward Love, toward Hope, toward Home.

There's room at the manger, there's room at the cross, there's room at the tomb, there's room at the throne just for you. Do what Mary and Joseph did and believe. Do like the shepherds and run. Do like the wise men and walk steadily. Do it 'til you find Him. Do whatever it takes but get to doing it. Get to Him. Get as close as you can. He knows your name. He gave you life. He has a plan. Choose Him. Believe Him. Worship Him. It's the old, old story of Jesus that brings new life on earth. It's the old, old story of the stable that invites the King's entry to reign in your heart. It's the old, old story of Jesus that brings the new you to life. May the old and the new explode in you today.

Tell me the story of Jesus
Write on my heart every word
Tell me the story most precious
Sweetest that ever was heard
Tell how the angels in chorus
Sang as they welcomed his birth
Glory to God in the Highest
Peace and Good Tidings on earth

Love in that story so tender
Clearer than ever I see
Stay, let me weep while you whisper
Love paid the ransom for me
1880, Fanny J Crosby

Continuous Christmas (2014)

The Chaotic Calm has come to an end
The Clean-up of Christmas now slowly begins
The memories now boxed but displayed in my mind
to ponder, to treasure, to reflect throughout time

The ribbon all wrinkled, the tinsel undone
the tree is dismantled, the garland unhung
the wreaths unplugged and lay unstrung
the house looks bare ... but not for long ...

For Christ is here and fills each room
with love and joy and peace a'bloom
HE sends HIS angels to surround this place
with light and joy and multiplied grace
HIS song HE sings aloud in our hearts
HIS promise reminds us HE never departs

Yes ornaments are gone
but THE CHRIST CHILD still lives
here, home with us, and continually gives

Dear Jesus, I thank YOU that
YOU can't be boxed
or lay unlit upon the floor

I thank YOU that YOU can't be contained
or become a clean-up chore

Live here with us for all of our days
teach us, O Father, to walk in Your ways
Let Your holiness dwell within these walls
and let our hearts always before You fall

Yes, Christmas remains for those who believe
that the CHRIST CHILD came so that we may live
that HIS birth, HIS death, HIS rising again
is THE CONTINUOUS CHRISTMAS LIFE.
Can I get an AMEN?

So if you have been raised with Christ,
Seek things above – where Christ is,
Seated at the right hand of GOD.
Set your mind on things above, not on earthly things. Colossians 3:1-2

The Magi (2005)

I'm sitting here at my kitchen table, looking at three small plastic wise men hiding in the center of a Christmas centerpiece. Just for today though. And it makes sense in this house. When Samantha Rose was two years old, I bought her a nativity set from Avon. Every year she selects a special spot to set the pieces in place. All except the wise men. Each year, the three plastic kings get moved daily all over the house, day by day, place by place, until finally on the morn of December 25, they end up at the manger. They travel all over the house – you never know where they'll turn up. We're not a family big on traditions – don't get me wrong, we like them – we just don't have many – but this one is truly a favorite. I love seeing these three on my mantle or in my kitchen window or on the back of the commode. You never know where they are, or where they've been, but you always know where they're going to end up. They'll be in the right place at the right time. Ten days from now their journey will be over, and they'll be at the manger's side, presenting plastic gifts to the Prince of Peace.

A little like us, don't you think? We never know where we'll be, we're constantly moving from one thing to another, one place to another, one event to another. Some places we get shoved into without our consent sometimes but praise GOD, because we are HIS, we will be in the right place at the right time. I'm planning to arrive, aren't you? Aren't you tired of the journey? At the precise time in history, a day already directed by Jehovah, a day fast approaching, the tribes and nations will emerge from their travels and be gathered there – not at a manger, but at a glorious throne. And we'll kneel in worship to present our gift to the King of Kings and Lord of Lords.

We are one day closer to meeting The Dayspring.

Purpose

Starting Again (2009)

The beginning of another journal. I've started quite a few over my 46 years; always with great ambition to start on the first page and scribble thru to the last; jotting down the lessons learned along the bumpy road of life. I have high hopes but poor outcomes. Rarely do I use every page, seldom do I see the back cover. I get mid-journal and lay it down. I walk away from a piece of me that must be. I walk away, thinking I can get thru it without it but knowing full well I can't. Thinking that the journaling piece of my life can go undone. I amuse myself at my own excuse. Over and over, I confirm that it can't. It must be done. It must be written. It must be. For it is me. So on some sunny day of my future, I circle back around, I sit myself down, I find a blank page, and begin to write. Today is that day. I've closed the book too many days now; the words have been vacant, few and far between. I can't live in that void. It's time for words. It's who I am. It's written in me. It's not that I want to write; it's that I MUST. I plead for the LORD's Blessing upon these words, upon these pages, upon these reflections. Let the words of my mouth and the meditation of my heart be pleasing to You and You Alone, my Rock and my Redeemer (Psalm 19). May my words reflect Him.

My life has seen many chapters, my life has lived many words. The words I speak out are sometimes far different from the Word I hear spoken within. It is a constant battle. My greatest moments are when those two are in sync … when my words are powered by His. The Word promises that what resides in my heart will flow out of my mouth. Sounds lovely in poetry but sometimes lives out quite hauntingly — depending on the purity of my heart. Eek. Sometimes I pour forth DIRTY WATER. That should not be. It's a constant battle keeping this "pen" on course. It can bless and it can curse; it can speak LIFE, or it can speak, well, you know the word that goes here. This should not be in the life of a Believer, in the words of a child of the Word. Today I proclaim — once again — on this Journal Beginning Day in the Life and Times of Robin Powell, that I want the Word residing in my heart; I want the Word poured out in my words. I want the tongue of the disciple, that I might sustain the weary with a word. I want to be the pen of the ready writer. I want my heart life to be clear and pure, refreshing and life-giving. To me, there is no greater joy than to be the ladle of the Wellspring of Life, handing cool sips of Living Water to the ones who have settled for less.

Even now, years later, I pose the same questions as written in journals before. I meditate silently within me, wrestling with my purpose, wondering if I know, wondering if I'm truly known. Saying in private that I want to be used for greatness and hoping in public that I'll allow myself to be. It is a great mystery that one can plan in private to be used with great ambition and boldness but fail so miserably at the task when opportunity knocks. Simply by not doing. Not being. By walking away when the LORD says COME. By closing the journal when the LORD says WRITE. We're all planted on earth for a season with purpose. I've missed far too much of mine. I refuse to miss more. I regretfully recall missed opportunities, disobedience, passive action which led to nothing. I don't want that to be the epitaph of my life. I don't want that written in heaven's journal regarding my days. I want no heavenly being to read the scroll of a boring, dull, effortless, fruitless, passive life. A tree planted by the water should bear good fruit. A child of the Word should write. To make the most of the Time. To say what I can while it is still called Today. My hope, my desire, my challenge, my goal, my proclamation today is this: "I'll do. I'll go. I'll help. I'll love it. I'll speak. I'll stand. I'll try. I'll write. I'll live." This time around, I will fill in the last page. *"Back cover, I'm comin' for ya'."*

In the beginning was the Word, and the Word was with God, and the Word was God.
In Him was life, and that life was the light of men.
John 1

This Old Cup

When I was growing up, one of the songs of the church was, *"Fill my cup, LORD, I lift it up, Lord, come and quench this thirsting of my soul ..."* I could sing it all in text for you, but I'll get back to the subject at hand. Cup. You are one, you know. Filled with (insert filling here). Shared with (insert whom here). I love using the word, whom, btw. Anyway. It's a time to pause and ponder. It's a time to inward dive. Go with me here ... What type of cup be thee? A dainty teacup or paper-thin Dixie? Styrofoam or plastic? A pricey Stanley or an off-brand remake fake that quickly breaks? I'm fervently praying you're not a red solo cup ... But no matter which, you're still a vessel to be filled. The container doesn't matter; it's the content that does. So, what is your cup full up of? Or are you bone china dry? No matter where we are in life, no matter how old, O Lord, the cups You've crafted cry out for You to fill us! Use us! Let us quench the thirst of those around us, ladling out Your gift of Love! You are the potter (as in Teapot), we are the clay (as in clay cup). Fill us, O Lord, today. Then line up the thirsty. We're happy to share.

Perhaps a little crackled
Perhaps a little dim
Perhaps a little faded
From the saucer to the rim

Perhaps a little broken
Perhaps a little stained
Perhaps it sits without a match
Or dribbles when it's drained

Perhaps it's lost its luster
Perhaps it's lost its sheen
Perhaps it still looks dingy
When one declares it "clean"

It lives behind the others
This old cup has met its end
Replaced by pretty patterns
Fancy china, newer trends

"You're older now, You're vintage"
"You're retired" they like to say
It used to be our favorite —
But now it's shoved away

But wait – hold on there, darlin'
Let's just think this thought on through
Just because we are now older
Does this mean we get shoved too?

Maybe we're chipped around the corners
Or just cracked around the rim
Perhaps we're dingy dirty
Or completely faded, dim

Does this label us as useless?
Just because we're now "with age?"
Just because we're chipped a little?
Oh, this thought fills me with rage!

Don't give us up to "vintage"
Just because we've aged a bit
Don't shove us to the background
Just because we're slightly chipped

We've so much more to do here
Don't let vintage slow you down!
Keep filling up your cup, my friend
Till it's traded for a crown.

The joy of the LORD is our strength. Nehemiah 8:10

Do not look at the outward appearance, for the LORD looks at the heart. 1 Samuel 16:7

Broken (2020)

We hold on to our broken things.

My dad bought me a small music box in the shape of a piano over 50 years ago. If I remember correctly, it was a Christmas gift the year my dad drew my name. And I'm sure our family drew names because Christmas would be a meager one. It played *Fur Eloise* so sweetly for years. And if memory truly serves me, it came from a store called Gibson's, the Walmart of its day. I could watch the metal stems create the soprano soundwaves as the roller with stubs rolled round and round. Ingenious invention. The mind of man. When I would lift the lid of the brass piano, the tune would play so rhythmically, so teenkily. Is that a word? Then, one day, it did not. Then one day, silenced. Stuck. Stopped. The roller wouldn't roll. The stems sat undisturbed. Still. Perhaps wound too tight or too often, perhaps the internal gears rusted, perhaps the tiny barrel of notches, once robust with power had now lost the strength to turn. Perhaps the Gibson's shelf life had finally expired. Who knew the reason? Maybe it had given all it had. This broken thing given by my dad.

Isn't that life? We're all broken, no melody to sing, some a bit rusty, some of us wound wayyyyy tooooo tight. Some of us with no strength left to turn one more day. Yet we go on. Day by day. Broken.

This music box has been stuck in drawers and on shelves, in boxes and trunks. It's been forgotten, ignored, overlooked – but always kept. Labeled, "UseLESS."

Isn't that life? We are all shuffled, stuck, ignored, overlooked, labeled "UseLESS" by the world that broke us. We've all been used less due to the life we've been living. Rendered mute becomes our norm.

43

My Steven just a few weeks ago found it, noticed it, picked it up. I told him its sad story while I watched with muted horror and without blinking as he surgically dismantled it, piece by piece – the inquiring engineer that he is. He wanted to fix it for the little girl in me. He loves me so. He suddenly disappeared for a few minutes, then returned. He set the music box on the table and lifted the trinket's 50-year-old lid. And I was then the one rendered speechless as I listened to *FUR ELOISE* play as if it were the first time for the roller to strike the metal stems in perfect pattern. Speechless is much different than silenced. The melody so sweet, the barrel of notches quickened to mechanical life. The rands ready and waiting, plucking each note into the air in perfect timing. Round and round and round. The gear once again oiled. The wands in rhythm happily doing what they were made to do. Whole. My Steven smiling.

40+ years, silence.
4 minutes later, song.

This is not just a story of my Steven nor of my earthly dad. This is a story of life. How our Heavenly Father created each of us to make melody to bring glory to Him. But sin has us broken. Silenced. Stilled. No one has been spared that wrecking ball. But HE in an instant – if we ask HIM – will make us whole; will fill us with the beautiful music HE always intended. It's never ever too late. We are all worth fixing. And HE never tires of waiting. He already knows what's broken underneath the hood. There's no hiding from Him. He's just waiting for you to surrender it to Him. Once our fists are open and palms laid out flat, The Restorer begins His work, inquiring Engineer that He is.

Don't wait 50 years. Jesus can heal, Jesus will heal. Jesus can and will make us whole. Jesus can and will compose our opus, our aria, our teenkily psalm. And as He repairs what is broken in the secrets of our heart, our lives begin to play His Song for all to hear. If we let Him.

Labor Pains (2004)

When God gives you a new idea or direction that you weren't expecting, and you surrender to that with obedience, you can then say you are expecting. The Lord has shown you the end from the beginning and He will use you to bring it about. Whatever that is – a new ministry, a new mission, a new talent – whatever it is. You are now expecting. Something has started to grow. Time will need to be spent in prayer and faith, preparing for this work the Lord has for you to do. It won't happen unless you are at the forefront making plans and forging ahead. Growing in excitement and vision. That takes time. Then after months of waiting, it's time to give birth to this thing the Lord has instructed you. Mark my words, preparing is one thing. Birthing is quite another. The birthing process is painful. It's not easy. It will take all your energy and won't let you quit halfway. Here you are, in labor, birthing a new thing in your life. The closer it gets to delivery, the more intense the pain. What do you do during the pain? Well, in labor, you BREATHE. You FOCUS. You PRAY! And when it's time, You PUSH. The closer the delivery gets, the quicker the pains. The deeper the pains. Pains that introvert you, encircle you, refusing to let you catch a breath in between. If the Lord has given you an assignment, there will be paralyzing pain in the process. But on the appointed day at the precise time, you will be told to PUSH HARD. And there it is. The pain is gone, the sweat is swiped, the old is gone, the new has come. The birth has taken place. New life. There it is.

The scary thing is that if you don't push, the birth won't happen and "new life" is stillborn within you. We don't want that.

I want to encourage as you birth this new thing in your life, during your contractions: Breathe deep. Pray at all times. Focus on the God who gives perfect gifts to His children, and at the appointed time, courageously PUSH.

Encourage

I'm reading a proverb a day; all about wisdom and gaining wisdom and praying for wisdom and discernment. I'm a little slow but I'm sensing a theme. ☺ Anyway, I know you are overloaded right now with things the way they are so I'm praying wisdom and discernment on both of us. Don't you worry one bit about anything, God has looked at the end of the book and knows the ending is going to be so good! He's smiling! He's the Author of your life and He's writing an incredible story. Sometimes the story is scary, suspenseful, sad. Sometimes a cliffhanger that you can't wait for the page to turn to see how it's going to pan out ... but as long as the pen is in His hand and your life is His journal, it's all going to end at the Way, the Truth, the Life. For when we are tired of watching the horizon for motion, He's going to round the corner from a new direction as a Knight in shining armor to rescue the damsel in distress. He's going to prepare a kingdom castle for the family to live and have all the townspeople know that the ragged handmaid is now in regal robes. Stay strong. Keep the faith. Forget the horizon, look to the hills. Good night, princess.

I will lift up my eyes to the hills, from where shall my help come from?
My help comes from the Lord, the Maker of heaven and earth. Psalm 121

The Passion (2006)

Go with me, if you will, to a small town, Matthew calls it a village, where there in plain sight is a mama donkey and her colt. Tied to a tree. They are bound and they are waiting. Did they know what was about to happen? Had the Lord told them how they would be used in the life of Christ? Do you think they are of the same lineage of another donkey some 34 years before, who carried the Savior to Bethlehem by way of Mary's womb? I don't know but my mind loves to think on these things. I love the story of the mama and her colt and what the Lord has shown me in it. I pray you see it for yourself.

Jesus told His disciples to go into the village, untie the donkey and colt, and bring them to Him. And then He added, "If anyone says anything to you, you shall say, "The Lord has need of them." And immediately they will let you go. Oh, the Power of the Word of God! Even if anyone had tried to stop them, the Word of the Lord would have freed them. Do you see that? Speaking to the enemy what the Lord had spoken to them demanded their release! Our Lord is POWER! Okay – back to the story – you know how it goes – the disciples went, they found, they untied, and they brought the two to Jesus. Just as He commanded. And all for this reason: The Lord had need of them. (Matt 21:3)

The Lord had need of them. The LORD had need of them. They were tied. The Lord knew it. So He sent His disciples to untie them and bring them. To HIM. For He had need of them. My friends, don't miss this, do not skip over the words, the pictures, the story. Today, this very moment, there are people everywhere in our lives, standing there, tied up. They're in the middle of the village in the middle of the day, surrounded by the hustle and bustle of life. People all around them are going on with their normal routine. Their can't-be-bothered lives. And there they stand in the midst, bound up. They are bound by something that won't let them go. Perhaps it's unforgiveness, perhaps it's unbelief, perhaps it's addiction, jealousy, hurt, pride, pain … whatever it is IT HAS THEM TETHERED. And the Lord knows. The Lord can see them … and He needs to send someone to retrieve them. For He has need of them. They have purpose! They have destiny! They have a future and a hope! But first things first: let's get them untied.

My friend, who is it in your life? In your village? Who is it? They're waiting for their freedom. They're waiting to be brought to Him. Where is the disciple that will go? Who will follow the instruction of the Lord and focus in on the freedom of? Let's obey Him! Let's say, "I'll go! I'll go get them, Lord!" Send me, Lord!"

And my friend of the Gospel, let me tell you ... when you go as HE commanded and begin to loose your friend, if someone, anyone, dares to rise up and stand in your way ... girl, girl, girl, you tell them what the Lord said to tell them, "The Lord has need of them!" and immediately they will let you go. The Word promises that. It's ammunition. Praise God Almighty.

They are tied. They are waiting. He sees them. He needs them. The time is running out. Who will go?

Our Lord and Savior, Jesus Christ, saw us tethered by our own sin, went into the village of Jerusalem and untied us by dying on a Cross. Through Him and because of Him, I have been loosed from the sinful chains that bound me. Oh, may I be faithful to share that freedom with someone who doesn't know. May I go and bring back the one the Lord needs. What an honor. What a privilege.

It's Passion Week. May the Passion of the Christ explode in your heart. How can we love Him more? I have an idea. Let's go untie somebody.

Faithful and True

I sat out on the porch after we hung up and prayed for you and your future, your destiny, the plans the LORD has for you ... for His protection and wisdom to be your hiding place. For those boys – for their lives to LINE UP WITH THE WORD OF GOD. Yes, and Amen. Thanking God for the miracle of loving a man so much that He would snatch him from the numbered days of death and place his feet on solid ground, restoring life to him, cleansing his heart and for that man's acceptance and desire to draw near to God. May the LORD complete what He has started in that Adam's life. Thanking God for my own miracle that I was in the midst of with a man who should not be living, but thru God's miraculous grace, is alive and well. Living in a house that should have been foreclosed on, but thanks be unto GOD, it is my home and I am content. Driving a car that should have been hooked up to a truck and hauled off, but thanks be unto GOD, it gets 25 miles to the gallon. I'm so thankful. And I'm at peace in that place.

I've learned a huge thing. In the past, I have thought that my "wonderful" testimony had to be communicated out to the masses ... for people to know what I'd been through and what the LORD has done ... I know that is important. But that is not what's most important. What's most important in my season of life right now is learning to accept the love of Christ, that He would love me so much that He would stand in harm's way to rescue me and

Steve out of every pit imaginable and bind us together even closer than ever before. To learn to live in the midst of a miracle, just my Lord, my Steven, and me. Strand of three cords. I don't have to let the world out there know that I've been to hell and back and I'm a stronger woman for it, although I hope that everyone I encounter can sense it. All I must do is accept His love thru this miracle, live every day in gratefulness, and pass His Love on, one by one.

That reminds me. Dear friend, hold out your hand. I have something to give you.

Buried

Good morning friends. I'm starting my day with **Streams in the Desert**. Following is an excerpt from today's reading. It seems a bit dreary but I guess that's just because that's "where I am" right now. I loved this portion of the reading. We all have had the floods come; we've all seen gold left behind. This is the story of the Cross. I can't help but relay this to what our friend is going through; and now another dear sister watches her brother struggle ... The floods most definitely come. Yes and Amen. Such is this life. But The LORD knows every water drop that touches His daughters; He knows every purpose for every "washing away." Our Keeper keeps us in the whirlwind for His eye is on the sparrow and He keeps us in the stillness of the eye of the storm. There is no earthly force that can snatch us from His eternal grip. When everything else is swept away, washed away, blown away ... we still remain. And something within us begins to shine like gold. Not because of us, but because of Him. And at the end, isn't that what matters?

Every person and every nation must take lessons in God's school of adversity. "We can say, 'Blessed is night, for it reveals to us the stars.' In the same way we can say, 'Blessed is sorrow, for it reveals God's comfort.' The floods washed away home and mill, all the poor man had in the world. But as he stood on the scene of his loss, after the water had subsided, broken-hearted and discouraged, he saw something shining in the bank which the waters had washed bare. 'It looks like gold,' he said. It was gold. The flood which had beggared him made him rich. So it is ofttimes in life." —H. C. Trumbull – Streams in the Desert

A List of Ys

LORD, What's it gonna take for me to
Understand wisely
Choose rightly
Pray nightly

Surrender totally
Commit wholly
Worship solely

Live purely
Reject worldly
See clearly
Give cheerily
Fall deeply

Believe boldly
Be totally
Complete holy

Yours.

My thoughts after reading Matthew 15.

2004

Perhaps my only role in this life is to aid a man, be Christ to a man that battles the stronghold of generations before him. Perhaps my greatest legacy will be to forgive him and be the good Samaritan to him, to see him lying in the ditch, go to him, have compassion on him, pour wine and oil on his wounds, bundle him up and bring him home. Believe me, in my flesh I didn't want any of that! But that is the life of Christ. When I held the mirror in front of my face I had to ask myself, "Is it just lovely lip service or does love truly serve?" This is a real situation where I can be the real Christ. I drop the rocks of "Why did you do this to me again?" and I allow Christ to fill me with compassion for a sick and hurting man. My truest love who is now unable to fight to live. For so long I've felt it was a lesson for him. Perhaps the only reason the LORD had me marry him was for me … for me to learn this lesson in my life. To teach me to be Christ. Lord Jesus, help me. I have so far to go. The love of my life needs me. Correction: Needs You. I know that Your grace is sufficient, for YOUR

POWER is made perfect in weakness. And Lord, today, standing in this closet, my face soppin' wet with tears, I am being made into the image of Christ. Let it be so, Lord Jesus.

Let the weak say, "I am strong"
Let the poor say, "I am rich"
Let the blind say, "I can see
What the LORD has done in me"
- *Reuben Morgan*

Pursue

The LORD Desires Us

The LORD desires us close to His heart, so much so that He placed us in a garden, an oasis of peace, a palace of Presence, in order to be close to Him. To be one. It's the reason the Garden was created – so that we could be close to our Creator God, One with one. This, my friend, was heaven on earth. True communion. The word Garden in Hebrew means "fenced." The Lord fenced us inside perfection, fenced in by His Glory. But our sin, the bite of the fruit as the separated serpent coached on, broke down the fence. In our awareness, we realized then ran from His Presence. We, His creation breathing with His breath, now separated from Him and sealed to the hell of sin. Two choices, once again. The closeness cut off. We were alone. Oh, but our All-Knowing God already had the only plan of restoration: through the sacrifice of His Only Son. The Blood of Jesus Christ. The Holy God of all creation hasn't changed. Never will. He wants us to want Him. He wants us to desire Him. He is jealous for our devotion. For the Garden. He longs for us to inch nearer and nearer back to Him, as we trust Him to lead our life. He wants communion with us. He rebuilt the fence. We just have to now choose The Gate. Why is it that we kick against Him with excuses? Why do we justify our laziness? Why do we ignore His plea? Why do we RSVP His invitation by ignoring it even exists? Can't we, shan't we, seek Him while He may be found? Why do we ignore His Presence? Have we become so numb, so callous, so scabbed over by the delusions of this world that we can't even hear Him call us in the cool of the day? Oh, how He wants us to know Him more intensely. He wants our intent to be intense. He calls to us in the cool of the day, in the dark of the night, in the heat of the hour, in the hit of the fight. He calls to us. Do we have ears to hear? Do we desire to hear? Do we choose to hear? The New Testament is filled with Jesus saying tenderly, "He who has ears, let him hear." Let that be your prayer today. The bundle of questions are ours to ask yet all are answered in our one courageous action. If we would just come closer.

Come Closer (2005)

I hear HIM say, "Come Closer
I have a place for you
A cozy spot, a perfect place
Room just enough for two"

I hear Him say, "Come nearer,
Come nearer unto Me
Press forward to the hidden place
A garden place for thee"

I hear Him say, "Come quickly
Pick up your feet and run
This place is good; it's full of love
Where you and I are one"

I hear HIM say, "Come closer
Come nearer even still
To hear MY heart, to hear ME sing
Allow MY breath to fill"

I hear HIM say, "Come closer
Come underneath MY grace
Lay down within MY nail scarred hand
And gaze into MY face

Just take the step and find MY wing
No matter what the cost
Let faith rise up and push you forth
Find Power in the Cross"

"The perfect place is closer still
Beneath the wing of Grace
I'm watching for you on the road
I long to see your face"

I hear HIM say, "Come closer"
I say, "LORD I'm afraid
This place I am, tho hard and bleak
Is where my bed I've made

My legs are weak
my breath is gone
I have no force to go
I'm frozen here, I cannot move
This place has held me so"

I hear HIM say, "Come closer"
I reply to Him "But how?
My eyes are blurred, I cannot see
I'm blinded here for now"

I hear Him say, "Come Closer"
But LORD, I say, "I'm tired
I'm weary on this lonesome road
My feet caught in the mire"

I hear Him say Come Closer
I finally say, "I'll try
I'll lift my foot, I'll force this move
I'll clear my blurry eye

I'll take the step, I'll find his wing
I'll stumble closer still
I'll rest in HIM
I'll stay with Him
It is HIS perfect will"

The perfect place is closer still
Beneath the wing of grace
I'm running down this dusty road
I long to see Your face

The sweetest place is
Closer Still
Where Face to face I'll see
The ONE Who with a hammer's blow
Prepared a place for me

Matthew 11: Come to Me, all of you who are weary and burdened, and I will give you rest.

When he came to his senses, he said, "How many of my father's hired workers have more than enough food, and here I am dying of hunger. I'll get up and go to my father and say to him, 'Father, I have sinned against heaven and in your sight. I'm no longer worthy to be called your son. Make me like one of your hired workers.'" So he got up and went to his

father. But while he was still a long way off, his father saw him and was filled with compassion. The father ran, threw his arms around his son's neck and kissed him.
Luke 15:17-20

Choose to Come (2006)

I'm going to type out some scriptures below and just see if your spiritual needle and thread can piece them all together with one certain stitch. Ready?

Come. Let us worship and bow down. Psalm 95
Weeping may last for a night, but joy comes in the morning. Psalm 30
Come now, let Us reason together. Isaiah 1
Arise, shine, for your Light has come. Isaiah 66
You who are thirsty, come and drink, and you who have no money, come, buy and eat. Isaiah 55
We have seen His star and have come to worship Him. Matthew 2
You who are thirsty, come to the water. John 7
Permit the children to come to Me. Mark 10
IAM the Way the Truth and the Life. No one comes to the Father except through Me. John 14
Come to Me, all of you who are weary and burdened, and I will give you rest. Matthew 11
If anyone wishes to come after Me, He must deny himself, take up his cross, and follow Me. Luke 9

If anyone wishes. It's a choice to choose.

The phrase that Jesus used is, "Come after Me." Don't misunderstand the phrase. He's not saying, "After I'm gone, then come. Be the next one." No – He's not saying that. Anyone remember playing chase in the yard at dusk with a passle of friends under the streetlights? One poor soul was sadly labeled "it" and all others had the great joy of running to keep from being caught. But there was always that one bold person who would look at the chaser and say, "Hey you, come after me!" And the chase was on. Hot pursuit. Until the two became one in the climactic collision of the chase. That's what Jesus meant. "Come after Me." Passion filled pursuit of His Presence in my frame of dust, only accomplished when I begin to chase His Glory Shadow, day after day after day. Colliding with His Presence, over and over and over again. The Lord Himself said, "You pursue Me and You find Me when you're runnin' with your whole heart." Passionate Pursuit.

Last but certainly not least, dare I say this last one might actually be the most one … John the Revelator, the only one who walked the whole way with Him. The only one not martyred (they tried but couldn't) so he was sent to exile for telling his testimony. The one who gave it all. The one who wrote down the words that Jesus said in the last book of the Bible, "IAM coming quickly" and it occurred to me – by the spirit of the LORD – that as we are "coming after Christ" at the very same time, He's coming after us. And one day in one moment, those two "comes" are gonna' climactically collide and we shall then be OVERCOME. We shall meet Him in the air and forever be with the Lord. Chase Over. Collision accomplished. Oneness once again. Glory hallelujah to the King of all the ages!

The close of Revelation ends with John's plea back to the Lord Jesus, "Come, Lord Jesus." Oh my Lord. As I come to You, I know You are coming to me."

There's really nothing more to add … other than I beg you to officially begin your "come," your hot pursuit, your collision course, to Jesus. See you in the sky. ☺

Run

This thing called Life. This happy, horrific, jolting, joyful, bountiful, boring, meaningful, maddening thing called Life. This breath we breathe, this heart we house, these days we live: Life. Some get so caught up in the chores that they miss The Chalice. Some fight so hard for trinkets that they miss The Treasure. Some see prestige in a worn designer label rather than choosing to put on the loveliness of Christ. Some run so fast toward pride that they miss The Peace. The Prize.

Then time runs out and they miss out. Called out. Cast out.

Where are you in this thing called Life? What do you strive for? Run toward? Hoard up? Board up? Let me help you make it simple.

Jesus. Is. Life.

All of this on planet earth is all about HIM. Let all the other puff-n-stuff fall away. Keep digging until you find the Pearl of Great Price. His Name is Jesus. Run toward Him.

Let us lay aside every hindrance and the sin that so easily entangles us and let us run with endurance the race that lies before us, keeping our eyes on Jesus, the author and perfector of our faith. Hebrews 12

The Night Sky

Looking up at a star-filled night sky is always a breath-taking marvel. Isaiah 40 says that "He leads them out, calls them by name, not one of them is missing." The stars. From earth with our necks craned back to see up, we see the stars as pin pricks in the floor of heaven, with the eternal radiance of the glory of God shining through.

When God looks down toward earth, perhaps He sees the same thing ... the darkness of this world but also the Light – God's Light – Christians aka "little Christs" - pinpricks in the darkness, shining brightly through each one of His own .... the saved ... the saints ... shining in this dark ... bought with the Blood of Jesus, filled with the light of His Love. A city on a hill that can never be hidden. The Glory of God. His brilliance in us and through us. Look up, look down, look all around.

Pin pricks in heaven's floor. The Glory of God above and below. One future moment in time in a twinkling, the thin barrier between the two will disintegrate, and the Glory will swallow up the darkness. And all that is left is LIGHT BRITE!

Oh my goodness, This Christ Light of mine, I'm gonna' let YOU shine.

Admonished to Trust

It all goes back to **TRUST**. (surprise! NOT.) Not trust in man, but in **THE SON OF MAN**. The very center of the Bible is Psalm 118, and the very center verse in the middle of that center chapter is a verse about trusting God instead of trusting man. I wish I could quote it but perhaps it's better if you look it up for yourself.

What does trust mean? So glad you asked. Trust is a process of building faith in One whom faith is warranted. It's the cement between the bricks that holds the Christian together. If there were directions on the trust bottle they would say something like this: Get out your Bible. Find the Promises. Believe the Promises. Live those Promises. Daily. Over time, you will find yourself in step with the Truth that you trust, the Way that you trust, and the Life that you trust. His name is Jesus.

o He said He came to give abundant life. That is His Will. Trust that.

o He said He came to wipe the slate clean and give you a fresh start. That is His Will. Trust that.

o He said that if you keep your mind on Him, He will keep you in perfect peace. That is His Will. Trust that.

o He said He has a plan for your life, a good plan with a future and a hope. Not to harm you but to prosper you. That is His Will. Trust that.

o He said He'd supply every need. That is His will. Trust that.

o He said that if you draw near to Him, He will draw near to you. He said resist the devil and the devil will flee. That is His Will. Trust that.

o He said that you are more than a conqueror and can do all things thru Christ Who gives you strength. That is His Will. Trust that.

Correction: Trust HIM.

The hardest part is trusting Him when you don't see Him. Trusting without questioning. (pretty sure that's called Faith but let me continue) … One of the greatest adversaries of Trust is Mr. **BWI. But What If**. That enemy needs slaying. Have you ever tried to make a decision for Christ then follow it with BWI? Guess what? That keeps you paralyzed, frozen in place, far, far away from trust. Just where the enemy wants us.

o Kick the devil in the knee and say with Job, "Tho He slay me, yet I'm gonna trust Him!"

o The Bible says to trust in the Lord with your whole heart. Lean not on your own stinking thinking. In all your ways, acknowledge Him. Then He will direct your path.

o The Bible says seek Him and His kingdom FIRST, then all the other will follow. That is His will.

That is a promise from Him. That is His Will for me and for you.

"TRUST AND OBEY, FOR THERE'S NO OTHER WAY
TO BE HAPPY IN JESUS, BUT TO TRUST AND OBEY."

Are you stalled at the intersection of Trust Avenue and the BWI round-about? I sense in my spirit to tell you these words: IT'S TIME. It's time to stop talking and start trusting. Turn right toward Trust and watch BWI fade away in your rear-view mirror. Now you're going places, baby. Driving that Kingdom Highway. Trusting Him at the wheel. That, my friend, is His Will.

Revelations

I've been chewing on Revelation 1 this past week. A quick synopsis of this chapter - John, the Beloved Disciple, the one who leaned on the chest of Jesus on the night of His betrayal; the one who never deserted; the only one recorded to follow from the garden to the cross; the one "Whom Jesus Loved" (as recorded in the gospel of John) finds himself in isolation, banned from society, imprisoned on an island called Patmos because of that love. Taking all of that into account, he had every fleshly right to be bitter, angry, full of self-pity and regret. But he was not. The chapter opens up saying that he was in the spirit on the Lord's Day. Wow. And in that moment, he heard a Voice behind him … and he turned to SEE the Voice. (ahmm, how do you see a Voice?) Now, I could go on from here and describe the SON OF MAN but I'd rather you go there and read the description of the Voice, the One that sounded like thunderous waters.

Once you read Revelation 1, I have a question. What if that were the only chapter of the Holy Word? What if none of the other words were written; only that one chapter by that one Holy Spirit inspired writer … would it be enough?

AHMMM …YES! I could go on and on about how personal the Lord is, how He meets us wherever we are - One with one. And His Presence is more than we can absorb. I could go on and on about how HE comes to us, sometimes from behind when we least expect it, as THE SON OF GOD AND SON OF MAN … ONE WHOSE VERY PRESENCE IS OVERWHELMING AND INDESCRIBABLE … but yet He comes as a friend and a brother, understanding our plight, and He lays His hand on us and says, "Don't be afraid." Yes, I could go on and on and on.

From that – be encouraged. Whatever your Patmos is, I admonish you, encourage you, desire you to be in the Spirit on the Lord's Day! And when you hear a voice behind you, **TURN AROUND!!** There's Someone to see!

Love and Blessings, Power and Strength, the Lord is the Storehouse for All.

Pressures

"IN THE WORLD YOU WILL HAVE PRESSURES, BUT BE OF GOOD CHEER, FOR I HAVE UNPLUGGED THE PRESSURE COOKER". – JOHN 16:33 (Robin White Feather's translation)

The World Would be a Better Place

Without

Blowers
Bullies
Weed eaters

Fire ants
Yellow Jackets
"Ma Skeeeters"

Ticks
Fleas

Fear

Snakes
Sharks
Spiders

Mean dogs
Mean girls

Lay-offs
Drop-offs

Rice Cakes
Tofu

Unwanted Hair

Jealousy
Humidity
Pollen
Pride

Wasps
Slugs
Scars
Sweat

Lost Children
Baby Caskets

Orange Barrels

Status
Labels
Lady-made Ladders

Tornadoes
Earthquakes
Hurricanes
Volcanoes

Fire Storms
Hail Storms
Life Storms
Hate

Selfishness

Menopause

Regret
Revenge

Inflation
Aggravation

Addiction
Abuse
Anger

Prejudice
Pressure
Pre-nups

Loneliness
Loss

Broken Bones
Broken Dreams
Broken People

Hunger
Sickness
Disease

Gloom
Doom
Despair
Delays

Death

We need a new world.
(Hang on, sister. We gonna get one! Sonday's comin')

> *2 Peter 3: But based on His Promise,*
> *we wait for new heavens and a new earth,*
> *where righteousness dwells.*

The following poem is the first writing I remember saving on paper. I was working at Vickers, Inc. at the time. I wrote it after a week or so of constant, unrelenting rain. I wrote it, printed it, and systematically hid it in my purse (aka my first nooked note). Later that week, I remember riding with Steve in the car. I pulled out the paper and timidly read it to him as he drove. It was important to me to know what he thought. He looked at me from the driver's seat and said, "Wow. You wrote that?" (Isn't it strange that I can still feel the seat and see his face and hear his words?) I was immediately reminded of that anonymous teacher's penned word, *"Good."* Later that same month, Vickers used it in their monthly newsletter. Truly a marker for me, a stone of remembrance, a pin in my life map, some 31 years ago. I was 29 years old.

The Bird and Her Father

The sky outside
Is dismal and gray
The birds are complaining
You can hear each one say

"It's cold out here
And it's wet in our tree
Why does this always
Have to happen to me?

There's nowhere to go
All the houses are filled
And I have no lumber
With which to build

Please give us the sun
We all want to fly
We can't when it's wet
Our wings must be dry!"

Then a voice from above
So calmly is heard
"Be still and listen
My sweet little bird

The rain is a blessing
From heaven you know
It's what the earth needs
To help make things grow

It seems like a lot
Right now on the land
But I assure you it's too small
For the palm of My hand

Remember Noah's day?
There was much more than this
Forty days it continued
Not one day it missed

So remember when you fuss
And when you complain
That you grow and are stronger
Because of the rain"

The bird remained silent
And as she did so
She looked up to her Father
And saw the rainbow.

*Matthew 5 – Consider the birds of the sky. They don't sow or reap or gather into barns,
yet your heavenly Father feeds them. Aren't you worth more than they?*

1 Peter 5: Cast all your cares on Him, for He cares for you.

Acceptance

It's hard to explain how this collection of words have been written. I have always journaled and some of these texts have been birthed there. But in most cases I would have to confess that I hear a whispering of a phrase, a cooing of a thought in my head that travels to my heart and relentlessly pounds at the door of my consciousness until I surrender and place it on paper with pen (or most likely screen with keyboard). The following was written early one morning at work … I kept hearing, "Acceptance is surrender." I finally surrendered, opened a blank page on my computer screen and jotted this quickly. Just an hour or so later, I received news that my husband had been laid off from his job.

All of that to say, when a word, or a phrase, or a thought is ablaze within you, perhaps you should remove your shoes and stand in silence, for you might just be standing on holy ground. Acknowledge the Voice. And I don't mean Blake Shelton. I mean The Voice of the Almighty. The Lord has something to say.

Acceptance is surrender
A letting go, release
A prayer of *"I can't do this,*
Here, Jesus, be my PEACE"

Come storm or sunny weather
Come wind, or fire, or rain
Come hurt or hard or happy
My prayer remains the same

There's wisdom in the knowing
When life is wimp or weight
To give it all right back to HIM
Like the passing of the plate

Let your graciousness be known to everyone. The LORD is near.
*Don't worry about anything, but **IN** everything, through prayer and petition*
With thanksgiving, present your requests to GOD.
And the peace of God which surpasses all understanding
Will guard your hearts and minds in Christ Jesus.
Philippians 4:5-7

Mama

Nothing can prepare you for a sick mama. Nothing. It's unthinkable, unfathomable, unbelievable that this pillar in your life is being jack hammered, maternal dust flying in every direction. Frantically trying to sweep up the pieces and glue them back together. This granite pillar daily drilled into grit. The once spark of joy that lit her eyes now dull and dim. The laughter silenced. The smile removed. The roles reversed. You're placed in her shoes far too soon, mothering her. The years of mama's sickness have many layers in me. A few of those layers I share here with you. My first real lesson to TRUST. You know, that Christianese word that every Christian hollowly pledges when they sing that trusted hymn, but when the rubber meets the road and the going gets tough, then the trust takes the backseat (and when you aren't looking, opens the door and bails). How can we trust Him in times of hurt and pain? How can we trust Him when life goes down the proverbial drain? How can I trust Him as I tuck her in bed, kiss her forehead, and drive home in the dark, with my mind screaming, "WHY!" This is real, folks. Life is real. Real hard. No one escapes unscraped.

But God.

The world starts and ends there. At His feet. His ways are not my ways; His thoughts are not my thoughts. All things that happen are filtered to me through His fingers. And that is the point of trust. Knowing that He knows and has allowed the "whatevers" that come, leaning hard into that mystery, stepping triumphantly or wearily into the next day, one day at a time, trusting His filtering fingers.

"Tho He slay me, yet will I trust HIM." - Job 13:15

"As for me and my House, we will serve HIM." - Joshua, June, and Robin

"Trust in the LORD and do good. Dwell in the land and feed on HIS faithfulness. Delight yourself also in the LORD and HE shall give you the desires of your heart. Commit your way to the LORD, Trust also in HIM and HE shall bring it to pass.... Rest in the LORD and wait patiently for HIM ... do not fret; it only causes harm." —
David, Psalm 37

Gwen (2016)

I'm sitting again at my desk in a roll-around chair, listening to *In Christ Alone* through ear buds. I felt the urge to just write some things down and needed "my three" to know. Sometimes it's okay to spill over, whether it be for good or for naught. Perhaps sometimes a cracked pot just needs to leak. I think that's where I am today.

I don't write for sympathy or "I'm so sorry for you" return emails. I truly already know and trust your heart for me. I know there are prayers abounding for me. I lean on that. Believe me, I do. I just need a sounding board today and "my three" are the lucky ones. (I chuckled as I typed that, just so you know. Poor you.)

Jesus said, "Come to me – all of you who are weary and heavy laden, and I will give you REST."

Today I come. I am exhausted and frazzled and ready for REST. Today I come.

My brothers and I continue to rally around mom while trying not to lose our minds in the midst. Every day is a different day with her. The majority of her legal needs are now complete; we have power of attorney over her healthcare and financial matters. I still have to get to the courthouse to get a deed for her home and call Oklahoma to get a deed for the mineral rights she owns from her childhood farmland. But that's another day. In the meantime, mom rollercoasters between reality, paranoia and unfortunately severe nausea. I still feel that I can talk some sense to her in those moments and help her see logic but it's a lot like exerting all my energy to punch air in the dark. Just last night when I talked with her, she told me that she had lost so much weight she looked like a refugee from another country and she needed a new doctor to go to in order to figure out why she's skin and bones (she's not skin and bones). She also is now refusing to take her meds because she is convinced her meds are killing her. Pray for Roger. He truly gets the brunt of it all since he's there with her 24/7. He came and got me yesterday to go get some wedding décor for me in his truck. While we were talking about everything that has happened, is happening, and the thought of what is sure to happen, he said, "I know this is hard to hear, but I just hope the LORD will take her while she's sleeping." Ok, just typing that has punched me in my gut again and I am grappling with the enormity of the mount Evertest we currently climb.

This past week was the first time I've cried about this. I was at Regions Bank (which was originally Deposit Guaranty back in the day – where mom retired from) and I was standing there with the kindest teller named Gwen, explaining our situation and looking over mom's accounts. She suddenly reached both hands over the countertop to hold mine and said, "I am so sorry for your family." In that moment, I was whisked away to 1972 when I would get off the bus in Rosedale at the bank where mama worked. I would go next door to get a potato log and a coke, then go into the bank's break room and wait for mom to take me to piano lessons. Mom was the teller behind the counter, serving each customer with kindness. She was the "Gwen." In that moment this week, I saw her again, sitting there. So beautiful. And I began to cry.

This life is truly a vapor. A blink. A flower that blooms at sunrise and withers at sunset.

The Lord gave me the gift of Gwen this week. An angel stranger who helped me unlock a door that had been closed far too long. I've been so caught up in the shock and horror of this diagnosis, combined with the wedding planning frenzy, that I had pent up all the emotion behind that locked door. Gwen turned the key. I'm thankful today for Gwen. God bless her.

2 Corinthians - Comfort in Suffering
3 Blessed be the God and Father of our Lord Jesus Christ, the Father of mercies and God of all comfort, 4 who comforts us in all our tribulation so that we may be able to comfort those who are in any trouble, with the comfort with which we ourselves are comforted by God. 5 For as the sufferings of Christ abound in us, so our consolation also abounds through Christ. 6 Now if we are afflicted, it is for your consolation and salvation, which is effective for enduring the same sufferings which we also suffer. Or if we are comforted, it is for your consolation and salvation. 7 And our hope for you is steadfast, because we know that as you are partakers of the sufferings, so also you will partake of the consolation.

Lord Jesus, help me. Us. Please help us.

To my friends who have lost their moms, those who walked this road, felt this fire, and endured this ache that I now carry, I now know your loss. And I trust that each of you had a Gwen at some point in your season of suffering. And I have to believe the God of All Comfort intervened to see you through. You're still standing. You made it through.

And now, I'm on the road, trailing far behind. With that visual, please reach behind you from time to time and drag me forward. Whether I be limp and lifeless or kicking and complaining, just drag me forward.

Thankful today for you. Thankful today for Gwen. Thankful today for Junie Bug. Thankful for the unwrapped yet to be found treasures hidden somewhere in this horror.

Sifted (2004)

Something I am learning through my bible study is that the devil has to ask permission to "sift you like wheat." Permission is given by Christ when there is something within a believer that definitely needs the sifting. It's never done out of anger or revenge or "I'm gonna get you for that" by Christ. It's because He sees something in us that needs to be removed. It's because He sees beyond that removal to something remarkable. The Word also says that Christ prays for us during the sifting. So He gives permission for the sifting but just like He told Peter, "WHEN you have returned, strengthen your brothers."

I feel like I've been sifted this week. I know Steve feels it. I'm sure you have felt sifted too at some point in your journey. I just picture a wheat field, blowing in the wind, and then a sickle coming through and cutting down a section of wheat at the base of the stalk. I can see the wheat fall. But the LORD is reassuring both of us that it is for reason and for purpose and for when (not if) we have returned, we are to strengthen others. "Returned" takes place the moment I "get the lesson" or when I see the miracle or when I truly believe that God is able. I think this week has been a testing of my faith / a "what are you going to do with this, Robin" kind of week. I have learned that forgiving Steve because The LORD forgave me is a very humbling thing. The LORD said that I should forgive "Seventy times seven." There are no "what ifs. Forgiveness covers everything. And if I choose to turn a cold shoulder to my husband, to act holier than thou and become self-righteous, then I have sinned against him. Which sin is greater? Sin is a level plain at the foot of the cross. So, I have to be very careful to be obedient to HIM by forgiving him. That's real wordy but it's what I'm learning.

I haven't been able to wear my rings this week. I have worn my small gold wedding band, but no diamonds. My rings have always been a symbol to me; the ones I wear are ones that Steve gave to me after hard times. The one that is most precious to me is the one he gave me after our year from hell in 1997. I can't wear that one right now for sure. I feel like this simple gold band means that I have to "go back" and remember the covenant. Take away the glitz and the shiny and figure out what is still left. Still standing. The covenant. Not sure when I'll be able to put the diamonds on again. And that's ok. Until then, the single gold covenant is enough.

Pieces

Roger

(2007) I saw Roger last night at River Oaks. He is in ICU for the time being; will probably be moved into a regular room today. This was done to watch him as they decreased his blood pressure quickly using some drip meds. The nurse let me back (even though the sign said NO to visitors) which I thanked GOD for … he is in ICU #8 … the number of new beginnings. I got to tell him that I loved him, and that GOD has shown grace and mercy to him over and over again … the fact that he is alive is a gift of mercy from GOD. He agreed. I got to tell him about a new beginning that God was giving him … he agreed. He was very calm and at peace and "surrendered" to his situation.

Okay – I have to show you … he is in I C U (I see you!) The LORD sees him … He is Jehovah ROI, the God who sees. And there is a new beginning for him thru this.

(2019) Roger passed away on Sunday morning, June 30. He was 55. Born January 7, 1964, Roger's childhood days were filled with hunting, bike riding, "anni-over," tennis, riding horses, and friends. Many, many friends. So many nights were spent playing kick-the-can under the streetlight with all the neighborhood kids. He pitched baseball for a time and could throw that ball with arrow precision. Come to think of it, he could throw a rock too and hit his mark on a moving target every time, in case he had a reason to. He could definitely hold his own, even though he was the youngest of four kids.

As he grew older he turned to music and writing. Not sure when he started playing the bass, but he taught himself well. He had a natural talent to "make that bass sing" and enjoyed hours a day, playing music, up until last week. He played with several bands over the years, one of which entertained at the Phoenix Fling for three years in a row. This made him happy. Oh, and mowing - that really made him happy. He loved to mow on his riding John Deere. So much so that he not only mowed his grass, but any needy neighbor who didn't mind him helping. Like the widow across the street. He just did it for her because he knew she needed it.

Roger had a heart of gold, despite his heart problems diagnosed in 2005. He loved his family with a fireproof love. Especially his nieces and nephews. He loved them fierce and showed them so with boxes of ice cream each time he arrived at the house. He was there whenever we needed him with whatever we needed. All we had to do was call. He was only happy if we were. He always put himself last. Our many trips to Disney as a family are a perfect example ... he would make sure the family was lined up like ducks and he would fall in behind, keeping watch on the bobbing heads in front. That was his job and he did it well. Keeping watch over the flock.

He had a quick wit and was very intelligent, even though he wanted you to not know that. He could write stories, songs and poems like no other. His brain was always working a story out, and when he was satisfied with it, he'd share, with that twinkle in his eye. Who can forget his tale of the "meatloaf biscuit" franchise? One of the songs he wrote for the girls years ago was, "Ole' Blue." They would sing along with him and laugh and laugh. Mission accomplished, Uncle Roger.

And speaking of, "Ole'," he loved his Ole Miss Rebels, beginning with Archie as quarterback. He went to games as a kid with his brothers and dad, but as an adult, he and Randy made game after game after game, dressed in their red and blue, supporting their Rebels. When Samantha chose to go to State, he had to first give her a good talking to, to ensure she was in her right mental state. He finally relented but kept up the "my team is better than your team" banter, again with that twinkle in his eye. Our Brooke now plays flute in the Ole Miss Pride of the South and Uncle Roger, my bookend brother, swelled with pride every time she took the field. On the morning Jess was married, they pulled in the parking lot of the church on two wheels because they were traveling back from the Sugar Bowl 2016, supporting their Rebs. Knowing that Case had applied at Ole Miss for the Fall 2020 was just the icing on the Fins Up cake for him.

Most importantly and most assuredly, Roger was a believer in the Lord Jesus Christ. He made a childhood profession of faith and was baptized but in later years our mama had many talks with him, ensuring his salvation. His gruff exterior was the housing for a tender heart that loved deeply, cared deeply, and showed that love through service.

Because of that, his heart has been made new. His heart has been made whole. And ours are forever shattered. I pray there's grass in heaven, and I pray he's been handed the keys to a green and yellow John Deere.

"Therefore, if anyone is in Christ, he is a new creation. The old has passed away.
The new has come." 2 Corinthians 5:17

To Roger, from Randy (July 5, 2019)

As is customary when a loved one dies, you somehow are whisked through the motions, ending up at a conference table planning a funeral. At a time when you can barely breathe, a time when your senses are shut down, you don't have the energy to think, your insides are screaming NO, but yet you have to return to being a sane person and schedule a service to honor the deceased. Numb and null, you begin to figure it out and write it down. When the question was asked, "Who will do the eulogy?" I immediately looked at Randy and said, "You should do it. You have to do it." No one knew Roger better than his best friend, his brother. Roger didn't let a lot of people inside his bubble but Randy had a lifetime pass. The bond my bookend brothers shared was sacred, strong, sure. And now silenced. Through his grief, Randy delivered the following from the platform to honor Roger's life. Roger would not have changed one word and he would've patted me hard on the shoulder and snickered at every topic in his story.

Good afternoon everyone. My name is Randy and I'm Roger's big brother. First, thank you all for coming out to spend just a few minutes celebrating and remembering, Roger…Thank you for coming. A special thanks and welcome to our family members watching live stream from their homes in Oklahoma and Texas…We love you and we miss you today. I'd like to take a few minutes and talk to you about my brother, and the things that meant most to him, and share some of our most precious memories. Now I'll only take a few minutes, because I promise you, a few minutes would be all the time Roger would allow us to sit around and talk about him. He was extremely humble, he avoided any spotlight, he did not seek attention. He did not like being the focus of a conversation. And so, if he could talk to us right now, at this very moment, he'd probably be saying something like "Dangburn Yall hurry up and get on out of here. I love you too, but let's wrap this up and go to the house. And don't forget to go by the Dairy Queen and try that new caramel blizzard, dadgum that thing is some kinda good!"

We all loved Roger, but what and who did Roger love? Well, for starters, he loved that beard he was growing. That long gray monstrosity on the end of his face. Did anybody, besides Roger, love, or even like that beard? Uh. No. But Roger loved it, and don't ask me why because I don't know. It was just him doing him. He combed and trimmed and waxed that thing always making sure it was in pristine condition before he left his house. Roger loved his beard.

Roger loved music. He was a very good musician. He started playing bass guitar way back when he was around 14 years old. And he worked on his craft and he worked on his craft. And he got good, and he got really good. He was a bit of a perfectionist, always grimacing and immediately apologizing anytime he missed a fill or a single note. We played together in several country and rock bands over the span of our lives and we even played together as members of the Worship Team at Southside Assembly of God for a time. Those were very special days. He loved his bandmates and he loved the music. And he was not married to any particular genre. He would call me in the middle of the night and ask me if I'd been listening to any Tom Jones or Tina Turner. And I'd say "What?...No!" Yes, imagine Roger sitting in his dining room with his guitar resting in his lap and Tom Jones going wide open on the stereo. You kids go home tonight and google Tom Jones. Roger loved music.

Roger loved to cut grass. I don't know why. Maybe because we mowed yards when we were kids. And we'd push our big ole lawn mower down the street with a milk jug full of gas all the way to somebody's house and we'd cut their grass and they'd give us $2 and we'd push that big ole' lawn mower and a milk jug half full of gas back to the house. Maybe that's how it started. Have you ever seen a TV show called "King of the Hill?" Well, if you haven't, the lead character is a guy who admires and adores his riding lawn mower probably a little too much. That guy reminds me of Roger Ammons. Roger took painstaking care of his riding lawn mower and he kept it at peak operating efficiency, and it never got dirty...never. And just like Hank Hill from Arlen, Texas, he probably admired and adored that thing a little too much. I remember one summer on Peach Orchard, he started cutting the elderly lady's grass across the street just out of kindness, and because he liked to cut grass. Within 2 weeks he was mowing 4 yards running full blast up and down that street on his riding lawn mower, and he loved it. Roger loved to get on that lawn mower and cut grass.

Roger loved Ole Miss. He and I used to sit by the radio on Saturday afternoons in the Fall when we were little kids and listen to the Ole Miss football broadcast. And Ole Miss had this guy named Archie Manning playing quarterback. And Roger and I had never seen or met Archie Manning, but he became our childhood hero. Archie, you had us at "Hello." Our Dad took us to an Ole Miss football game in Oxford in 1974. Our allegiance would never be tested and it remains unbroken. As we grew older, Roger and I became football season ticket holders and every Saturday home game we'd make the pilgrimage to Oxford. We had a game day process and a system that was tested and true. We had the pregame meal at a certain restaurant, the tailgate, the game, the post game meal at a certain restaurant, and the ride home. We did it the same way every single Saturday and Roger loved it, and I did too. Now, when you think of tailgating at Ole Miss you think of thousands of people streaming through the Grove like a turned over ant bed, and tents with chandeliers, and music and food on silver platters. But for Roger and me, our tailgate consisted of 2 lawn chairs, an ice chest, and a boom box, 50 feet from a port-a-john in parking lot E on the campus of the University of Mississippi. We never went to the Grove and we never missed it. We enjoyed our little 2 man tailgate in the parking lot away from the turmoil and bedlam. This was our time together and it was always special. Now, unfortunately, our game attendance did not lead to any Ole Miss victories. If a game was ever going to be decided by fan excitement and involvement, Roger and I would've been pivotal in Ole Miss winning 15 consecutive national championships. However, that ain't how it works. I am pleased to note that we didn't cause Ole Miss to lose any games. Now, when Roger learned Brooke was attending the University of Mississippi and would march in the Pride of the South Band, he was overjoyed to the point of tears. She was completing a circuit for us. She was fulfilling a dream. She was answering a silent prayer. And when Roger learned that Case would be a Rebel in the Fall of 2020, he again was overwhelmed and elated. You see, Roger loved Ole Miss.

Roger loved our country and his momma. I don't know how he felt about apple pie, but he loved this country and he loved his momma. He was very patriotic. His American flag is sitting by his front door right now ready to go into its holder at the front of the house. He was truly proud to be an American and he loved just being a big ole country boy from Bogue Chitto, MS. Roger was the primary caretaker for our mother when she became ill several years ago, and he served her and protected her until it was no longer physically possible to continue. He deeply loved and cared for his momma.

As we are obligated to do after a loved one's passing, we went over to Roger's house on Tuesday afternoon and began the difficult chore of looking through all that our brother had accumulated. I went through Roger's wallet, and there I found true evidence of what Roger loved and what he treasured.

I found this business card from the Little A'Le'Inn, a one horse, rinky dink diner in Rachel, Nevada, tucked away for safekeeping in the wallet. You see, back in 2008, he and I made a bucket list trip. We flew to Las Vegas, not to gamble, but for the buffets and to simply marvel at the giant buildings. We left Las Vegas and drove to Hoover Dam, toured the Dam, and drove to the Grand Canyon where we spent the night. The next day we drove through Monument Valley all the way to Moab, Utah, where we stayed and visited Canyonlands and Arches National Parks. Then we drove to Springdale, Utah, and visited Zion National Park. Then we drove to Rachel, Nevada, the absolute middle of nowhere in the absolute middle of nothing, and this was all Roger's big idea, to get a t-shirt and a hamburger from the Little A'Le'Inn, which, in fact, is a double wide trailer and a street light sitting alone in the barren desert. We drove back to Las Vegas, ate some more buffets, saw one of our favorite bands perform, and flew home. Look, if you really want to get to know a person, put him in a car and drive across Arizona and Utah and into the middle of the

Nevada desert with him. You will find out all kinds of stuff. We had the greatest time together, just me and Roger, on this trip, and we would reminisce about our fun journey on occasion, both glowing and laughing about our wonderful adventure. Roger loved to take trips, but he was especially fond of our family vacations. I think our trip to Wyoming and Yellowstone was among his all-time favorites. The beauty of the amazing scenery and vistas were stunning to us all, but especially to Roger. And I'm sure he'd like me to remind everyone that, during that trip, he got stuck on top of a mountain and he pulled a Code 10 on a Teton…He would want me to tell you that.

I found this in Roger's wallet. It's a ticket to Dollywood in Gatlinburg, Tennessee. What is this doing here? As I said earlier, Roger loved family vacations and, for us, a family vacation usually meant a theme park. We went to Dollywood one year and stayed in a cabin in the Smokies. Now, at Dollywood they have this large enclosure where they house American Bald Eagles. And they have a little show, a little demonstration, where one of the animal caretakers brings out a majestic eagle perched on his arm and he shares with the audience all the details about the life of the American bald eagle. Well, me and Roger were sitting there listening to this guy with an eagle on his arm go on and on about it, then all at once, and for no good reason and without any warning, the guy just started singing "I'm Proud To Be An American" by Lee Greenwood at the top of his voice. We looked at each other wondering what we were supposed to do…stand at attention, join in singing, or just continue to stare at the guy with a puzzled look on our faces wondering what was going on. Roger asked me "Hey, is that guy having a stroke or something?" We laughed and laughed about that every time Dollywood came up.

But usually, if we're talking family vacations with my brother Roger, we are talking about a visit to the happiest place on earth, Walt Disney World. We went there every single year without fail. And Roger loved Disney World. Yes, Roger. The big ole 6 foot 2, 260 pound, truck driving, country boy, Roger Ammons, loved Disney World. Just like me, and just like the rest of our clan. Roger had a tough, hard, Kevlar exterior, but deep inside his chest there was a big ole bowl of wet oatmeal. He loved Disney World. But not for any particular ride or attraction. Yes, he was fascinated by the technical wizardry of the place and the efficiency with which it runs. He marveled at the way they keep the grass cut down there. Most of all, Roger loved the family atmosphere and the joy he saw in children's faces at Disney. His absolute pinnacle was seeing Brooke glimpsing Cinderella's castle, watching Nick strap into Rock-N-Roller Coaster, sitting beside Jess and Sam at Mickey's Philharmonic and smiling as they grabbed for the floating diamonds and rubies. That is the Disney World experience that Roger Ammons loved. And he went again and again year after year just so he could capture those special moments.

Finally, in Roger's wallet I found the little plastic holder where the pictures are stored. There were no pictures of Roger in there…no pictures of me or Robin. There were only little school pictures of Roger's nieces and nephews. Roger, most of all, loved family and he deeply loved Jessica, Samantha, Nicholas, Brooke, and Case. There is not one single thing he would not do for family. You know, for an old, crusty bachelor, he certainly turned out to be a pretty good family man. He devoutly loved his family.

My friends, these are just a few of the things that Roger Ammons loved. My brother had an enlarged heart. I'm not talking about a medical condition. I'm talking about the size of a man's heart and his ability to care and to give. He loved the people in this room right now. And his heart was so big, there was room enough for us all.

Loss (2019)

Randy and I want to thank those who gathered with us in 2019 as we said "bye for now" to Roger. He lived with CHF and had been through many close calls, but he always came through. Until he didn't. The family always believed he'd outlive us all. Oh, how I wish that had been truth. His death was unexpected, definitely unwelcomed. We are still gasping for air at the loss of our brother. Your presence that day gave us strength, gave us love, gave us family. I don't know how we can ever return the gift so I'm praying that the LORD will do so for us. We love you and we thank you. We will never forget the gift of your presence that day.

Seems I write about water a lot these days. It's the word picture in my mind that truly portrays where I am in this grief. And perhaps it's because water is my greatest fear. I don't like water. I never have. Perhaps that's where I feel the greatest compromise, the greatest insecurity, the greatest WHAT IF. The total release of control. And perhaps that's why I write it out. It helps me work it out. For those who are riding the rapids or flailing in floods, I pray this is a buoy thrown in your direction.

For Roger.

Two Rivers

I'm stuck somewhere 'tween
Grief and greet
'Tween part and meet
'Tween sorrow and sweet

My brother gone
My grandson born
My heart in twain is rent
Black Night creeps on yet
Spring has sprung
"God, is this what You meant?"

It's safe to say
A heart can house
Two rivers inward flowin'
One's rapids filled with sadness, grief
With me on string a' towin'

It yanks me down its stream of hurt
It jerks me under pain
It slams me on the bank of WHY
It sucks me near the drain

I bubble up for bites of air
I hold on tight for hope
While life speeds on, me far behind
Tight clenching slippery rope

The other river – cloudless day
Its waters – tranquil sea
We float on blue, a brand new hue
The birds glide carelessly

My grandjoy sits beside me
We dreamily rock along
Boat motor purring softly
Singing rhythm, humming song

We take in all the quiet
Our hands stroke gentle waves
We strum along down river
Beneath the sunny haze

Two waters are my life now
One boat from bow to stern
Two channels underneath me
from both I try to learn

Is it forward I should focus?
Or should I stare behind?
Which way to go? I do not know
A captain I must find

To navigate these waters
I will daily give the wheel
To the Author of the Oceans
Whose Voice can make them still

Who knows the wave's direction
Who set the northern star
Who pens me in the rapids
Who heals this shattered heart

The Captain of this vessel
With The Lighthouse on the shore
And The Spirit's weighty anchor
Would I ever need for more?

I will trust Him on this voyage
Whether wave or calm it be
He'll see me safely homeward
From sea to shining sea.

They pushed me hard
To make me fall
But the LORD helped me.
The LORD is my STRENGTH and my SONG
HE has become my SALVATION.
Psalm 118:13-14

Grief

Yesterday was Roger's 56th birthday. I went to the cemetery at lunch. Standing there alone, with all the horizontal lives silently 'round me, as if I were the center of a compass and the needle was spinning in every direction as I circled completely around, looking at the lives of the past. All the headstones quietly reminding me of the fate to come for us all. The stone at our head. I stood there, staring at the words chiseled into my brother's marker, "*His heart had room for us all.*" I placed some flowers, pulled some weeds, sat sideways on the seat of my truck in silence. Thinking back, remembering when, wishing only if. Treasuries of memories trapped in my mind. The time came too soon for me to drive back to work. Caught up in my thoughts, wrapped up in my grief.

As I drove out of the cemetery, David Jeremiah was on the radio telling the story of how this famous football player was at training camp when his brother unexpectedly died. The athlete was of course heartbroken at the loss of his brother. He returned home, planned the funeral, then returned to training camp. Time passed. When the brother's birthday rolled around, the athlete went to the cemetery (ahmm, at this point I was wide eyed as I listened) but he couldn't find the grave! (Well, at least I know where my brother's grave is, I thought to myself.) The man was in the cemetery crying his heart out and praying, "LORD, help me find him! Help me find my brother!" And very quietly he heard the SPIRIT's whisper, "Why look for the living among the dead?"

I turned the radio off immediately just to catch my breath and absorb what I'd just heard. Not in my ears – in my heart. I needed to grab hold of the hope that the LORD had just given me. I had not been alone in that cemetery. Amid all that horizontal silence, the once horizontal now vertical LORD was there the whole time. He heard my thoughts and saw my tears. He understood my sorrow. He had a message for me, and He used a radio preacher to give it. Right. On. Time.

Roger's sudden death was my own "hell on earth." I'm still wrecked by the loss. I still limp from the grief. But Roger is not dead; he's just not here. He's alive and well and waiting for me there, that coming day when I'll have a headstone of my own. And when I see him, I will run, a'hoopin' and a' hollerin', to hug him, slashing silent separation forever.

There was a well-known tv commercial years ago that said, "Beef. It's what's for dinner." I'd like to introduce you to the same tag line, only exchanging the word "Beef" with "Grief." Yeah, it's so daily. It hits you right in the stomach. You can't go around it, you can't go under it, you can't go over it. You have to go through it. I thank GOD for the provision of my friends. Jehovah Jireh, God Provider, did good when He circled me with them. My few sister friends I have who stood with me in silence when words couldn't be found; who laughed with me so hard that we couldn't breathe. The two that sat quietly on a vinyl couch with me, lights turned off, while I sobbed into a washcloth. They have encouraged me, spurred me on, cheered me forward. My very own steel magnolias. They have given to me, over and over and over. They've held my hand, hugged me hard, giggled like girls, given like saints. They've forgiven my imperfections and strengthened my faith. They walked me, dragged me, coached me through. They've reproved me when I was off center. I love them. Not many women have what I have but every woman needs what I have - a platinum circle of women with arms locked at the elbows and faces set like flint. Oh, my truest sisters, you know who you are. May the GOD OF GODS, LORD OF LORDS, KING OF KINGS, clothe you today with strength from ON HIGH. May HIS RIGHTEOUS RIGHT ARM hold you up; HIS WONDROUS PEACE keep you calm. May HIS LIGHT AND LOVE direct your path; may HIS WISDOM AND HOLINESS be your joy. May HIS ETERNAL FAITHFULNESS anchor you to hope.

Always remember, whether we're up close and personal or a faint echo from a distance, you are greatly loved by this sister in the circle. I love you more than my luggage. And when your evening meal is grief, I'll pull up a chair right beside you, quietly, hand you a wash cloth, and pick up my fork.

And to our Mantha, who walked quietly into the piano room with all the lights off, quietly sat down beside me, said not a word, as I sobbed. Who showed up at the funeral home to help with the planning of the service and picking of the casket. Her Uncle Roger, so adored by his nieces. Mantha represented all three that frozen, dark day.

Dark Swim (2020)

I swim in deep, dark ocean
With eyes searching for shore
The tide sucking me outward
I cannot touch the floor

I swim in deep dark waters
I swim but can't see where
The storm it howls above me
And below me, liquid air

Not sure how long I've been here
Not sure how long I'll last
Not sure if land is out there
My fight is fading fast

Alone in middle ocean
The water crashing high
The creatures circle 'round me

I do not want to die

I scream above the tempest
I scream above the howl
I scream with all that's in me

"OH GOD,
WHERE ARE YOU NOW?

Is this the course YOU set for me?
Is this the plan YOU wrote?
(Seems to me on Galilee
YOU got to have a boat)

And here I am trying to swim
In waters way too deep
I've cried and prayed and prayed and cried
That my soul you would keep"

Yet silence from the heavens
No word from Heaven's throne
No rescue in my vision
I'm still out here, all alone

Then suddenly it hits me
Then suddenly I think
My God is God No Matter
If I swim or if I sink

He's bigger than this ocean
He's stronger than this tide
He's smarter than the creatures
That circle every side

He's the writer and the planner
He's the captain of the sea
He's the warrior and the wordsmith
He's the hand that buoys me

He has the power to scoop me
From the dark and deadly storm
He has the power to rescue me
To pluck me safe from harm

If HE does then HALLELUJAH!
If HE does then PRAISE HIS NAME!

And If HE doesn't?

Well then shouldn't
My response be still the same?

HE is GOD and that's enough
HE is GOD and so I rest
HE is GOD and Wise eternal
Only HE knows what is best

If I swim from now to doomsday
With no land ever in sight
I will praise HIS NAME forever
I will praise HIM THROUGH THIS FIGHT

I will trust HIM in this tempest
I will trust HIM as my boat
I will trust HIM and HIS mercy

I will lie back now and float.

Isaiah 43: "When you pass through the waters, I will be with you, and through the rivers, they shall not overflow you. When you walk through the fire, you shall not be burned, nor shall flame scorch you; FOR I AM THE LORD YOUR GOD. THE HOLY ONE OF ISRAEL. YOUR SAVIOR."

Goliath

It's been a challenging week. Mom's disease (alz) came out of the corner on Monday - fully energized, gloved and ready. It immediately took to boxing us - every one of us - until the final ring of the bell on Friday. No one got a hall pass; everyone got a punch. Round after round, on the verge of a K O. We returned to our corner, bruised and spent. Just being honest. This disease is relentless. It's a Goliath, screaming threats and taking prisoners. Where is our David? Where is our Deliverer? When will this Goliath lay motionless, headless on the ground?

Paul wrote that we are hard-pressed on every side - YET WE ARE NOT CRUSHED. We are struck down - BUT WE ARE NOT DESTROYED. Watching my mama struggle is a perpetual gut punch. Below the belt. Hard press. Struck down. I struggle, tangled in the ropes of the unknown. Yet I hear the faint whisper of a Redeemer Champion. I feel the tingling breeze of a Mighty Rushing Wind. I trust that the Presence of the LORD is here. Right here. I can't give up, I can't give in, I won't give over. I'm still here.

I've written the following for anyone out there that might be on the verge of a K O by life. I remind myself and I exhort you to TRUST IN THE LORD with all your heart. Regardless. As believers, we must trust. Lean not on your own understanding. Goodness knows, dementia makes no sense. Let's acknowledge HIM today. Let's let Him take over the fight. I read somewhere that He's already won. I'm keeping my eye on the Prize. Much love. Stay strong. Keep going. Goliath's going down. Our David is in the valley, taking our place.

When it doesn't make sense
When muscles stay tense
When all strength is spent
I'll trust Him

When tears steady fall
When emotions are mauled
When I'm slowed to a crawl
I'll trust Him

When I want to scream "WHY?"
When I silently cry
When my joy is drained dry
I'll trust Him

When the road fiercely turns
And the waves darkly churn
And the fire closely burns
I'll trust Him

When all seems so lost
When I can't pay the cost
When I'm tumbled and tossed
I'll trust Him

When I trail behind hope
When I struggle to cope
At the end of the rope
I'll trust Him

When there's nothing but pain
When there's nothing but rain
When it all seems insane
I'll trust Him

When I've done all I know
When I have no control
When dementia still grows
I'll trust Him

When my heart's filled with sorrow
Tho I beg, plead and borrow
When I dread the tomorrow
I'll trust Him

When prayers seem unheard
When life seems absurd
I'll stand on His Word
I'll trust Him.

"Tho He slay me, yet will I trust HIM." - Job 13:15

Watching Mama Bye (2016)

I'm losing her.
Little by little.
Day by day.
She slips a step
Deeper
Into unknown.
The not known.
Alone.
A place I pray I never go
While pleading all the while to be her companion
Into the abyss.
Today she knows her daughter.
Today she stays on task.
Tomorrow she will wonder
At the woman at the door.
She doesn't know order.
She can't remember why.
All the while
I'm watching mama bye.

All your waves and billows have gone over me. The LORD will command his lovingkindness in the daytime. His song shall be with me in the night. Psalm 42

Mama (August 2018)

INCH
by inch
I watch her
stripped
Bare

STRIP
by strip
Till she's no longer
There

SHRED
by shred
Torn reckless
Apart

LED
by the med

She's lost in
The dark

SKILL
After skill
Has been stolen
Away

STILL
Eerie still

Day
After
Day

FROZEN
In ACTION
She struggles
To eat

SLOWLY
But surely
She shuffles
Her feet

CAUGHT
Like a fish

SIFTED
Like
wheat

WEAKNESS
Cursed weakness
Encompassing
Rain

BLEAKNESS
This MADNESS

This SPIRAL of pain

Night after night
I recite my case

Fright upon fright
I stand in her place

Time after Time
I lift up my voice

I lay it before HIM

I've no other choice

Prayer after prayer
For Mama,
For grace

Prayer after prayer
I render my case

Hear me
Please hear me
For Mama
I plead

Hear me,
Come near me
MY MAMA NEEDS FREED!

Rend NOW the
Heavens
LORD JESUS
I cry

I KNOW THAT
YOU SEE HER
JEHOVAH
ROI '

JESUS
I BEG YOU
APPOINTED TIME -
COME

LORD JESUS
I PLEAD FOR
A MIRACLE CRUMB

YOU've allowed
For some purpose
This disease to tread prey
Yet mama still trusts in the
LIFE and the WAY

So Hope, LORD,
I hope LORD
Your Mercy WILL
Tug

The Love String
Of Heaven

And free
Junie Bug

On a Sunday (2019)

She slowly glided in her chair. Back and forth. Back and forth. Rhythm. I sat beside. Shoulders almost touching. We listened. The Bill Gaither Homecoming sang through my phone (thanks, Pandora) ... "To the old rugged cross, I will ever be true ... its shame and reproach gladly bear." These are the songs she and I would clean house to every Saturday morning. But in those days, it was heard through a stereo record player and big 33 LP ... Mama and I locked eyes ... unable to join in, she listened as I sang, "Then He'll call me some day to that home far away where His Glory forever I'll share ... "I belted out the chorus while her eyes intently watched me sing, "So I'll cherish the old rugged cross ... till my trophies at last I lay down ... I will cling to the old rugged cross ... and exchange it someday for a crown." My voice crackled, especially on the high notes (thanks, thyroid surgery) but I belted it out, strained it out, refusing to stop, refusing to look away. My eyes locked with hers. Shoulder to shoulder. Back and forth. Just her and me. I'm not sure what she was thinking, but my mind was seeing all my days with mama, all the "just her and me" moments, all jumbled into one second of time. I said, "Mama, we're going to heaven one day." Quiet. So quiet. Back and forth. Back and forth. Her eyes searching mine, she finally said, "That suits me." (Thanks, Jesus.) It suits me too, mama. It suits me too.

The radio shifted to a new song. This time I didn't sing. Not that I didn't want to. It was my turn to listen.

Farther along, we'll know all about it
Farther along, we'll understand why
Cheer up, my (mother)
Live in the sunshine
We'll understand it -
(Alz)
by and by

The Day Room (2018)

I don't know her name. She was sitting in front of mama in a glider rocker, bent forward, talking to herself. Rocking back and forth. In her own reality – far, far away from mine. I couldn't help but watch her. She sat up, turned and made eye contact with me. I handed her a doll. She smiled with her whole face, like a child on Christmas morning. She cradled the doll so gently and began to mouth, "Sweet, sweet baby."

I'm always looking for purpose in this season with mama. God wouldn't put her through this without doing something through this.

Today, He did. He did something for this lady whose name I do not know. But mostly, He did something for me.

When the Saints Came Rollin' In (2018)

There's a baby grand in the dining room. As I told you before about me and a piano, it's steel to magnet – I have to play. While visiting mama, we'd stroll around there to it and without permission from staff, I'd sit down and begin. Whatever came to mind. Whatever song I thought would prompt a memory for her. She there on the bench beside me, this woman who paid for all my piano books and sewed the dresses for all my recitals, sat there quiet. I just kept on playing, believing in my heart that even if her body wouldn't allow her to react, that her heart was singing with fierce passion. Checking her face from time to time for some sort of connection. As we continued, slowly and surely, wheelchairs would begin to creep toward the hymn sound wave… each pulling themselves with the leg strength they could muster, turning the big wheels with houseshoes on tile, one pull at a time forward, headed toward the music down the hall … steel to magnet they were. They would roll in to hear songs like "When the Roll is Called Up Yonder" and "Unclouded Day." It would always send shivers down my spine but I'd keep on playing, knowing full well I wasn't the best player in the world but I would never stop this chain reaction of grace I was caught up in, there on the bench, watching these saints marching in. I remember distinctly beginning to play The Old Rugged Cross. When I got to the chorus, I looked up to see a crumpled, little man, almost balled up in his wheel chair … eyes closed … arms drawn up to his chest … singing loudly every word. Every word. I am tearing up now just remembering him in his praise. A secret moment I was gifted to witness. We may have been sitting in a sterile, fluorescent lit cafeteria, but in our hearts we were on the porch of heaven. I will never forget.

I feel certain that crumpled, little man is now free from that chair, strong and mighty, boundless and free, yet still singing that same old chorus. Only difference is that now he's at the feet of the nail pierced King.

The Gospel Bearer Wears House Shoes
(2019 on a Sunday)

Today I was honored to sit on a vinyl couch under too bright fluorescent lights, holding my mama's hand, listening to one of the purest sermons I've ever heard. The preacher man – a 92 year old resident from the other side of the facility – his house shoes on the wrong feet, his ankles swollen purple, sitting on the back of his walker, frail in body but fervent in spirit. He preached compassionately and without stutter from Matthew 11 – "Come to Me all you who are weary and heavy laden, and I will give you rest." As Mrs. May rhythmically "a manned" in her glider, I tried so hard to take in what I was experiencing, here in this little day room of rockers, filled with the aged, listening to the Good News. As I sat shoulder to shoulder with mama, I thought about sitting beside her on so many pews in our past life, with knee socks and dresses that she had sewn. Listening to the same Good News then as it was proclaimed right here, in this secret church. When it was over, I squeezed mama's hand and said, "How do you feel?" It took her a while to answer, which is common these days. Finally she whispered, "I feel free."

Tis so Sweet and Sweet Petite (2018)

I gave my mom a hymnal this morning. She loves to thumb through and read whatever you give her. She came to "Take the Name of Jesus With You." I started to sing the first verse to help her remember. As I sang, the sweet petite lady beside her dozed. BUT when I got to the chorus, Sweet Petite woke straight up and started to mouth the words, barely making sound, "Precious Name, oh how sweet, Hope of Earth and Joy of Heaven." We sang the remainder of the chorus together, smiling all the while.

Then mom turned to the back and found a reading … you know if you were brought up Baptist, it's those readings at the back of the hymnal where the preacher reads then the congregation joins in when the text is bolded. The one mom chose, #637, stunned me, but she read it slowly, accurately. Word for word. Sweet Petite was back asleep.

Sometimes you wonder if GOD is near. When I walked into the dayroom, I hoped I'd find Him. Well, let me assure you, He was present and accounted for, there on a couch with me and mama and Sweet Petite.

Baptist Hymnal Reading 637

To everything there is a season, and a time to every purpose under the heaven
A time to be born, and a time to die
A time to plant and a time to pluck up that which is planted.
A time to kill and a time to heal.
A time to tear down and a time to build
A time to weep and a time to laugh
A time to mourn and a time to dance
A time to throw stones and a time to gather them up
A time to embrace and a time to avoid
A time to search and a time to count as lost
A time to keep and a time to throw away
A time to tear and a time to sew
A time to be silent and a time to speak
A time to love and a time to hate
A time for war and a time for peace.

What does the worker gain from his struggles? I have seen the task that God has given the children of Adam to keep them occupied.
He has made everything beautiful in its time.
Ecclesiastes 3

Can I ask you, what time is it?

No Mores

I am very tired. I have been mentally making notes of things that are NO MORE as the dementia takes my mama. First it was no more trips to Kroger with her – after the time she refused to get in the car in the parking lot (and the police were called, but let's not remember that). Then it was no more movies with her – after the two times I took her and she said it was way too loud. I have called her pretty much every day all of my life; last night I was driving home and thought, "I'd love to call her but I can't." (no phones in the room and she can't operate a cell). So, I've added this sorrow to my NO MORE list. I carry this sorrow in my heart. Those of you who have lost your mama know the weight. One day I will take the time to grieve, but between work and running hither and thither, that's a time yet to come.

Dementia will continue to take her until she is completely NO MORE.

But then, gloriously, joyfully, amazingly, there will be new NO MORES … NO MORE tears. NO MORE takes. NO MORE death. NO MORE dementia. NO MORE sickness. NO MORE sorrow. NO MORE empty. NO MORE vanishing. To be absent from the body is to be present with the LORD. Our HOPE is in Jesus Christ, the author and **finisher** of our faith. He is the FIRST and the LAST. He has the first and last word. By golly, He is THE WORD. IN HIM all things move and breathe and have their being. My mama is IN HIM. Dementia can't take that.

Habbakuk had a GOD moment when he said –

> Though the fig tree does not bud
> and there are no grapes on the vines,
> though the olive crop fails
> and the fields produce no food,
> though there are no sheep in the pen
> and no cattle in the stalls,
> [18] yet I will rejoice in the LORD,
> I will be joyful in God my Savior.

¹⁹ The Sovereign LORD is my strength;
he makes my feet like the feet of a deer,
he enables me to tread on the heights.

Can't wait to one day meet up with him and say, "Me too, Hab. Me too."

A Daughter's Father (2004)

The following writing is definitely my biggest wrestling. I shall end this section with this finale'. I have contemplated whether or not to even include it. For now it's included. I may remove it at some point later and you will never know. Time will tell.

These are my notes from a time I spoke at a women's conference. Perhaps you can relate.

God has impressed on me a word that He wants me to share that I have entitled "A Daughter's Father." God is obviously wanting to do a work in my life because this area of daughters and fathers is a very tender and protected, private area of my life. It has become clear in the past few days that the LORD wants to heal this old wound. To make myself vulnerable to receive that healing. It scares me to open up this territory in my life because I've hidden it for so long. Subconsciously, I have protected this part of my heart. I have pretended it away. But now I realize He is waiting to heal that real wound. All of the prayers I have prayed to become more like Him, He has obviously taken seriously. Imagine that-Ha. He has pulled back layers of my life and healed me, piece by piece. I know in my innermost being that this is the message He wants us to hear and use it to heal. I pray that for each one who reads about this daughter's daddy.

I grew up the daughter of a pastor. People called him Brother Bob. He preached in small country churches, places where he always had to have a second and third job to make the household ends meet. I was the third of four children, the only girl child. Our length of time at any given church was three to five years. Everyone loved Brother Bob. He just had a charisma about him and an energy and excitement that was contagious. He was a spiritual magnet. God used him in many, many ways.

Brother Bob was a man who could do anything he put his mind to; and he put his mind to a lot. He was a man who loved words. He loved to preach the Word and I loved to hear him preach. Growing up in a traditional, country

Baptist church, we always sang a few hymns. The one standard that opened every service was the Doxology.

Praise God from Whom all blessings flow
Praise Him, all creatures here below
Praise Him above, ye heavenly host
Praise Father, Son and Holy Ghost.
Amen

My daddy loved music. He wrote songs. He had a gift with words and could easily put his poetry to music.

He was a boy scout leader and I was an honorary boy scout troop guest so that mama and I could tag along wherever they went. (Please note we had our own tent.) If the youth of the church needed a trip to Florida, Brother Bob would first find a bus to use, then drive the bus. When a group of kids wanted to learn how to shoot a 410, Brother Bob went through the process of becoming certified with the Fish and Game Commission so he could come back to the youth and teach us how to shoot, then get us certified. He was always asked to preach revivals at surrounding churches. He put a gospel group together called "The Delta Singers" who traveled the state and even recorded an album in Memphis. He later returned and recorded a solo album of his original songs.

Brother Bob was a good father. He loved his kids. He loved doing things with us. He loved to play his guitar and sing. One of my earliest memories is of him lining the four of us up and forcing us to sing, "Daddy Sang Bass." I always got to sing solo the "Mama sang tenor" line. He'd also taught us the song, "Those cottonfields back home." Why? Who knows. The only line I remember from that one is "when those cotton balls get rotten you can't pick very much cotton." Today I read that and think, "What in the world was that about?" Anyway. I'm not sure why he had us singing that. He always took time with us. I remember the day he came home with my first kitten (the first of many critters). He found her in the road driving home from Louisville and took the time to stop, rescue her from the highway, and bring her home to me. Sunflower was her name. She was the matriarch to many kittens. I remember the day he brought home the mini bike. The trampoline. For some reason, he always thought we needed a horse in our life, so we had horses. We always had a dog. He loved to take us fishing. He loved to take us on vacations where we slept in KOA camps in sleeping bags and tents. (And lived to tell about it. I'm sure physical therapists and chiropractors have made a fortune from adults with childhoods like mine.) Daddy really loved that, although I'm not quite sure my mother joined him in that sentiment. I never knew until years later that the Christmas we had our picture taken with Santa at the Sears store, that it was actually my daddy in the Santa suit. He worked at Sears part time and ended up being their Santa. (Spoiler alert – Santa should never keep his red suit in a big box under his bed.)

Anytime there was an accident or medical emergency at my house (and there were many) my daddy always knew what to do. Please understand my three brothers daily tried to kill me. I don't know why but for some reason they thought their purpose on earth was to remove me from it, and I have the scars to prove it. No matter what those three did to me, my daddy always fixed me up. Whether it was the BB out of the nose, the fishhook out of the knee, or the day I was "accidentally" pushed off the back of a car as we were driving along the levee in north Mississippi. Daddy's the one who picked me up from that fall, dusted me off, helped siphon out my mouthful of levee dirt, then made me sit in the front seat of the white Comet with him. The three offenders were still happy go lucky on the trunk, oblivious to my near-death experience. I was thinking the other day how STUPID it was for a parent to let us four kids ride on the back of the car, along the levee in the first place, but praise God there was no car behind us when I went tumbling. God is watching all the time – can I get an amen!

He was a wonderful man. He was a powerful preacher, a compassionate pastor, a great daddy. He loved his kids. And this daughter knew her father's love.

Some of my favorite memories of him and me are when the lines of preacher and daddy mingled together. When we were at church and he would say something about me from the pulpit during the sermon, my pride would swell. My parents had me in piano lessons as a young girl. Every time he needed someone to play a hymn, he'd ask (force) me to do it, encouraging me to do my best and always telling me I did good (even when it was very evident I didn't). Always encouraging me. Always building me up. Training me up. Anytime I got to church without my Bible, I knew I could just run to his office and ask him for one. I'd feel so special going back to Sunday school with it, knowing that no other child in the room had that power.

Thinking through all this, I figured out my most favorite memory. My most favorite memory is when I would be at church and would get cold, I would ask daddy for his suit coat. Daddy always wore suits at church. He was a big man, tall with broad shoulders. A John Wayne kind of man. Whenever I would get cold, I would just ask him for his coat. He'd immediately give it, and I would wrap my little boney self up in it and go lay down on a pew. I could get all of me inside that coat. I can remember how it smelled – a sweet, salty, sweaty smell mixed with a little cologne. Let's face it, it smelled like my daddy. Now of course, it would completely swallow me and I looked ridiculous in it, but I felt 10 feet tall when I had it on. I felt privileged and special. A lot of times I wouldn't even be cold when I would ask for it. I learned there was recognition in that coat. I wanted people to see that Brother Bob had a daughter, a special daughter that got to wear his coat. I wanted to be set apart from the rest of the girls in the congregation. I wanted to be claimed as his. That is my favorite memory.

I loved my daddy. I was secure in the fact that he loved me. I respected him and was oh, so proud of him. I looked up to him. I depended on him. I believed in him. I knew without a shadow of a doubt, that he could solve any problem that would come my way. I found rest in that. When a storm blew up, as long as my daddy was there, that storm was going to pass over. Anything that was broken, he could fix. Or semi-fixed. :/ (Duct tape and hangars were his toolbox.) I felt like all my friends were jealous because Brother Bob was my dad and not theirs. I know that's not true but that's how this daughter felt. That made me feel special and set apart. I had his last name. And his name meant something.

Then tragedy struck our family when my oldest brother was killed in a car accident with his two best friends. I remember being picked up from school early that day by some of the church members. I remember Roger in the backseat with me. The church members didn't speak to us on the drive home. I remember seeing all the parked cars along our driveway and along the road outside our house. I remember walking into a house full of people, being led to the den where my mom and dad sat, crying. Randy was in the side chair, crying. They explained to us that Butch, Ross and Jimmy had died on their way to school.

Later that day when most of the company had left, daddy took Randy, Roger and me on a walk. He gathered us up in a little circle to talk about Butch and about heaven. He asked us to get on our knees there in our backyard, and through many tears, daddy prayed for help to get our family through this unspeakable tragedy.

That happened three days before my 11th birthday. My daddy was 36 years old. I watched over the next decade or so how my daddy began to change. How a hardness came over him. How the hurt in him never healed. He still cared for and loved his family, but this big, strong, powerful daddy now had a limp. Not on the outside but a limp on the inside. I look back now and see that he never truly recovered from Butch's death, he didn't know how to deal with it and besides who does a pastor go to in 1973 when he has a problem? When the congregation's counselor needs counseling, where does he go? Where does he turn?

Years passed. I became a teenager, a high school senior. 1980. Our home life began to change. I knew something wasn't right but didn't know exactly what.

I learned that my dad had made some very bad choices that involved another woman in the church. Now, in my mind I was thinking, "Wait a minute. Not MY daddy. This man who took me fishing, who held the reins on the pony and led me around the yard, the one who would wrap me up in his Sunday coat. The one revered by all who knew him." Shaken trust, stolen love, broken belief. That's what this little girl had then. And Shame. Let's not leave that out. Everything I thought true of him wasn't true anymore. I couldn't depend on a man who would choose another woman over my mama. I didn't know that man. I didn't want to know that man.

I was 17 years old. My dad was 42. I graduated high school, my parents divorced, my mom, brothers and I moved to Jackson. Scarred from the scandal but determined to survive. In that season, my daddy stopped being my daddy. He more or less dropped out of my life. I no longer had him to trust, no longer had him to depend on. I was a given-up girl. I saw him from time to time but from that point on, it was never the same. It was as if someone else had taken over my daddy's body, and I didn't know who this new person was. I no longer felt safe with him. I didn't trust him. I didn't even like him at that point. The anger within my heart toward him seared. He had hurt my mama, my brothers, me. He couldn't fix that. He had made a choice and walked away from his own family. We had been left in his dust.

He moved in and out of my life from then on. When I became engaged and married, he came to the wedding long enough to walk me down the aisle, then immediately left the church. When I had our Jess, he drove to see her as a newborn. I have one picture of him holding her. He never met our Mantha. His visits became less and less frequent, his calls became seldom. I learned to live without a daddy. More than that, I learned to close off that area of my life. I learned how to wall in that section of my heart. My hurt. I pretended to not have a daddy. I learned to not need him.

That went on for 17 years or so. It's amazing to me as I write this that from the age of 1 to 17, I had a wonderful daddy; then for the next 17 years, he disappeared from my life. AND that as I write this, my daughter is 17 years old.

Around 1995 or 1996, I hadn't heard from daddy in a few years, and I began to have a daily faint needling in me that I needed to write him a letter. I needed to first find him, then open the lines of communication. I wanted to try to bridge back to some sort of relationship. By that time I had two children; one he had met as a newborn; the other he had never met. I knew he was living in Oklahoma with his sister. I would think through the mechanics of writing the letter, what it would say, how I would say it, mailing it to my aunt's home and asking her to give it to him. I rehearsed the content of the letter over and over in my mind, the lover of words that I was. A gift I got from him. It was a great plan. But I never wrote it on paper. I thought it through a million times, I just never followed through with the actual action of it. That was 1996. On October 7, 1997, my daddy died at a truck stop in Terrell, Texas. He had died within me 17 years before; but now his physical death took away any chance at restoration. My hope for reunion was gone.

I lived 17 years of my life with a wonderful daddy, followed by 17 years of desertion. The same man both loved me and left me. The same man both believed in me and betrayed me. He encouraged me then excused himself from my life. I couldn't think through any of that at the time, so I made the passive decision to just not think of it at all. To pretend it never happened. To erase all memory – both good and bad. To not think about it and maybe it will go away. To place it all, the good and the bad, in a Tupperware container, place the lid down tight, lock it in (#tupperwareburp), and hide it away.

I have found out today at the age of 41, that God will bring all hidden things to light, sooner or later. In His perfect timing. Things just don't go away. God knows my innermost being, He knows every wound, He knows every bondage, He knows every sorrow. The LORD knows when to say it's time to reveal the hidden things. He knows when it's time to open up that Tupperware. To stop pretending. The LORD has told me that it's time to bring this out in me and out of me so that healing can come in. For some reason, He is doing it in front of you. I have to believe there are other daughters who need healing as well.

Because of my relationship with daddy, I had a skewed picture of God, the true Father. In the Trinity He is God the Father, God the Son, God the Holy Spirit. I knew God the Son, Jesus Christ. I was saved as a 9 year old girl and learned the New Testament growing up as a child. My whole Christian life was based on Jesus Christ. In 1997, when my husband's horror was happening and my dad died in the midst of it, I got the privilege of meeting God the Holy Spirit. I have grown in my relationship with Him and am learning to hear Him and move with Him throughout my days.

But the LORD is now taking me full circle to meet the first member of the Trinity. God the Father. God wants me to know that He is my Father. My Daddy. My Abba. To understand fully that I am His daughter. Not just in my head, but in my heart. To somehow find the courage to trust a Father again, to call Him Abba and truly know what that means.

Can I trust Him as a daddy? My Father says I can trust Him with my whole heart.

Will He desert me? My Father says He will never leave me or forsake me.

Will He remain constantly faithful to me? My Father says that He is faithful and even when I am unfaithful that He remains faithful for He cannot deny Himself.

Will He make a bad choice that will affect me? My Father says that the plans He has for me are for my good and not evil, to prosper me and not to harm me. To give me a future and a hope.

Can I depend on Him? My Father says, "With man it is impossible, but with Me, all things are possible." And then He backs that up with, "Cast your cares on Me, for I care for you."

Is there a chance He will wound me? My Father says that a bruised reed He will not break and a dimly burning wick He will not extinguish.

Will this Daddy decide to change? My Father declares that He is the same yesterday, today and forever. He will not, cannot change.

He loves me. The Bible says that there is no where I could go that would separate me from His love. No height, no depth, no width could measure the greatness of His love toward me. The Bible says that He sings over me with joy. The Bible says that He is enthralled with my beauty.

It's my choice. All of this time as a saved woman, I have not known Him as Father. I have said it hundreds, perhaps thousands of times in prayers, "Our Father in heaven." I have read it in the Word but I have not believed it for me. My idea of a father was modeled by one man who walked two roads – that of daddy and deserter. A good man of bad choices. A man who started with charisma and ended with chaos. A man who made mistakes that rippled down on top of a whole slew of people. That's my perception of "Father." Calling God Almighty "daddy" is almost too intimate for me to do, because that is touching something in me that hasn't been touched in a very long time. Something that I had hidden away (and Tupperware doesn't leak). But the LORD wants all of me. It is His desire for me and you to know Him as Abba.

Abba loves His daughters. He wants us to trust that love. He wants us to trust Him, believe Him, depend on Him, know Him. God knew when He created families that the man would be a symbol of Him. He knew we would always fall short of His perfect plan but He wanted man to imitate within his own limitations a picture of God. Now I'm not trying to rake anyone over hot coals or point fingers or place blame, all I am trying to understand for myself is how am I going to open that hidden box in my heart so that God – my Father – can heal it? I don't have that answer yet but I am on the journey. And what God starts, God finishes.

I'm reminded of Eve. I just realized for the first time that she was the last of creation. And you know what we say, "He saved the best for last." But then I also realized that the last thing created – woman – was the first to sin. Bummer. There the two of them were, Adam and Eve, naked, bare, hiding in the trees as God was walking in the garden in the cool of the day. God called out to them, "Where are you?" He already knew, He just wanted confession at that point. Of course, when they were found by Him, all they did was blame another so that they wouldn't look guilty. But what they looked like was naked. They couldn't hide from God. The Bible says that when God saw their nakedness, He made coats of skin for them to wear. He clothed them.

He put a coat on them.

I told you earlier that my most favorite memory is that of wearing my daddy's coat. I told you how special I felt in that coat, how it smelled like him, how warm it was, how secure I felt in it. The LORD wants me to know and wants you to know that He has a coat for us to wear. He wants us to know that He has prepared it for us and we will feel special when we wear it, we'll be secure within it; it will set us apart, it will make us smell like Him. In order for us to wear His coat, we have to come out of the trees. We have to stop hiding, stop pretending that nothing is wrong. We have to hear Him call our name as He passes by, and we have to respond to that call. We have to come out of the trees and we have to confess our nakedness to Him. We have to hand Him the Tupperware. He has a coat waiting for us. He's prepared it, tailored to our inches, for He knows our frame. Perfect fit.

I want to know Him as Father. I want to be able to call Him Daddy. I want to be healed from the hurts of past years and be whole. I want all of my nakedness to be covered up with the coat He has for me. I want to hear Him call my name. I want to be a daughter again. I want His aroma on me. I want to trust Him completely, be secure in His love for me, be totally dependent on Him.

I don't know what your relationship with your earthly father has been. I pray it has been wonderful, steady, always healthy. I hope that if your father is still living, that you'll make a point to tell him how thankful you are for his indelible impression on your life. If your relationship with your daddy is severed, I would challenge you to ask the Holy Spirit for restoration. That is between you and the Holy Spirit. For many of us our fathers have already passed away and talking with them is impossible. I regretted for many years the fact that I never wrote that letter. I have asked and received forgiveness for my passiveness. My fear. My disobedience. I am learning to remember both the good and the bad – and not be afraid or ashamed of either. I am learning to have a relationship with my Abba Father. I want to know Him more, to love Him more, to be fully dependent on Him.

But most of all, I want to always wear His coat.

Psalm 23 (2010)

I need
Your calm and Your comfort
Green pastures, quiet waters

Your rod and Your staff
Your strength and Your guide

Your presence and power
Protection and peace

Your hand and Your hold

I need to lay down and rest
As You watch, on alert

To fall back with eyes closed
On the meadow of safety
Fully trusting my Keeper
With the chaos of life

I need restoration
From complication

I need to eat from the bounty
Daily set on Your table

To drink in the water
To inhale the grace

To watch from this pleasure
As the enemy is thwarted
Re-routed, removed
Cut off from my life

To dwell in the knowing
That You are the Shepherd
And I am the sheep

As long as I follow
The path You have chosen
Your goodness and mercy
Will passionately pursue, quietly lead me home.

This is all I need.

Power

HE'S More Than Just a Hobby

HE'S more than just a hobby
Or a medal on the wall
He's more than just a love note
Or a late night distress call
He's more than just a bell boy
Or a t-shirt that we wear
He's more than just a chorus
That we sing from padded chair
He's more than just a symbol
That is hung around our necks
He's more than just the driver
Taking wheels, preventing wrecks
HE'S GOD ALMIGHTY
EL SHADDAI
JEHOVAH
ELOHIM
EMMANUEL
THE LORD OF HOSTS
TO WHOM ALL ANGELS SING
THE GREAT IAM
THE KING OF KINGS
THE GLORY AND THE GRACE
THE PRINCE OF PEACE
THE HOLY FIRE
NOT HELD BY TIME OR SPACE
THE LIVING WATER
LIVING WORD
THE GOD WHO NEVER FAILS
STRONG TOWER
INFINITE POWER
THE GOD WHO TOOK OUR NAILS
GIVE HIM HONOR
GIVE HIM GLORY
GIVE HIM ALL HE'S DUE
GIVE HIM WORSHIP
GIVE HIM PRAISE
GIVE HIM ALL OF YOU.

Am I Faithfully Fearful or Fearlessly Faithful?

I was saved as a little girl. What I mean by "saved" is that I had heard the Gospel – the Good News - of Jesus, I had listened with my heart's ears to the message of salvation. I had heard it many times before, but that time, the Fisherman's net caught me. In that moment I understood a decision for my eternity needed to be made, and I made the choice. My choices were one of two – to accept or reject Jesus. Your choices are the same, by the way. (Please choose The A Way.) I decided to ask Jesus to live with me through this life and be the Lord of my life. Now I didn't understand that at the time, but that's what the decision meant. That was my beginning. My daddy was my pastor and I remember running down the aisle to him with tears on my cheeks. I remember being wrapped into his embrace. I can still smell that sweet, salty-hot smell, his woody cologne mixed with sweat. Wrapped up in the dark of that daddy hug at the end of that aisle, in front of the knotted pine communion table, I asked to be saved. For Jesus to ask the Father for me. I didn't understand the eternity of that decision or all the disciplines that were to come or all the lessons I would endure as I grew in my faith. I just knew I had been convicted to run to Jesus. The run was my first step. The aisle, my first journey. Daddy's arms, my first destination. I wanted Jesus in my heart. Since then, I have had a relationship with Him. Now, in utmost honesty, my relationship with the Lord hasn't always been up close and personal. Spiritual binoculars have had to be used at times in my Christian walk to see the true and living God in my life. There've been times when I've run senselessly away from rather than clung desperately to. Choices always filter down to two, don't they? My prodigal adventure would last for a time, but never at the point of too long. The Holy Spirit wouldn't allow that to continue and was with me wherever I wandered, wooing me back (Psalm 139). Once you are the Lord's, you are.

The poem ONLY was written in April 2003. I don't remember the messy situation that I was neck deep in. I do remember scrawling these words in a journal with tears in my eyes at my kitchen table. I was obviously remembering my faith in the midst of the mess and staking yet another claim for Christ's authority in my life. Another pin in the map. I was 41 years old.

Only

Only through the blood of Christ
Only through His Sacrifice
Only in His bleeding side
I hide myself in Thee

Only when I'm feeble, still
Only when I break my will
Only when I lay it down
I crown HIM LORD of all

Have I bled with willing blood?
Have I stood amidst the flood?
Have I drunk from that same cup
He offered up for me?

Can I live after I die?
Can broken wings give lift to fly?
Can I soar into the sky
With my Savior as my all?

All I was is now no more
I find in death an open door
With nothing left, I walk toward
My LORD who died for me

I tell HIM there is nothing left
All is empty now
Lifeless
He holds me to His beating chest
"Now Rest, my child in ME"

"Through death alone
Your life is new
I've waited all this time for you
To die the death, to bear the cross,
To suffer loss
for ME

And now I give you all I have
For every wound IAM the salve
I fill your mouth, I quench your thirst
But first - you had to die

Abundant life to you I give
I died so that you too can live
You've died the death
now LIFE has won

Arise, my love, in ME."

I have been crucified with Christ and I no longer live, but Christ lives in me.
The life I now live in the body, I live by faith in the Son of God, who loved me and
gave himself for me. I do not set aside the grace of God,
for if righteousness comes through the law, then Christ died for nothing.
Galatians 2:20-21

Sisters, Remember

I love you. God reigns. Just wanted to remind you that His ways are perfect and so much higher than ours. I wanted to ensure you remembered that His plan and His purposes are exceedingly, abundantly more than we could ever fathom them to be ... and that our legs are becoming like hind's feet so that we can stand on our high places. Don't ever forget that He led us out so that He could lead us in. Ewe, sweet sheep, know His voice and follow close.

I need to implore you to know that God is faithful even when we're not; He's worthy and He's righteous and has given us the gift to be called the children of God. Don't forget that He suffered and died but that death couldn't contain Him. Think on the fact that He walked the road, The Way walked all the way to the end. He completed His mission. He could've called 12 legions of angels but like a sheep before the shearer, He opened not His mouth. Remember that we want to know Him, in the power of His resurrection and in the fellowship of His suffering. Meditate today on the truth that He lives, resurrected in power and all authority is in His hand. Marvel at the truth that He's seated right now at the right hand of the Father, and we, clothed in the righteousness of Jesus, are seated with Him. Never forget that He intercedes for His own - and that includes you and that includes me. He knows our name. It's written on His hand. Revel in the excitement that one day He's coming from on high, we will be changed in a moment, we'll meet Him in the clouds and forever we will be with the Lord. On that day, there'll be no more tears, no more night, no more pain. There'll be no more violence, no more hatred, no more prejudice, no more selfishness. There'll be no more wealthy, no more poverty, no more darkness, no more hunger, no more fatherless, no more governments, no more loneliness, no more sadness, no more sickness. No more tornadoes, earthquakes, tsunamis, floods. No more landslides, mudslides, suicides. O GREAT JEHOVAH GOD, FATHER OF ALL, we look forward to that GLORIOUS DAY.

Today, regardless of sickness or situation, no matter the problem or pain, cast off the crisis and chaos because we have Jesus, the Hope of Glory. We are His and He is ours. He is for us, not against us. He is our shield and our rear guard. He is the one who is closer than a brother. Having a bad day? Sometimes you just need to lay hands on yourself and anoint yourself with Truth.
Not convinced? Read it again.

The Blood. The Wine. The Water. The Vine.
(2003)

During a beach trip, I sat on the sand staring at the endless ledge of H^2O, just spending time in quiet meditation. I asked the LORD to talk to me about the water. Ask and you shall receive (I read that somewhere). Over the next couple of days I would sit on the balcony of our condo and look at the vastness of the ocean. The endlessness. Aquaternity. With my Bible in my lap, God took me to many different verses in scripture and dropped this "knowing" into my spirit.

The first miracle in the Old Testament the LORD performed with water is when He turned it into blood. You can read all about it in Exodus as He was fulfilling His plan of freedom for His people through a man named Moses. The first miracle in the New Testament the LIVING WATER performed was when He turned the water into wine at a wedding in Cana when man's wine ran out. (You can read all about it in the gospel of John.)

Water.
Water to Blood.
Water to Wine.
Water.

We can't get the true wine without first going through the Lord's Blood. Everything we go through here on earth, we must first pass through "the blood" to get to "the wine." To come to the LORD, you must go through the

Blood of Jesus; He will then open up to you the eternal supply of The Best Wine. For HE is the Vine. Every trial, every pain, every gritting of the teeth here on earth is part of the molding process ordained by Him. When you walk through the Blood of Jesus, when you take His cup and drink, the LORD will then serve you the wine. What is the wine, you ask? His Presence. An awareness of His Presence, His Goodness, His Love. His Wing of Safety. The surety of eternity. At first we sip cautiously, then as we trust Him, we gulp it in. AW Tozer wrote, "He has both satisfied me yet left me thirsty for more." His cup is ever full, perpetually overflowing. Yes, the trials and pains continue on this orb of sinful sod but we as His children are to, because of His Blood, focus only on the wine He has offered. And we, with the attendees at the wedding in Cana will proclaim, "Where has this been all my life! This is so much better than the man-made bitterness I drank before! You have certainly saved this best for my last!" As believers, this is indeed part of our inheritance.

Don't give up – persevere! Hope in Him! This pain – this blood of sorts on earth – will pass. The wine – the sweetness, the goodness, the satisfaction, will come. Believe the Vine when He says, "This is My Blood which is poured out for you."

Come, Taste and See that the Lord is good.

And He took the cup of WINE and said, "This is MY BLOOD."

Jesus, our Bridegroom, has entered into a wedding filled with the Bride (His church). They are fellowshipping with each other, drinking something made by man. Second best. Adding ingredients along the way, spicing up the recipe, coaxing their audience to drink. And like all things made by man, it eventually runs out. This causes panic with the head of the household, the one in charge of the counterfeit, dust-made festivities. Watered down gospel is not the Gospel. Ever trying to please, now his cover blown. He is bankrupt. Empty. Finally empty. Enter the Lord Jesus. Staring at the empty vessels, His heart broken with compassion, knowing that He Himself is our wine. He instructs the servants to take six pots (the biblical number of man), fill them with water, pour it out, drink it up. The miracle. The water is now the superior wine. He took the ordinary and made it extraordinary. The old is gone, the New has come! Man exclaimed, "This is better than the first! Where have you been hiding this? Why did we have to drink that other concoction! This! This is the best!" And they guzzle it down.

Anything, A N Y T H I N G the Lord Jesus does is better than what flesh man could ever possibly do. Christ's sole purpose for His three years on earth was to pay the penalty of man so that man could drink from this new wedding cup. The original recipe (by The Way).

111

Now the dilemma is, "Which wine is in our cup?" Is it man-forged or miracle poured? Has our counterfeit supply run out, leaving our mouths dry, wanting for more? Oh yes, that first sip was so sweet, but it didn't take long for its flavor to turn, exposing its own sour, bitter fake in our mouth. Are you drinking that?

Or have you switched your cup to the Miracle Maker Who satisfies the very depth of your thirst? Have you drunk your fill to find your cup full still? Ahhh, how our Lord loves to fill things. And if we have tasted this miracle wine, who are we now pouring and passing it to? Who needs it? If it's never poured out, it's not a miracle. If it's not shared, no one knows the difference. It's only when the clay pot is tilted over and poured out for someone who has never tasted, someone who doesn't know, the one who believes he's tasted all there is. He is the one who needs this new cup. Only then does the miracle occur. Father God, pour us out on those who need a taste of heaven. Pass us around, cup by cup, to the ordinary and let them exclaim, "This is extraordinary … I never knew … this is the best wine! You've saved the best for last! Jesus, save me."

Let the miracle of Cana continue through us, cup by cup, as we wait for our Bridegroom to take us home to the marriage supper of the Lamb. (The Saved have a seat. Will you sit by me?). ☺

Rock

The needs in our lives are constant. Seems like we get over one stone just to find a boulder waiting on the other side. Roadrunner and Coyote. Incoming anvil. FORE! Every day. Over time, that gets exhausting. (And painful.) I am praying today that the **ROCK OF OUR SALVATION** will intervene in each of our lives and will shatter the teeth of the enemy on our behalf.

The various episodes currently streaming into my life seem overwhelming. However, I have seen an OVERWHELMING GOD at work and so I will not fear. He's got this whole world of mine in His Hands. And yours too. Whatever you're dealing with in your own world, the LORD is at work … perhaps in ways you can see, perhaps in ways you can only trust. But HE is there and HE is on your side. I know you believe that.

I pray that HE shows HIMSELF strong in each of our lives today. He is an awesome God. We watch for Him, for He will surely come; He will not delay.

The God of RE

The prefix, "Re" is defined by Webster as: to do again, <u>repeat</u>, go back, <u>return</u>

Our God is the God of RE
- REpairer of the Breach
- REsurrection and the Life
- REwarder of those who trust Him
- God of REcompense
- REfuge
- REdeemer
- REscuer
- REnewer
- REvivor
- REstorer
- God Who REmembers

To REceive Him, what must I do?
- REpent.

The Animals' Business Meeting

"Ok, ok, everyone here? Good. The question in heaven today is, "Why are you here?" So, with that, let's get started. You there, you go first please."

"I gave Adam and Eve clothes" *baa'd the sheep.*
"I helped Noah find land!" *Cooed the dove.*
"I replaced Isaac on the mountain" *rumbled the ram.*
"I helped change Jonah's mind" *bubbled the whale.*
"We didn't eat Daniel" *roared the pride of lions.*
"I carried Jesus to Bethlehem so he could be born!" *Heehaw'ed the donkey.*
"I carried Jesus to Jerusalem so he could be killed" *squealed the donkey's colt.*
"I helped build Peter's testimony" *crowed the rooster.*

"And you. Why are you here?"

"I'm waiting for the saddle." announced the majestic white stallion, while pawing the ground in his stall.

Be the Beam

May the LORD bless you with constant Christmas – before, during, and long after. Eternally. I heard a song this morn on Moody radio that said, "when all the angels bow down, and the saints receive their crown, then it will be, FOREVER CHRISTMAS." Yes and Amen. We are one day closer to our reality.

I pray the truest love of Christ be truly known by you. I pray that the Beam of Heaven shines anew into every crack and crevice, every dark place, every hidden place be filled afresh with knowledge of CHRIST. Let our dry patches become drenched puddles. Let streams overflow in our deserts. Let the BEAM be. It cannot be contained, stalled or stilled. The nails couldn't stop it.

It must MOVE.

And so must we. We must move. Say the words, do the deeds, show His Love, **BE THE BEAM.** There are three types of BEAMS that come to mind – 1) a ray of light (*for sight*) 2) a balance bar (*for hind's feet*) and 3) a foundation piece (*for anchor*). Again, I say, BE THE BEAM. There is no time to waste, to rest on our laurels, to pass today's assignment to "tomorrow." In this hellish, angry, evil, violent, maddening black darkness in which we live today, tomorrows are not promised. BE THE BEAM today.

And you, *beloved*, are the light of the world. A city built on a hilltop cannot be hidden. Similarly, it would be silly to light a lamp and then hide it under a bowl. When someone lights a lamp, she puts it on a table or a desk or a chair, and the light illuminates the entire house. *You are like that illuminating light.* Let your light shine everywhere you go, *that you may illumine creation,* so men and women everywhere may see your good actions, *may see creation at its fullest, may see your devotion to Me,* and may turn and praise your Father in heaven *because of it.* – Jesus Christ, The Sermon on the Mount (Matthew 5-7, The Message Bible)

Wisdom (2020)

In the book of Proverbs, I have studied through to chapter 8. I am reading it through The Message version. Here are a few side notes from Robin White Feather:

King David wrote the majority of the Psalms, the book just prior to Proverbs. The Psalms is a book of praise to our God. Was David a perfect man? Nope. Did God use him? Yep.

Solomon, David's second son with Bathsheba, wrote the Proverbs. Just following praise comes the manual to wisdom. Was Solomon perfect? Ahmmm, double nope. His father, David brought in one woman, Bathsheba. Solomon brought in hundreds of 'em. Hundreds. Do you see how in just one generation, things can multiply? Be they good or be they bad ... hmmm ... BUT GOD still used him. Yep. He built the glorious gold temple. He wrote the Proverbs.

A person filled with PRAISE (psalms) and WISDOM (proverbs) can't be shaken. Or I think the scriptures say, "can't be greatly shaken." I heard Jack Graham say yesterday, "We are always in the middle of the griddle." Loved that. And none of us are perfect but He uses us anyway.

A thought to percolate: Wisdom and Insanity, polar opposites, are portrayed as women all through the Proverbs. They are given she/her pronouns. Why is that? Could it be because only women can birth something through them, into the next generation? Is LADY WISDOM calmly, quietly waiting to fill me so that I can birth wisdom? Is LADY INSANITY screaming at me to come close so that I can birth its heir? Each is wanting my companionship. Each is wanting a relationship so that it can be continued through me, through you, to your kin. A multiplication of something to someone else. Hmmm ... and so I get to choose.

Here are a few of the excerpts from the Message version that struck me:

Proverbs 1 – "A manual for living. The first step in learning is bowing down to GOD." "Carelessness kills. Complacency is murder. First pay attention to me (*wisdom*) and then relax. Now you can take it easy – you're in good hands."

Proverbs 2 – "Search for (wisdom) like a prospector panning for gold." (how great is that)

Proverbs 3 – "Don't lose your grip on Love and Loyalty." "Listen for God's voice in everything you do, everywhere you go." "Never walk away from someone who deserves help; your hand is GOD's hand for that person." (wow) "stupid living gets the booby prize." (hahaha)

Proverbs 4 – "The ways of right living people glow with light; the longer they live, the brighter they shine." (loved that – need to recharge my batteries) "Keep your eyes straight ahead; ignore all sideshow distractions." (Boy, am I distracted these days!)

Proverbs 5 – "Mark well that GOD doesn't miss a move you make; HE's aware of every step you take." (and that's not lyrics from the 80's band, The Police)

Proverbs 6 – "So how long are you going to laze around doing nothing?" (whoa) "Can you build a fire in your lap and not burn your pants?" (no you can't – don't play with fire)

Proverbs 7 – This proverb made me think of another thing Jack Graham said … "At first sin fascinates. Then it assassinates." (whoa)

Proverbs 8 – "I am Lady Wisdom; and I live next to Sanity. Knowledge and Discretion live just down the street." (I loved that neighborhood) (this next verse is speaking of how WISDOM was there at the beginning) "Day after day I was there (at the beginning) with my JOYFUL APPLAUSE, always enjoying HIS company. Delighted with the world of things and creatures. Happily celebrating the human family." HOW BEAUTIFUL IS THAT! The banner over us is LOVE AND WISDOM OBVIOUSLY! Then the proverbs goes on to say, "Mark a life of **discipline** and live wisely; don't squander your precious life."

Mark a life. Squander a life. What shall we choose?

The Beginning and the End (2004)

God chose a poor, humble righteous man named Joseph to be the first to hold Jesus's body as he helped Mary bring the Savior of the world into the world. God chose a rich, humble, righteous man named Joseph to be the last man to hold Jesus's body when he took HIM down from the Cross. One Joseph laid Jesus in a food trough. One Joseph laid Jesus in a newly hewn, never used tomb. Two men. Same name. One LORD, who came out of both.

The wise men, on their search for Jesus, asked Herod, "Where can we find The King of the Jews who has been born?" The birth on earth of Christ. On the last day of The King's life on earth, Pilate wrote a sign that hung above Jesus that said, 'The King of the Jews," and nailed it above His bleeding body. The wise men were the first to call Him King at His birth. Some 33 years later, Pilate was the last to declare it so at His death.

Ain't (2005)

I am praying harder than ever before. I am eating scripture all day long. I am learning to stand in shoes of faith. To speak my faith. To put those soundwaves out there for the spiritual realm to hear. I want what I say to shake the foundation of evil. I am past my broken-down place. My heart is broken but my spirit is rising up. I will choose to believe that whatever hard thing I have to walk through, that there are good things on the end of it. I had declared this year as my year of Jubilee, and I have believed that July 7, 2005 (7 7 7) was my Jubilee date. I believe that all this mess I am living in right now is in direct relation to my Jubilee, as weird as that sounds. Perhaps the way I see Jubilee and the way God sees it are different. This has been one of the scariest, darkest weeks of my life, but Praise God, I lived through it and He made me strong. I am not giving in to the devil and I refuse to give up my family to the devil. I am a woman, standing in faith today, on behalf of my husband and kids. In the spiritual places I am running to the edge of this earthly veil and I'm screaming into the spiritual realm, "HEY! You can come against me with sword and spear and javelin, but I'm coming against you in the NAME OF THE LORD OF LORDS AND THE KING OF KINGS. I declare my faith in Jesus Christ today and I am covered in the BLOOD OF THE PASSOVER LAMB. Every death angel – take notice – you have to pass over. The King of Kings is my Father and I am in covenant with Him, declared holy and righteous and a part of His family. The righteous will never be forsaken nor will I beg for bread. My family is blood bought and grace grown. Every spirit from hell, take notice – I demand you, through the authority of JESUS CHRIST AND THE BLOOD HE POURED OUT, to return to the pit of hell empty handed. You ain't taking nothing from this family with you. You tell your defeated master that your time has expired and the ONE WHO HAS THE KEYS will bind you up and lock you up in the hell of hells. My family will endure and prosper and live out the good plans HE has for us. I am sitting down at this table HE's prepared for me today and I want the enemy to watch me eat.

It's unsure at this point what we will have to lose materially to get through. It is unsure what tomorrow will bring. But this I know, that the GOD, who began a good work in me, in Steve, in my home, will see that good work to COMPLETION. And I will live in my JUBILEE.

It' ain't over till HE says it's over.

No Matter

Believing God. A measure of faith. Looking the enemy in the eye and telling him to GO and be gone. Reminding yourself, your family and the spiritual places who you are IN CHRIST. Saying to that mountain, MOVE! And refusing to take no for an answer. I had to make a choice. To be a woman of God. To pray my family through. I had to make a choice to believe GOD for Who He says He is and that He'll do what He says He will do. I had to be the one in my household to grab onto the hands of my family and say to them, "Do not fear! Do not be afraid!" I could either back up or back down or I could hunker down and stand up … I could dig my feet into the earth and stand. And that is what I've tried to do. To live my faith. To speak my faith. To believe in THE ONE Who is my faith. That doesn't mean I haven't cried a million tears or laid in my bed and "what if'd" my life. I started on this journey with phrases like, "The LORD is gonna make this right and make that right" and I've ended up in a place that says, "No matter what happens, no matter what I lose, no matter what I go through, I will be safe from harm, for I am in His Hand."

Faith pleases God. It gets His attention. He is the Rewarder of those who diligently seek Him.

Yes, today I could choose to fall away. Or I could choose to faith the day. Today, faith has my focus. One day at a time.

Rocks (2004)

I told everyone I wouldn't be at work today but then got up and came in anyway. He's home asleep. He was up most of the night. I was too, but for a different reason. I journaled and read my bible on forgiveness. God broke me and made me "drop the rocks." Remember the story of the woman in the circle of men that were about to stone her? Jesus said, "Those that are without sin can cast the first stone." He convicted my heart last night and told me that I had to drop the rocks. So I drew rocks in my journal and wrote words on them

– anger, revenge, uncaring, self-pity, hopelessness, hatred, hurt, wounded, you know, hard rock words that had bouldered in my heart. I had to stay up until I could pray to forgive him. Then, I had to stay up until I forgave him. I had to stay up until the avalanche fell. And praise God, it did. I found my oil and anointed the house. At midnight, I went in the bedroom and anointed him. I told him the LORD had told me to do it. He weakly said, "Go for it."

We're going for it.

David said to the Philistine: "You come against me with a sword, spear and javelin, but I come against you in the NAME OF THE LORD OF ARMIES, THE GOD OF THE RANKS OF ISRAEL. You have defied Him. Today, the LORD will hand you over to me. Today, I'll strike you down, remove your head, and give the corpses of the Philistine camp to the birds of the sky and the wild creatures of the earth. Then all the world will know that Israel has a God, AND THIS WHOLE ASSEMBLY WILL KNOW THAT IT IS NOT BY SWORD OR BY SPEAR THAT THE LORD SAVES, FOR THE BATTLE IS THE LORD'S. 1 Samuel 17: 45-47

The LORD is THE LORD,
The Only Wise God (2010)

HE

sees the broken
hears the cries
soothes the pain
seeks the lost

knows our name

heals the sick
blesses the poor
clothes the naked
redeems the forsaken

forgives us all

showers His mercy
displays His power
grants His grace
restores the years

119

holds all things together

calms our fears
guides our feet
shoulders our burden
bridges our gaps

makes us strong

opens broad doors
shines great light
breaks old chains
removes high mountains

builds our faith

names the stars
chastises the winds
clothes the lilies
paints the skies

carries the lambs

took the stripes
took the nails
took on death
rose with life

wrote the Book.

reigns in power
holds the keys
sits by Jehovah
waits for His bride

HE   loves.

HE   lives.

HE'S LORD.

The War Drobe *Ephesians 6*

You raise a shield of faith daily that protects you from the wiles of the enemy. You wear a helmet of salvation that protects your mind. The insignia on its front declares to Whom you belong.

You wear a breastplate of the righteousness of Christ. What on earth could pierce you through? *#nada*

You wear a belt of Truth that keeps you balanced. Stand. Firm.

Your shoes are sized with the gospel of peace. *#donttakeemoff*

Your sword in your hand is the Word of God. It can slice and dice every enemy quicker than any 3 a.m. infomercial. Need proof? Hebrews 4.

Your spear of prayer is clutched in your fist for protection, constant and alert. The LORD Himself is your rear guard. Nothing can sneak up on you from behind when the Warrior is on watch. Which is always, by The Way.

Our enemy is not flesh and blood. We war against the principalities, the authorities of the darkness. As believers, we have been given weapons for our WARdrobe and we suit up every day and fight the good fight. In JESUS' NAME.

Don't believe me?

I remember clearly one particular Fall day in 2005 when I needed my entire ensemble oiled and ironed and ready to go. Steve had been in the bed 24/7 for some time due to extreme depression and anxiety. I had recently begun a new job and appeared at work every day, all smiles on the outside, all clenched jaw within. I called home at lunch to find that Steve was in pure panic. I raced home, not knowing what I would find once I got there. In those situations when anything is unfortunately possible or plausible, time stands still. The rest of the world falls away and your only goal is to get to him. All thoughts scrambled through my mind like a roller coaster ride as I drove the streets to home. I had no idea what I was walking in or out of. Steve was there, and all I can really say to describe the situation in my house was that it was under attack. There was a tangible foreboding. Steve was not himself … he was completely out of control … I knew in my spirit that I wasn't dealing with something that a pharmacist could fix. I knew that little ole' me had come up against a big old devil and he was waging war right there in my home. You see, I believe in the spiritual forces that this earth contains. You can read all about them in

Ephesians 6. The enemy wanted Steve's life, just like he had wanted and victoriously taken Steve's dad's and grandad's lives. Steve was next to take.

BUT GOD.

I praise GOD for the CHAMPION JESUS in our life, because in that moment I knew that I had no choice but to fight. I dropped to my knees and began to pray for help … screaming out for help from the Sanctuary. As the prayer progressed, it turned into a demand that the devil had to get out of my house. I began in my prayer on my knees, cutting every demon I could think of off Steven … anxiety, depression, self-loathing, addiction, hopelessness … As I did that, Steve began writhing in the bed, and as I cursed every devil, demanding the devil out of my home, Steve began to beat the headboard of our bed with his fist and scream … I knew I knew I knew I wasn't fighting Steve, I was fighting the enemy and he was angry. And I knew Steve was joining me right there in the fight. I continued to pray … really honestly not knowing how to but knew with every fiber of my being that this moment was meant to be and I had been given a task. Lord Jesus was in control. As I continued to pray, the LORD gave me words to say … in the moment … Steve's life was hanging in the balance and the generational curse on him was angry. That went on for some time … I don't know how long … but as I continued to demand the devil out and invite the Blood of Jesus in, Steve became peaceful and quiet, very still, almost to the point of drowsy sleep. I then began to thank GOD for taking over, winning over, all over again.

There is Power, Power, Wonder Working Power in the Blood of the Lamb. In the precious Blood of the Lamb.

Have you ever read the beginning of Job? It says that the devil went to the throne room and asked to implode Job's life. Do you get it? He had to ask permission to attack. The LORD in eternal wisdom gave the devil access to Job that came with a boundary – the devil couldn't take his life. The LORD ALMIGHTY knew that Job would be faithful through whatever the devil thwarted him with. So the devil did everything he could to inch his toes right up to that boundary of death, but he never crossed over. Why? Because he was told he COULDN'T.

I believe the enemy had asked for Steve's life. And he put up a pretty tough fight. I'll give him that. But I believe God gave the devil a boundary and I believe his toes were right up to the line in the bedroom of our modest home. BUT GOD. Praise God Almighty for the war our Champion had already won on the cross for us. Praise God for the timing of it all and for giving me in that moment the clarity and courage I needed to usher His Presence in. Devil, you can exit, stage left.

Why am I telling you this? I didn't intend to … but for some reason, I just pictured all that in my head … I guess mainly because I know that, here on earth, we are not fighting a person … we are fighting the stronghold, the generational curse that has chained itself to a leg in each of our families. Don't believe the lie that you are the exception. And please don't think you're alone in the fight. Everyone on earth is daily duking it out with the very real unseen. What is it in your life? In your family? Are you going through the day with smiles and clenched jaw? I get it. And as long as you pretend daily that all is well, go ahead and clink the chain around your ankle because one day, unbeknownst to you, that chain is gonna' get yanked. Hard.

That happened years ago. Right here in 2023, my life has been riddled with anxiety. The trauma of losing my brother and my mother surfaced and the physical effects of it have been, well, horrendous. For the past year, I have been to doctors and pharmacists; I have been to scriptures, counselors and books. I have had daily anxiety attacks that I thought would take me out. Some days I actually wished it would just so it would be over. My husband has held my hand and prayed over me in the middle of it all. He's walked the floors with me, quoting Psalm 23. We've lain in bed in the dark and recited the Lord's Prayer. My husband is now fighting for me, alongside me. And we together look up to the One Who will see us through. Again.

And Job said, "Tho He slay me, still I'm going to trust Him."

Our address has changed since 2005, but our trust has not.

If there is any direction I could give that would have power, it is this:

As a believer in the Lord Jesus Christ, take time to walk thru your home and speak out loud who you are in Christ. Speak out loud what Christ has done for you and thank Him for it. Confess your sin and ask forgiveness. Stand in the place of the Matriarch for your family, and ask for forgiveness for any and all sin … the ones you are aware of and the ones you are not … then once that's done … stand in a place of spiritual authority over your home and begin to declare and decree … demand that your household be FREE IN CHRIST … tell every demon to take notice that the time of their bondage is OVER AND EXPIRED and they can return to their pit empty handed … Just start naming the spirits … even if you don't know their names … as you speak, the LORD will tell you their names … and tell them to GET OUT OF YOUR HOUSE AND OUT OF YOUR FAMILY LINE. Get some oil (Wesson will work) and start anointing doors and windows, bedroom doors, beds, everything in your house … anoint it for the LORD. Do a HOLY CLEANSING and set it apart for the HOLY SPIRIT. Invite the Holy Spirit inside, make room for Him in your home.

Now some of you are saying, "Whoaaa Robin, that's a bit on the other side. You done gone too far." Yep, you're exactly right. And every day we fight that other side, whether we acknowledge it or not. Ask the LORD to open your eyes to see and your ears to hear. Then walk the borders of your home and proclaim it as The Lord's Territory. Then dare those demon toes to cross over.

Father, in the Name of our RESURRECTED SAVIOR AND LORD, JESUS CHRIST
I ask for YOUR HOLY INTERVENTION
That YOU would come and INVADE each of us
With YOUR PEACE, YOUR EXCELLENCE, YOUR JOY, YOUR STRENGTH.

Lord, we know that it's not by power, and it's not by might
But it's BY YOUR SPIRIT
That things are accomplished

So, HOLY SPIRIT we welcome YOU here
Be the Shekinah Glory, encamped over this rooftop
Dwell within us and help us
Bless the work of our hands
Guard us with YOUR perfect peace as we set our hearts and minds on THEE.

There is NOTHING TOO HARD FOR YOU, NOTHING IMPOSSIBLE FOR YOU, DEATH COULDN'T STOP YOU ... OUR FUTURE'S SECURE.

As YOU offer us our daily bread, we ask that YOU enable us to discern with YOUR wisdom, rest in YOUR JOY, and walk in YOUR favor this day.

IN JESUS NAME we pray – amen.

Back to 2005. Months after that, Steve and I were sitting on the swing on our front porch. The swing had been his mama's and she had gifted it to us. We sat there in silence, watching the sky changing its colors at dusk. Steve started to talk about all that had gone on before, and when he had finished, I said, "We shall speak of this no more." We held hands, watched the sun set, then went into our Blood Fought, Blood Bought home.

The Name of the LORD is a STRONG TOWER.
The Righteous run into it and are saved. Proverbs 18:10

Good Friday (2018)

Today Oh LORD I think of YOU
Upon that bloody hill
Your blood soaked down
Your thorny crown
The hate screamed, "**Kill, Kill, Kill**"
The spikes, the screams
The robe with no seams
The gambling at your feet
The soldier's spear
The mob's gnarled sneer
It seemed that LOVE was beat.
BUT OH - NOT SO
THEY DID NOT KNOW
THEY PLAYED RIGHT INTO PLAN
YOU, PERFECT ONE,
GAVE YOUR ONLY SON
TO REDEEM EARTH'S DIRT FILLED MAN
The Death of Christ
YOUR Sacrifice
The Blood flowing from YOUR side
The mob knew not
At the very same time
Heaven's door swung open wide
Don't tarry! Come!
Believe in HIM!
The Blood covered even your sin!
Upon that Hill
the Blood flows still
It steadily whispers, "Come in."

*Let us run with endurance the race that lies before us, keeping our eyes on JESUS, the
SOURCE and PERFECTOR of our faith.
For the joy that lay before HIM, HE endured the cross, despising the shame,
and sat down at the right hand of the throne of God. Hebrews 12:2*

*For GOD so loved the world that HE gave HIS ONLY SON,
that whosoever believes in HIM shall not perish but have everlasting life. John 3:16*

*He was oppressed and afflicted, yet He did not open His mouth.
Like a lamb led to the slaughter, and like a sheep silent before her shearers,
He did not open His mouth. Isaiah 53:7*

Zion (Easter 2012)

HE rode a colt toward ZION
With palm leaves waving high
Amid the crowd's *HOSANNA*
HE knew HE'd come to die

HE taught them in the temple
HE passed the bread, the cup
HE tried to help them understand
HIS life HE'd soon give up

HE cried out in the garden
Drops of blood poured down
HE prayed as friends were sleeping
Then A Kiss, a Court, a Crown.

HE bore the beams through ZION
HE fell beneath the weight
The mob in anger waved their fists
He loved them thru their hate

HE laid down on the splintered wood
HE let the hammer fall
HE hung upon my sin full cross
HE died there. ONE. For all.

A struggle in the darkness
A hellish battle raged
The BLOOD dropped on THE MERCY SEAT
Then FATHER said, "It's paid."

HE rolled the rock that caged HIM
HE walked back into view
HE looked out over ZION
BEHOLD, ALL things are NEW

HE now sits by The FATHER
THE KING OF KINGS IS HE
MY HIGH PRIEST smiles, with keys in hand
HE did it all ... for me.

He exercised this power in Christ by raising HIM from the dead
And seating HIM at HIS right hand in the heavens
Far above every ruler and authority, power and dominion,
And every title given,
Not only in this age but in the one to come.
Ephesians 1:20-21

Then THE ONE seated on the throne said,
"LOOK, I AM making everything new."
Write, because these words are faithful and true.
I AM the ALPHA and the OMEGA, the
Beginning and the end.
Revelation 21

Blood (2012)

Today is the Passover. I hope we each will take the time to remember that our Passover Lamb died so that death would pass on over and we'd be birthed into eternal life. We were held in bondage, slaves to sin, chained to the evil one, until our Passover Lamb, with great compassion and power, died in our place so that His Blood could be painted on the doorposts of our hearts ... and we could be saved. What can wash away our sin? Nothing but the BLOOD OF JESUS.

He was led like a sheep to the slaughter, yet He did not open His mouth. He surrendered Himself to death, with me on His mind. He loved me so much that He did not want me to perish but have His eternal life. But He had to die for that life to come. And He walked the road of Golgotha to pay for my life. He fell under the weight of the cross, knowing that I had fallen under the weight of my sin. Oh, what a POWERFUL VICTORIOUS LORD WE SERVE. Thank You, Jesus. Thank You, Jesus.

While I was yet a sinner, He died so that I might have life.

The death angel has passed over. Arise out of the darkness ... for the LIGHT has come.

There is no GOD like our GOD. Praise His Name.

Blood (2006)

I'm still basking in the goodness and greatness of the BLOOD of Jesus. I've been singing a few oldies but goodies this week … "what can wash away my sin? Nothing but the BLOOD OF JESUS." And this one, "There is POWER, POWER, WONDER WORKING POWER in the BLOOD of the LAMB" and this one too, "There is a fountain FILLED WITH BLOOD DRAWN FROM EMMANUEL'S VEINS." Thank You Lord, for the Fountain that washes away all my guilty stains. Thank You Lord. I love the new praise and worship choruses, but I'm longing to sing the songs of the past. The songs that focus on Him. The songs that recall the SACRIFICE so that I could live. The songs that don't mix words or leave out details about the death on the Cross. I think we have forgotten its MAGNITUDE. I think we handle the BLOOD flippantly; I think we skim right over our guilty stains washed clean. The LORD has stopped me in my tracks on this one and I love HIM all the more, for the BLOOD that flowed from His veins to mine, when Perfection stepped in, got nailed down, and gave me a second chance. Oh how I love Him and want to know Him. I put a charge before you tonight: spend some time singing the old hymns, retelling the Only Story worth telling, describing an old, rugged cross on a hill far away. Then tell me what happens. I am telling you now … you will OVERCOME by the BLOOD OF THE LAMB and the WORD OF YOUR TESTIMONY.

I am with Paul who said, "I count this world as loss ... I want to know Christ." Knowing Him is the greatest blessing; having walked with Him and talked with Him through the good and the bad, through the light and the dark, through the thick and the thin ... I have learned to be content in any circumstance ... as long as He is with me and for me. With Him and Through Him, I can do all things ... He is my strength and my song, my joy and my delight. I live in the Goodness of the LORD in the land of the living ... He has turned this desert into dessert ... and I walk with Him in the cool of the day. He is Real and He is Mine. He is the Passion of my Life ... and what I cannot comprehend is ... I am the Passion of His.

Do you know Him?

I speak RAIN OVER YOUR HOUSEHOLD ... SHOWERS OF BLESSING ... Oh, that today they would fall.

Proverbs 16:3
Commit your works to the LORD and your plans will be established.

Peace

The Feather

I don't remember cutting the alarms off – 6:15 and then again at 6:30 – this morning but I guess I did. Woke up again at 7:20 a.m. and JUMPED into action. STARTLED AWAKE, HIT THE GROUND RUNNING. HURRY, ROBIN. YOU'RE LATE. Shower, hair, make-up, a swab of deodorant, all the while thinking of things to wear that didn't need ironing. Rush into the closet fussing at myself in my head for not yet being a better morning person, stepped into a beige skirt, disgusted with the stomach roll that I now have to contend with, turned again to the hanging clothes and AHA – that's wrinkle free - I yanked out my green turtleneck and scramble to get it over my head ... then stopped in my tracks ... this .... the white feather was literally embedded in the stitching of the sweater and I had to gingerly fight to get it out. How long had it been there? How did it get there? When did I wear this last? Who knows. Only He knows.

The intermission of this story is that for years, the LORD has given me the gift of white feathers. In some of my most perplexing moments, I would find a white feather in the most unlikely spot, somewhere near me. It became so constant that I knew it was a symbol of the presence of the Lord in my life. I even started collecting them. Somewhere in this house is a Ziplock bag full of white feather gifts from the Father who crafted them Himself. Each one says to me, "I am with you. Do not fear."

Dear Jesus, I want to stop in the midst of my madness and thank You for stopping me in my tracks. Thank You, Lord, for the millionth time, for reassuring me of Your Presence and Your thoughtful, gentle, watchful care. I want to give You glory for being the extraordinary Father who delights in showing up in my ordinary day. That in the midst of my self-created chaos, Your Presence brings calm assurance that YOU are ever watching, delighting over me with Your love. Thank You Father for loving me so much and for reminding me of that love at every crazy twisted turn of my life. This year has had so many of those. Your Word says that every day of my life was written before one of them came to be. Thank you for writing today. In rush and in rest, I honor you Lord Jesus. Amen.

After Mama's Abdominal Surgery

Junie Bug is mending, slowly but surely, faithfully as God has promised. She took her first unassisted chair bath yesterday - a **huge** accomplishment – applause accepted right now, wherever you are – just stop and clap your hands. I'll take her to the surgeon follow-up tomorrow. Hopefully he'll answer our journaled questions and she will continue to progress. It has certainly taken the wind out of her sails but not out of her hope or her joy. It's been a privilege and an honor to serve her these past few weeks, making memories that I will never, ever forget. I wouldn't trade a second of the time I've spent with her. I'll hold them close like Mary did and ponder them in my heart.

I shared this with a friend on the morn of mom's surgery. She had dropped by the hospital to pray with me and mom prior to the operation. Because I have praying friends. I want to share with you now how the Lord talks with us, so plainly, throughout the chaos of life. That morning for my scripture, I had read Psalm 23. I had read it over and over, just seeking peace and rest and surety in the midst of that horrific morning, knowing that I was about to watch my mama undergo surgery and the pain that was sure to follow. To prepare for that as best I could, I found myself in the 23rd Psalm. With that scripture fresh on my heart, on the way to the hospital that morning, the Lord reminded me of a scene from *The Bible mini-series* (have you seen it?) where Jesus was beaten and flogged, barely alive. He had fallen to the ground on Golgotha and was being tormented by the Roman soldiers. He was literally crawling, covered in His own blood, toward the cross to lay down on it willingly so that they could continue the horrific act of crucifying Him. As that vision flashed in my head, the Lord whispered, **"I will make you lie down in green pastures."** It was as if the Lord was telling me that the cross – to Him – was a green meadow. The link between Psalm 23 and that scene memory reminded me that nothing this earth could do could snatch Him from the Father's Hand of covenant love. There I sat by a stainless steel bed with a sedated mama, holding her hand, waiting for the team to wheel her away. The room smelled like alcohol. The machines buzzed and beeped. The sound of the entrance curtain being yanked back down the hallway, over and over again, was like nails on a chalkboard. Was this a green pasture? It is, if I choose to trust Him so. No matter what we face on this earth, no matter how ridiculed, tormented, harmed we are, wherever we find ourselves on this planet earth, it can spiritually be our planned green meadow. If we choose it to be. I know I'm preaching to the choir right now but be encouraged. The Lord is with you; His rod and His staff, they will always comfort you. You will sit down at the table in the presence of your enemies and you will be anointed with oil. No. Matter. What.

Goodness and mercy shall follow you in hot pursuit all the days of your life, and you shall dwell in the house of the Lord. Forever.

Find a green meadow in your circumstances today. Roll around in the clover of the Goodness of God. Take in the smell of fresh air while immersed in the chaos, the crisis of life. He is there. He is here. He is mine. And I am His. Nothing, nothing, nothing can separate me from the love of the Father which is found in Jesus Christ our Lord.

The Lord is my Shepherd. I shall not want.
He makes me lie down in green pastures. He leads me beside still waters.
He restores my soul.
He leads me in the paths of righteousness, for His Name's sake.
Yea tho I walk through the valley of (_____)
I will fear no evil
For THOU art with me
THY rod and THY staff – they comfort me.
THOU preparest a table before me in the presence of this enemy.
THOU anoint my head with oil.
My cup overflows.
Surely, goodness and mercy shall follow me
All the days of my life
And I will dwell with
The LORD
Forever.
Psalm 23

Afternoon.
I feel inclined to tell you that
I love you,
through and through,
up close and personal
or gazing from a distance.
In times of many words
and in times of stark silence.
In both light and in dark,
I love you.

Praying GOD'S LOVE will
BLOOM in your life
And the BEAUTY
of the BLOSSOM
Would fragrance the air.

Little Me (2004)

As I journaled this morning, I wrote about my trip to Gunnison, when I traveled to the church where my "wonder years" were lived. As I wrote, I realized that in the halls of that church my very being was being founded, grounded, sanded, and rooted. That the little girl running those tiled floor halls was happy, deliriously happy most of the time, a girl with shy confidence, a backwards girl naive enough to believe that every day of my life would be just like a day in the Delta. Running free. That little girl had courage and compassion, kindness, a simple way of thinking. A girl that had many friends, a family of friends that she shared time with. A girl with a daddy that I could look up to, run to, be confident in knowing that he would fight for me. A girl with a humble servant heart mama, quietly in the shadows behind each of her kids. And that I now, a 41 year old mama, some 30 odd years later, was given the gift of going back into those hallowed halls and sitting with that little girl for a while. God gave me the gift of pressing "pause" on my current reality, and gave me the chance, the gift, the incredible gift of walking back into the place where that little girl met me, and reminded me who I am and why I am. She stirred up in me things that had become silent. I spent time with that little girl there. And I came away complete.

Well (2007)

Hey friends. I wanted to tell you about a moment in my home last night. With all the chaos of no air (our air conditioner is broken), calls to repair people, the storm rolling in, Jess being sick, tv noise … Samantha, in the midst of that, invited a friend over to practice for their choir talent show. They went to the back porch to practice. The two of them stayed out there for the longest time, then came in and said, "Listen to us and see what you think …" (I'm going to cry just typing it …)

The two of them stood there in the living room, in the heat, the sickness, the worries, the chaos of that moment for our family, and began to sing in their angelic soprano …

When peace, like a river attendeth my way
When sorrow, like sea billows, roll
Whatever my lot
Thou hast taught me to say
It is well, It is well, with my soul

I was overcome.

Isn't God something? In the midst of all the sea billows that were rolling inside my house, He ushered in a song of peace. That's what the two of them chose to sing for the 4th period talent show in their choir class. Glory to His Name. Glory to His Name.

We slept with the windows open, Jess slept off and on, sweating with fever. She is up this morn and has eaten breakfast. I'm praying she'll take a shower and this will all be over for her … I have prayed all night for God's Hand. Then somewhere in the middle of the night, I began to pray for parents whose children are terminally ill, who cry out to God over and over and over, and situations don't change. Diagnoses remain the same. Perhaps even fatal. How do they bear it? I pray for their faith - that no matter what sea billows roll thunderously thru their lives, that they will find His peace like a river in the midst of their sorrow. Let it be so, Lord. Let it be so.

Wordless August 10, 2006

I'm short on words tonight. I've been near wordless for a few weeks now. It has frustrated me so because I am a word person, a person in love with words. It puzzled me to no end for some time but I think I've finally heard the answer. It's humbling to have to admit but the LORD needed me to STOP TALKING FOR A WHILE. And that's where I remain. Mute. It's not a comfortable place nor an easy place, but for whatever reason it's a necessary place in my life. I continue to try and surrender to it. To let HIM have HIS way even when it's bumping up against my way (which is most of the time, let me tell you!) Although my tongue is still, I am still urging my mind to do the same. To still. To quiet. To rest. To listen. To be void of constant chatter. To be clear of mental clutter. That is the hardest battle – a quiet mind.

And then to truly hear. It's very hard to hear in a noise filled world. I resisted it for a while but am now trying to discipline my very flesh to conquer it. Silence. Quiet. I'm learning that it's near impossible to take something in when I'm constantly pouring something out. Hmm. I'm learning that to everything there is a season. And this is a season of quiet. It's as if the LORD Himself is saying to me, "You've said it, Robin. I heard you speak it. You've told the folks you needed to tell and for a time I let you. Now is the time to stop. I now have something to say." And there is an interlude between me stopping and HIM starting. A space between the two that isn't comfortable but that links the two together. And I'm on the bridge in between. A quiet road.

With my mouth shut and my mind quiet, I can truly see. Truly hear. I can truly feel. I can breathe. I can treasure these things, like Mary, and ponder them in my heart. With all at peace within me, I can almost sense that something is coming. No wait – I mean SOMEONE is coming. Someone who deserves my full attention. Someone who wants me to know it is HIM, so HE's closed my mouth and opened my eyes. And it makes me nervously excited at the very thought. I'll watch and I'll wait. I'll look and I'll listen. One day I will see. When my eyes behold HIM there will be no words to describe Him. So perhaps I'm in training now for that moment then. Learning the art of quiet preparing my heart to dance. I'm ready. I'm watching. I know HE's coming.

Surely I have composed and quieted my soul like a weaned child rests against her mother.
Psalm 131:2

Passion

She is thirsty

She awaits Him.

She has never met Him. Yet she knows Him.
She has never seen Him. Yet she sees Him.
She has never heard Him. Yet she hears Him.

She awaits Him.
She knows He is coming. Her Father told her so.

   She spends her time preparing.
   She sits down at her mirror and stares at her reflection.
   She sits down at her vanity in her vanity.
   She asks her Father to see her through and through.
   She asks Him to help prepare her to meet Him. He gladly
   consents.

      She bathes her body. He forgives her sin.
      She paints her lids. He beautifies her vision.
      She paints her cheeks. He graces her with modesty.
      She paints her lips. He purifies her words.
      She adorns her ears. He clarifies her hearing.
      She dresses in her gown. He clothes her with Christ.
      She covers her head. He covers her with anointing.
      She puts on her shoes. He teaches her to walk.
      He teaches her to dance.
      She adorns her jeweled bracelets. He removes her
      shackles.
      She binds her waist. He binds her to Him.
      She smiles. He smiles.

   She watches for Him. He watches over her.

Suddenly

She sees Him. He sent Him.

   He has journeyed for her.
   He has never met her. Yet He knows her.
   He has never seen her. Yet He sees her.

He has never heard her. Yet He hears her.
He knew she was here. His Father told Him so.

He finds her. He beholds her.

He hands her the cup.

She drinks.

The Circle

The LOVE of our LORD. How to tell it? Where to start? When to stop? A circle has no beginning nor end. Such is His Love. I would stand on the street corner with a bullhorn, proclaiming with earnest to the passersby about His love that never fails, never exhausts, never depletes, never wimps out, never lets go, never gives up. I would climb the towering heights and proclaim into the wind at the top of my lungs that His love shields, protects, matures, embraces, reveals, honors. I would travel to the middle of a desert plain and, using my foot in the sand as a pen, spell out word for word His Love as peace, health, hope, help. I'd swim to the middle of the ocean and sing with the whales how His love is power, light, wisdom, purpose. His Love encompasses all ... for the true definition of Love is (are you ready for this?) Jesus! Will we ever have enough words, enough time, enough breath to describe Him? Will we ever fully understand? I think they call that ETERNITY.

Knowing now this iota of a fragment of His nature, how could we ever doubt His Love? His provision? His shelter? His wisdom? His care? His guidance? All encased in His love? How could we ever see for ourselves this PRINCE who would never leave us or forsake us because He loves us, then flippantly turn our heads back to the warty frogs of this eroding swamp?

Don't settle for the toads. Don't believe that the toad is your future or your hope. Jeremiah 29:11 does not promise warty frogs. But, let's face it, the plagues of toads do come from time to time. Attacks come. Creatures invade. Crisis commences. All of them – warty frogs. Whatever your "toad" is today, it's not toadal (see what I did there?). It's just hopping through, hoping for a home. If you give it one, sooner or later, you'll croak. Don't kiss the frog. Instead, look into the eyes of the TRUE KING PRINCE and wait for His entry. The reptile is already under His feet. The Prince is right now watching His timeless clock. And your deliverance is coming. Because He loves you.

Frogs, you've been warned.

Take this in, slowly, steadily, and with surety - The LOVE our LORD has for us circles back around to Him as LOVE we have for our LORD. Read that again if need be till it gets into your marrow. Round and round. No beginning, no ending. Just like He planned it.

May the circle be unbroken.

Love (2003)

What. Is. Love. Is. What.

The word is so common, so boringly used without thought … I love pizza, I love sunsets, I love him, I love her. I love it. It's used as a verb. Is it? What word can I substitute the word "love" with? If the word "love" fell off the vocabulary train, what word could I go to that would mean the same thing and stay on the right track? That, my friend, is my question.

Of course, for a saved person, our first target is the Bible. The Word tells us that God is love. Well, that's unexplainably simple enough, don't you think? Love is God. Okay, that's a limitless answer. I can't really put my hands around that because God has no boundaries, He is limitless, He is overwhelming, He is powerful, He is all sufficient, He is everything and then some. With a boundless, infinite, limitless love. An overwhelming, powerful, forgiving, sufficient love.

A love that covers.

1 Corinthians 13 tells us that Love is
Patient, kind, never envious … *oops, first strike against me.*

Love does not brag, is not arrogant, does not act unbecomingly, does not seek its own … *I do this all the time. Second strike.*

Love is not provoked, does not take into account a wrong suffered, does not rejoice in unrighteousness. *Well, third strike. Bat down. Head down. I'm out. Dug out.*

Love rejoices in the truth, bears all things, believes all things, hopes all things, endures all things. *GUILTY AS CHARGED.*

But, to the Praise of our Jehovah God –

Love. Never. Fails.

Wait, wait, wait. You mean to tell me that if I have been impatient, if I have been unkind, if I have been jealous, true Love still stands because it never fails?

If I have bragged, if I have been arrogant, if I have sought my own selfish way, Love still comes out the winner?

If I have complained about what I've had to bear, if I have refused to believe or hope, that His Love for me still stands? It never fails? He never moves one increment away from the LOVE position? The LOVE decision? He never turns His back? Love looks over my failures because of His Unfailing Love?

Oh my goodness ... oops- another mistake, I mean, OH **HIS** GOODNESS!

Does that confirm the scripture that says that He loves me (and you) so much that while I was still a sinner that He sent His Son, Jesus Christ, to replace me on the cross? That He knew I couldn't or that I wouldn't ... that I would mar the perfect love with my earthly grasp of it ... so He became one of me to do it perfectly? My substitute? That Jesus was God's Love in the flesh? That He loved me so much that He sent His only begotten Son to die for this world of sinners?

Imma' havta' stopa' minute. This is too much. Seems my cup is spilling over at the moment.

He loves me. His love is everlasting, it has no beginning and no end. Limitless. Boundless. Boldness. Forgiving. Accepting. Powerful. Protecting. Calming. Securing.

Safe.

In other words,

Love is God is Love is God is Love is God is Love is God is Love is God is Love is God is ...

Now these three remain: Faith, Hope and Love. And the Greatest of these is Love. What does that mean? Let's look at Faith – my faith is in Him. Let's look at Hope – my hope is in Him. Let's look at Love – it's not my love in Him but (oh I'm so excited to type this) it is HIS LOVE in me! For me! I didn't love Him first – He loved me first! Hmm. That IS the greatest. Not what I've done or do, it's what He's done for me that is called Love. 1 Corinthians is right. Love is the greatest because He is the greatest.

The only way to truly taste and know the meaning of love is to try and get a grasp on His love for me. That in spite of myself, in spite of what I've done or not done, in spite of what I've believed or not believed, no matter what others have done for or against me, He loves me. In spite of me. He delights in me. He dances over me. Can I understand that? No, because it is not my nature to love like that. Can I grasp that? No. It boggles my mind. Can I accept that? I want to. But that would mean taking my hands off everything I've known about love, opening the gate so to speak on the fence that I've built around my knowledge of love, and letting me walk through the boundary I've created into the openness, the vastness, the limitless, the unending territory of His Love. A new territory that travels beyond the horizon, as far as the eye can see. And then some.

That's the love I want. I want to be loved that way. I want to be consumed with it. I want to literally taste it. I want to be unable to contain it. I want my heart to explode with it. I want to dance with it! I want to be speechless because of His boundless love on me, in me, for me. If He is for me, who can be against me? He loves me. Can I deserve it? Never. Can I repay it? There's no way that my tainted blood can parallel to The One and Only Begotten Spotless Lamb. Can I accept it? I want to. And most importantly, He wants me to too.

I'm thinking of Eve. She was created in the garden of Eden, born into the perfect love of God. She could actually walk with Love every day. She didn't have to do anything to acquire it other than be ribbed into it, and even in that, she didn't have to choose. Until the day she did. And she chose her own way. Until the day she separated herself from Love when she separated the fruit from the tree. We don't know much about her after that, other than she tried to hide her nakedness from the Father, she didn't want Perfect Love to see her imperfections so she hid herself from Him among the trees. From Shalom to shame. We do know that later in life after Abel was killed and Cain sent to wander, the Bible says that "Adam knew her again and they conceived a son named Seth." I wonder if she ever "knew again" the perfect Love God had just for her? I wonder, after seeing two sons of hers taken, if the love of God was reborn within her with the new birth of Seth. I wonder if she died of old age with the complete knowledge of the boundless love of God … that even though she made some pretty catastrophic mistakes, she was intensely loved limitlessly by Him? Or did she continue to try and manufacture her own life, walling herself into a love that was man made.

Hello. My name is Eve.

I, like Eve, have separated the fruit from the vine. I, like Eve, have seen things precious to me taken away as consequence of my actions. I've tried to hide myself from Him, tried to make life work my way. And in spite of these mistakes and my earthly grasp on this thing called my life, He loves me. He has not moved one iota from that place of Love. He cannot be moved from that place. It is solid ground. I on the other hand can run into the trees and try to hide, I can make choices that bring **grave** consequences, but He never moves. He stands in His love for me. When am I going to learn to stop hiding and start standing?

God loves me. God is love. God wants to pour out His love on me and in me. He wants me to love others for Him. How can I do that? I'm an Eve! I made my own choices and have suffered the consequences! How can I, in my sinful state, love others with a pure love? A true love? Only by allowing Him in me to do it through me. I can't do it. I can't obtain it. But I can let myself die to myself and allow Him to resurrect me. New breath. Allow Him to overwhelm and overflow me. To remake me. To rename me. I can release all authority over myself and become the bondservant of Christ, which brings me into the storehouse of blessings, the greatest of which is Love.

The song I sang in Sunday school was, "Jesus loves me, this I know, for the Bible tells me so." All those years of singing it and never knowing it. All those years looking at the words on the page, and that's where they remained, printed on paper. I never knew them for me. I never experienced the love of Jesus in my very being, from the bottom to the top. Through and through. Full to overflowing. Now, all these years later, I come back to Him, like a little girl, with a hurt heart from life, with shattered dreams and broken promises and a pocket full of used out excuses, with a hungry heart for something pure, something complete, something real. I sing to Him, "You love me, yes – You love me The Bible says you do so please do!" Then in my brokenness, let the love of Jesus be poured into me like the Balm my wounds so desperately need, let the love of Jesus be applied to the brokenness and make me whole, let the love of Jesus fill my empty cup to overflowing. Let the love of Jesus in my life quench this thirsty child, let the love of Jesus feed this hungry soul. Reknit me, Sweet Savior. Let my mind be renewed in the rebirth of Love within me. The true birth of pure love, limitless love, powerful love, God's love. God. This is my heart's desire. To know love. To know Love. To know LOVE.

Think about His Love
Think about His Goodness
Think about His Grace
That brought me through
For as high as the heavens above
So great is the measure of my Father's Love
Great is the Measure of my Father's Love.

The Love of God (2006)

He loves me.
Despite my mishaps and messes
And desperate guesses
Of what love's supposed to be

He loves me

Despite my sins and "my bads"
My haves and my hads
My happies and sads

He loves me

Day in and day out
Through complaints and through pouts
Midst turmoil and doubts

He loves me

Night after night
My wrongs and my rights
I can count on His light

He loves me

I don't understand
Why He'd be a man
And lay down His life
Just for me

I can't comprehend
The weight of my sin
That killed Him on
Mount Calvary

I do it so badly
Yet HE loves me so gladly
He's patient, He's kind, He's true
He offers it freely
I say to Him, "Really?"
He smiles back
And says, "I do"

This thing called Love
That comes down from Above
Is a thing I can never repay

The Love that He gives
That makes dying things live
Grows greater with each passing day

His love never fails
His love never ends
His love is a great mystery

He never looks back
He doesn't keep track
He hasn't stacked it all
Against me

He chooses to see
The girl I can be
And He'll love me through
Till I'm she

Perhaps you, like me
Are just starting to see
A glimpse of His great love for you

I hope that today
We'll have courage to say

"My Abba, I do love You too."

1 John 4
We love because He first loved us.

1 Corinthians 13:12-13
Now we see only a reflection, as in a mirror
But then we will see face to Face.
Now we know in part, but then we will know fully, as we are fully known.
Now these three remain – Faith, Hope and Love.
And the greatest of these is Love.

The Love of God

This past week I've been studying 1 Corinthians **13**. The LOVE chapter. The most excellent way. God's Way. God Himself revealed in **13** verses. (and who said 13 was unlucky? It's LOVELY!) I've read this passage hundreds of times over my lifetime, usually rushing thru it, way too familiar with the words, but far, far away from the truth of the text. I've disciplined myself to stop this week and meditate on the LOVE of GOD. To hear the words as if for the first time, valuing the scripture for Truth, mulling over the very essence of LOVE from the Father. Holding the diamond of His Love to the Light of His Word and seeing a million dazzling facets … each one a new vision of His Love. For me. Sensing Who He is through His passionate perfect Love. Sensing who I can be if I allow His Love to be funneled through me. His Love is patient and never forces its way. His love is whole and perfect. There is nothing lacking, nothing tarnished, nothing prideful about His Love. His love rejoices in truth. His Love bears all things. His Love believes all things. His Love endures all things. His Love never fails. Not too long ago in my own life, I clung to this scripture as a roadmap in my daily journey … knowing that the Covenant of Love that I was bought with was able to bear anything this world threw my way; knowing that the power of Love could endure every dark night and every hellish day. I learned one of the greatest truths about our God in a time in my life when I really needed to know it … His Love NEVER FAILS. He cannot lose, He will not lose, His Love will have His victory. And because I am His, His victory is mine. Praise His Name.

Oh my friend … if you are battling what seems to be a hopeless situation, if you are facing what you think is an unconquerable foe, if tonight you are seeing life with broken vision, and your ears of faith have dulled to a whisper, if you feel crippled under the burden that is weighing you down … let me, an unlovely sinner that God snatched up by His gorgeous Grace, cleansed by His Blood and filled with His Presence, remind you of the Banner that flies over you today. The Banner of His Love. A Perfect Love. A Powerful Love. An Infinite

Love. Stand strong under the Love of our Lord and Savior, Jesus Christ. Stand strong in the faith that His Love will see you through. Stand strong in the Hope of Glory, Christ Jesus. Stand Strong in the knowing that He will not fail. That He will endure. That. He. Will. Get caught up in the wonder of how our Lord, the Son of God, loved us so much that He became the Son of Man, that He walked the road of Golgotha, fell beneath the weight of a cross, poured out His Treasured Blood, crossed over into death and conquered it so that we could have life. Because He loved. Oh, the Hope of our Lord … how He lavishes us with His Love; how He pours on us the Oil of His Joy; how He equips us each day with the robe of His Love. How He completes us with an overflowing cup of His Goodness and Mercy. I pray today that you will join me in the quest to know His love, to be His love, to share His love. For this is His Plan for our lives.

Love Bears All Things
Love Believes All Things
Love Hopes All Things
Love Endures All Things

Love NEVER fails.

1 Corinthians 13: 7-8

Grace (2018)

I think about the soldiers
Who fight on foreign soil
I think about the farmers
Who sweat in muddy toil
I think about the nurses
Who work throughout the night
I think about the mamas
Tryin' hard to raise 'em right
I think about the prisoners
Who can't walk through the door
I think about the servant who is
Caring for the poor
I think about the rich man who
Is generous to all
I think about the player who is
Focused on the ball

I think about the brother
On whom you can depend
I think about the sister
Who always seeks to mend
I think about the friend
Who is always there on time
I think about the desperate
Who just committed crime
Just people going through their day
Each one in his own place
With nothing else in common
Except our need for Grace

#JesusisHisName

"My Times Are In Your Hands" ... Psalm 31
He gives greater grace ... James 4:6

For you are saved by grace through faith
And this is not from yourselves – it is GOD's gift ... Ephesians 2:8

Lord, Let Me Be A Towel (2016)

Lord, let me be a towel
An ordinary thing
A simple cotton square of cloth
Folded, neat and clean

Just waiting for the moment
When someone, right on cue,
Reaches out to find me
To do what towels do

Perhaps someone will need me
To dry away their tears
Or hold me close for safety
To pry them from their fears

Perhaps someone who's dirty
By sin that's left caked mud
Will need me to find beauty
With just a little scrub

Perhaps someone who's drowning
In life's chaotic storm
Will tie me to the Cross Tree
To pull them safe from harm

Perhaps someone who's freezing
Who's shivering in dread
Can use me as a blanket
To warm them with my thread

My thread of light
or thread of cheer
For sure, the thread of love

The thread of hope
Or thread of help
Each woven from above

Lord, let me be a towel
Like the cloth one night You squeezed
And willingly washed their grimy feet
While bending on Your knees

Lord, let me be a towel
A humble, lowly thing
A simple cotton square of cloth
Folded, neat and clean

Just waiting for the moment
When someone, right on cue,
Reaches out to find me
To do what towels do

So HE got up from supper, laid aside his outer clothing
Took a towel
And tied it around Himself.
Next HE poured water into a basin
And began to wash HIS disciples' feet and to dry them with the towel tied around HIM.
John 13:4-5

He comforts us in all our affliction, so that
we may be able to comfort those who are in any kind of affliction
through the comfort we ourselves receive from God.
2 Corinthians 1: 4

150

Pointers, Sisters

To The Wives Coming Behind Me,
I Write This For You.

Our wedding took place today, 36 years ago. Trace Ridge Baptist Church at 1:00 p.m., Ridgeland, Mississippi. He wore all white, from head to sole, the rented tux hung on him perhaps a half size too big. I too wore all white and lace - lots and lots of lace. I wore all white, except for the delicate satin baby blue ribbon hugging tightly just inches above my left knee cap. The veil was patterned after a beekeeper's hat (not kidding) and of course, I wore satin ballet slippers. The hat - the envy of the 80's. The ballet slippers - everyone knows I'm tall. Heels are waiting for me in heaven, but until then, it's flats, baby, all flats. The wedding was small, meager, no big fanfare, my recently single mama did the best she could on a very tight budget, and it was enough. My older brother, just back from basic training, stood with the groomsmen. My younger brother stood and sang, "IF" by Bread. My dad came long enough to walk me down the aisle then he left the church. The only song I made sure was played by the pianist was "Bridge Over Troubled Water." My mom set everything up before and cleaned it up after. It was enough. Nothing more than that. Enough to become Mrs. Powell.

Let the marriage begin.

Since that day of all white garments, I have put on a variety of outfits over the years ... such as shiny boxing shorts with matching gloves (the better to hit you with, my dear), camouflage cloth from heart to toe (the better to hide from you, my dear), sack cloth and ashes (the better to purge pity from you, my dear), a dirty maid's outfit (the better to scream at you, my dear), a judge's black robe (the better to build my case, my dear) and last but certainly not least, martyr's chains (the better to seem better than you, my dear). Oh, the outfits I have worn during my years of wife life. All of them sewn by me in an effort to so show him up.

For the wives coming behind me, I beg of you, stay out of that closet. Learn from me, my friend. I. Speak. Truth.

The garments of marriage that are beautiful are not sewn by human hands. Our personal Designer beckons us, draws us, challenges us, implores us to change our style. He wants us to take off the self-made worn-out hand-me-downs given to us by generations before and don His exquisite couture. His one and only perfect style perfectly stitched for you, for me. Here's what I've learned after 36 years. As wives, we are to:

152

◊ Wear love every day. EVERY DAY. (It never gets dirty)

◊ Button up our shirt with kindness and

◊ pull on pants of compassion.

◊ Wear shoes of forgiveness and

◊ socks of encouragement.

◊ Put joy in all our pockets.

◊ Tie service around our waist.

◊ Put on the sweater of contentment and

◊ the scarf of happiness.

◊ Zip up the back with romance.

◊ Put on glasses of desire that focus only on him.

◊ Try on the hat of humor (I promise it will fit).

◊ Put bangles of peace on our wrists and

◊ Slide on rings of gratefulness.

◊ Wear the gold necklace of order ... God first, hubs second, children third. Keep this necklace in order or you'll end up in knots.

Once dressed in the Designer's couture, your hubs will come alongside and cover you with his coat of protection, his covering of security.

This is how the Designer intended marriage to be. Don't be afraid to admit your clothes are self-sewn, handed down and patched up by wives that have gone before. Don't be afraid to change. Yes, you'll feel stripped for a bit, but have the courage to look in the holy Three-Way mirror of grace and see truth. What are you wearing? Is it time for something better? There's a closet of vulnerability with your name on it. Step in and strip down. Your eyes will then be opened to precious garments galore at your fingertips, each with your name hand-stitched on the label. Eternal style.

Let's face it, the clothes you wear will be yours or HIS as you walk this marriage thing out. I hope these words have challenged you to examine the fabric of your life. With that, I ask you, "What's in your closet?"

"For All The Married Ladies" - By Beyo / I Mean Robin Powell

If Beyonce' can give advice to the single ladies, I'd like to sing out a few nuggets of advice to the married ones (although I can't dance a lick). After 32 years, I've learned hard lessons the very hard way; I've messed it up and almost given up one too many times. But my marriage has survived. I give GOD all the glory for that. I don't claim to be a wise soul - just a grateful wife. I'm very aware that good marriages do fail; they fall through the dark cracks; and I hurt for the fallen. There are far too many that slipped through that dark. Believe me, several times my own was in that downward spiral, but just in time was grabbed by the Grip that won't let go. Why us pulled through the grate? I am humbled by that Truth.

The most important key to marriage is a true relationship with Christ, Who teaches you the second most important -- how to out-love your man every day. Here are a few do's and don'ts I've learned over the years. It's not rocket science, but it will rock your marriage in the best kind of way:

1. Take him water when he mows.

2. Hold the hammer when he's hanging curtains.

3. Rub his feet when he's tired.

4. Talk soft when he's sick.

5. Make him laugh when he's mad.

6. Say please, thank you, and I love you every day.

7. If he loves Italian cream cake, learn to make Italian cream cake.

8. Forgive him.

9. Kiss him, hug him, and speak love words to him where the kids can hear.

10. Sit close and hold hands on the couch.

11. Flirt with him - and only him.

12. Pray for him.

1. Don't blame him for everything.

2. Don't store bad memories in your mind's arsenal, shooting him with words when he least expects it.

3. Don't put the kids first. If you do, chances are you'll be left behind with them.

4. Never ever humiliate, belittle or degrade him in front of other people. If you must complain, do it in a dark room behind a locked door on your knees.

5. Don't try to prove him wrong. If he's wrong, he'll figure that out eventually.

6. Don't wear gym clothes to bed.

7. Don't keep secrets from him.

8. Don't eat without him at the table.

9. Don't take him for granted.

10. Don't try to change him.

11. Don't ignore him.

12. Don't stop praying for him.

Fool proof? Fire proof? Unfortunately, no. But with God's help, my married ladies, it might just help you keep a ring on it. :)

Wives, submit to your husbands as to the LORD
Because the husband is the head of the wife as
Christ is the head of the church.
Ephesians 5:22

Husbands, love your wives. V25

A Letter to the Next Generation (2009)

Congratulations! Your wedding day draws near. I can just imagine your joy, your nerves, your anticipation of the life that is to come. A blessed life. A marriage life.

I was asked to join a circle of women, tasked with journaling bits of wisdom regarding love, learned through the covenant of marriage. I will try my best to pen a description, as I've come to understand it. What an undertaking; what a challenge. Not that I know in full, for the boundaries of Love are limitless, it is ever widening and infinitely deep. The power of Love is unstoppable. There is no way to measure it, no mind to conceive it, no scholar to define it. And certainly no equation to solve it. It is a great mystery. When we are young we think we feel it. When we are old, we realize we are overtaken by it. It is taught to us over time, infused into us through joy and great sorrow, through peace and through storm. It is the greatest of gifts. The eternal gift. What little I know of true love I've learned through my relationship with the LORD and my beloved Steven.

Steve and I met in the Winter of 1981. We married in the Fall of 1982. I vaguely remember two best friends – two energetic, light hearted youngins' holding hands and looking life square in the face. We thought not of the troubles we would encounter. We thought only of the life we planned to make. Our love, an inch deep at the time, began us on this thing called life.

And life came. Our 26 year marriage has encountered great joy and blessings. Too many to count. Horrific nightmares and messes. Too scarred to forget. The LORD has allowed the dark seasons to prove that true love never fails. That it is patient and it is kind. And that it holds NO RECORD OF WRONGS. Had it not been for the darkest of nights, I would never have tasted that Love is not jealous, nor is it boastful or self-centered. That it fights for the weak and it cares for its own. That it lays down its life so that others might live. It was there in the dark that I learned that it powerfully holds the feeblest ones in its clutch. And it never lets go. I now praise GOD for the storms that have taught me this truth. This day, I love my husband with a force that can't be reckoned with; can't be defined nor can it be penned; a love that cannot, will not be destroyed. True love made strong in the dark by a God FILLED WITH LIGHT. It is the Power of Heaven. And it is filling me.

So, my only treasured heirloom that I pass down to you is this: when life becomes hard, love becomes strong. In the dark seasons that you and your beloved will face – refuse to give up, refuse to throw in. Never ever walk away. Set your face like flint, fight for your beloved, stand strong in the grace of the Lord Jesus Christ. Be molded by the Potter being filled with His Love. It is the Greatest of Gifts.

Mothers (2006)

I had a friend jokingly say, "By the time my children rise up and call me blessed, I won't remember who they are!" I've always loved that little jab at Proverbs 31, because that Proverbs 31 woman never lived with these folks I live with or dealt with these folks I deal with. Or so I think. And if she weren't enough competition, I grew up watching mamas like Carol (The Brady mama), Caroline (the Prairie mama), Samantha (the magic mama), Edith (the looney mama), Lucy (the hilarious mama), Ruth (Lassie's mama) and who could forget Aunt Bea (the stand-in mama). All of these mamas, along with a slew of others that you can see nightly on TV Land, always had the right answer, the right recipe, the right outfit, the right hairstyle, the right people. And most always performed their duties wearing a strand of pearls. They always used their time wisely, always saved the day, always had food on the table and a jar of hidden cash, gave insight and wisdom freely without restraint, usually made pickles at some point, and even smiled their way through their family's 30-minute crisis. They had a perfect little family in a perfect big house (except for Caroline's one-roomer, thanks to Charles) ... why can't I have all that? Makes me feel real bad about not always having the right answer or knowing anybody worth knowing or being lazy as all get out or completely failing at a task while burning up the supper in the oven or screaming my way out of a 3 month crisis ... why can't I be like Caroline on Little House and be content with a one room, one window house? Why can't I have an Alice in my kitchen and a butcher that delivers daily to the back door? Why can't I work for a chocolate factory with my best friend? Just once I'd love to follow a freshly brushed collie to an abandoned well and help pull Timmy out. Then immediately sew up the rip in his only pair of jeans. And what about a big front porch with a man strumming a guitar in a rocker while I stir up some homemade ice cream? If those mamas could live like that, why can't I? Please, I'm desperate to know – does anybody live like that? Raise your hand higher please, I can't see you.

Crickets.

That's what I thought. No hands. Because the answer is emphatically NO. We all realize those drama plots were fantasy life, not the real earth life. No one could ever fill the shoes written in scripts by Hollywood writers, but we were glued to the tube thinking we could. Those Hollywood stars symbolized an unreachable bar and we in our realness frantically leaped and repeatedly fell back down to the mat. Never quite good enough. Hollywood's height was not in this mama's sights.

When we come back down to it, no matter how tv portrays us, the reality is that we, as women, aren't called to be fake mamas. We weren't called to be

perfect. We were called to be present. We weren't called to always be right. We were called to always be real. We weren't called to always know the answer. We were called to know the One Who does -- and go to Him daily on behalf of those hanging onto our hems. We weren't called to demand in anger.
We were called to lead in love. We weren't ever called to control every action. We were called to comfort with assurance. We weren't called to be a nuisance. We were called to nurture. We weren't called to hover. We were called to cover. We weren't called to leave when the 30 minutes were over. We were called to leave a legacy when our life on earth is done. We don't always get it right and sometimes we wear that guilt necklace way too long. But Praise be to God, sometimes we do, sometimes we get it perfectly right, and there is dancing in heaven and joy on earth and tears stinging eyes when that occurs. And those are the moments most mamas strive for, live for, would die for.

And I'll take that joy over a butcher at the back door any day. Wouldn't you?

What a Mother Means (Mother's Day 2014)

being a mom means being

puked on
peed on
cried on

hid from
ran from
pulled from

lied to
tried to
drive through

spend all
mend all
know all

sewer, sower, and so on ...

counselor
caterer
candle lighter

mess with her kids?
WWF Fighter

cheerleader
child feeder
book reader

loudest clapper
shortest napper

lightest sleeper
best mind reader

first aid
perpetual maid
nerves frayed

growing pains
potty train
permanent stains

lover of gigglers
pincher of wigglers

softest lap
the church pew tap

silent pride
deep and wide
jugs of Tide

constant worry
constant hurry
tears make blurry eyes

beauty for ash
treasure in trash
she sings amid the cries

a mom is a woman
simple but strong
who loves her babes
her whole life long

from her last push
to her last breath
her love is fierce and true

She's strong and sweet
and provides retreat;
a solace right on queue

She's nothing to fear
She's nothing to dread
She's as soft as morning dew;

But heed this warning ...
you mess with her kids ...
AND SHE'S COMIN' AFTER YOU.

He gives the childless woman a household,
making her the joyful mother of children. Hallelujah! Psalm 113:9

Turning 40 Stinks. (2002)

I wasn't real sure which section to place this piece, but I think since we women have a hang up about aging, I'd end this section with this one. You know, down wind.

Birthdays, in general, stink. Why is it so hard to live through the day you were born, over and over again? You would think I would feel blessed that I made it to another celebration of the day of my birth, considering the alternative. And in a way, I very much am. But honestly, in the most ways, I am not. And it's because of the attention that this particular birthday gets. What is it about turning 40? Why is there such a negative connotation connected to it? Am I really older? Am I now middle age? Can I let kids in grocery stores now start calling me ma'am? Does 40 give me the courage to color my gray? Now that I'm the big 4-0, should I let my waist continue to slide down the slippery slope called pear shape of which I have come to hate? Is that why it's called the BIG 4-0? Does this mean, 40, that I am finally grown? Why are there little lines around my eyes? Why are there hairs under my chin?

I don't like being under the microscope. I don't like being enlarged in a group of people. I don't like being stared at, for no other reason except it's my birthday. Oh, and this really gets under my skin - I don't like being asked over and over and over, "What do you want for your birthday?" The greatest gift you could give me is to stop asking me what I want for my birthday. If someone wants to get me something – fine! But don't make me a part of the process. It's hard enough to get through this without having to coordinate part of it.

Does anyone out there understand what I'm saying? Anyone on my side? Is there a line in the sand – me on one side, my birthday audience on the other? I don't like being separated out, glared at to see if my words, deeds, moves will be any different on my first day of 40 than they were my last day of 39. Trust me. They won't.

I pray it's a beautiful Fall day. I pray I'll awaken tomorrow on November 4 and have so many grateful things on my mind and my tongue. I pray that I'll rise up and look up, thanking God for the past 40, looking forward with giddy excitement toward the next 40. I pray that I'll look around and see people who truly love me, who I truly love, and I will again thank God for the real gifts. And those I can't physically see, that God will bring them to my mind off and on all day long, and I'll whisper a "Thank You, Lord, for the face I just saw." I pray that my mind will not be foggy and depressed, but alert and active; ready to think of things I can do for others on a day when others feel obligated to do for me.

161

One question I plan to ask on my 40th year is this, "Is there anything left within me that hasn't been born yet? Is there any inkling of an idea that is waiting to come forth, burst onto the scene and bring life? Is there something I haven't done that I need to, something I want to do but haven't taken the time to, some piece of me that has laid dormant for 40 years, waiting for just this moment in history to be born?" I wonder. Would that be the greatest gift – to see what's been sleeping awaken?

The gifts I want can't be purchased at a store. The gifts I want can't be used up or worn out, lost or broken. My wish list looks something like this: I ask God to quicken my hearing, so I can really hear what's being said behind the words. I want stronger vision so I can see what's on the internal camouflaged by the external. I want broader hands so I can support a network of family and friends in an active way. I want swifter feet so I won't waste time but be the first to respond. I want courage to speak to a stranger; determination to help the desperate. I want a conscience that will increase its volume so I can clearly hear what to and what not to do. I want more compassion for my own children, more understanding for my husband. I want a bigger heart.

I want more memories. Good memories. But I've just figured out that to get those, I have to make good decisions today that will result in good memories tomorrow. Right now, there are some memories that, well, like birthdays, they stink. I wish I could erase them. I wish I could blot them out of my memory. But I can't. I can however learn from those and turn things around the next time I get a chance.

That's what I want. Another chance. Lord God, grant me another chance. Pick me up, dust me off, wipe my face, set me back on my feet and point me in the right direction. Let me fix what's been broken, heal what's been sick. For those who are bent over, give me words to say that will stand them up straight. Let me be glue that holds things together. Give me patience and stamina to get through tough days, especially tomorrow's tough Four-O day. Please just get me through this. For once tomorrow comes, I'm off the hook for another 364 days. Hallelujah.

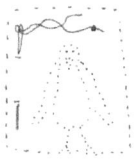

November 1, 2023

Fifty years ago this morning in a frosty Fall chill, the morning after old fashioned Halloween fun, an old yellow mustang with one bad tire filled up with three young boys and headed off down Highway 1 to school in Rosedale. Ross and Jimmy in the front, my 14 year old brother Butch in the back. Somewhere along the way on Highway 1, that one bad tire gave way. That was the morning our family's journey took an unexpected sharp left turn into unknown territory, never to return. No map included.

Three days before my 11th birthday.

I remember the funeral. Gunnison Baptist. Three coffins across the front. Overflowing pews, doors wide open with people huddled outside to hear. We walked between them to enter, much like the Israelites through the Red Sea. Waves on either side. Brother Butler speaking words of comfort. My dad bent over Butch's coffin, wailing in uncontrollable grief. My navy blue dress with red ric rac down the front. Sitting beside Uncle Wayne in the car as we drove to Shelby's cemetery. My first ride in a fancy car. Bits and pieces of memories.

I remember the days after. Seeing my mama in his room, going through his drawer contents, wailing in uncontrollable grief. Saying through her sobs, "Why couldn't it have been me?"

Many, many years later, during one of our annual trips to the cemetery, mama and I rode down Highway 1 in silence. She finally split the air with these words, "Stop here." We pulled to the side of the road, got out of the car with four good tires, and breathed deep. Stood still. Stared. Remembered. Thinking of where that unexpected sharp left turn into unknown territory had taken us. Much without our permission but all in the Atlas of God. Wondering what would've happened if that tire had been good. What would he have been? Where would our life had gone?

One of my favorite memories of Butch is when we took off for Oklahoma one year, all four of us little ones spitting and spatting in the back and we stopped at a gas station for a fill up and a bathroom break. We all piled back into the car – not sure how good those tires were, believe me, there's no telling – and we took off back down the road on our journey. A mile or so down the road, someone from the backseat blurted out, "Where's Butch?" And our first unexpected Uturn took place as we sped back to the gas station to find him standing there in the parking lot with the gas attendant's hand on his shoulder, watching the highway for his family's return. I'm sure my parents apologized for forgetting to count heads …. But we all laughed it off as we headed back down the highway to see our Oklahoma fam. Just another day in the life of our family.

Since 50 years ago today, Butch has been standing at the Gate with the Son's hand on his shoulder, watching the highway for his family's return. And it's been happening, one by one. Our family of six is now down to two. No tires involved, but I tell you, these two are tired. Randy and I are still traveling down the highway, making the best of every new unexpected turn midst the memories that never go away.

In three days, I turn 61. And today it dawned on me -- I think I've finally figured out why I don't like to celebrate my birthday. Because at some point in the day of birthday candles, I find myself back on a pew at Gunnison Baptist, swinging my knee socked legs under the pew, or on the side of Highway 1 with mama, staring in silence, the Delta wind whipping us clean through. All the while, wondering what would've, could've been.

Prayers

A New Year Prayer for Every Day (2001)

On the verge of this new year, I pray the Light of the World hovers over you so closely that you can see the brilliance of His glory, feel the brush of His wings, hear Him whisper your name, feel the beat of His heart. I pray He guides your feet with sure steps; holds you up with His arm; and moves you forward by His Spirit. Let every word you speak, every thought you think, every action you make, every step you take, be done in His power, His timing, His love, His grace.

Let there be showers of blessing on you and your family. Oh that today they might fall. When you see your reflection in the mirror, may you see the daughter of the Most High God, a pillar being carved to adorn the King's palace. May you see His ring on your finger and His robe as your dress. May you see your name on His Hand.

Our God is so good. For He is our Light and our Salvation. Whom shall I fear? For He is the Defense of my life. Of whom shall I be afraid?

We may be miles apart, worlds apart, but Praise God, as believers, we're not far apart. We're walking side by side, forward, in His light.

July 6, 2004

The joy of the LORD is my strength. In a dry and thirsty land where there is no water, You, Oh Lord, quench my thirst. You, Oh God, are the living water that takes away the ache. There is peace found only in You, and satisfaction only in Your ways. God, I love You today and I bless Your Name, for You alone are worthy of all the praise, honor and glory. Be exalted to the highest place. Let me not compare You to man on man's level, let me not compare You to man's standards or man's ways, continue to remind me that You are the highest of the high and Your thoughts are higher than mine. Let me not picture You as an ordinary man, but as GOD, high and lifted up, and the train of Your robe filling the temple. Let me give all glory and honor to You, for You are worthy and it is due. You are God Alone. You are the Author of my life, the One whose hand holds the pen. Write this story, Oh God, a love story back to You. A love story, a redemption story, a miracle story. A store of beauty from ashes. A story of redemption and restoration. A story of life. Life abundant. Write this story, Oh God. Let me, the journal, be open to Your

Hand as You scribe the words, as you finish the chapters and change the scenes. As You present situations and journey me toward discoveries, as You change characters and settings and plots, let this journal hold still, hold fast, and know that Your Hand that began this good work will complete it, in Jesus Christ. Let me never slam this journal closed as long as there is one more empty line left for You to write on, changing everything with the stroke of Your pen. Let this story unfold, Oh God. Let this journal be open until Your Hand is done. And then, when all is said and done, when the last word is written, when the problems are solved and the challenges overcome and the victories won and the damsel rescued. When the new territory is discovered and the monster slain and the new home is lived in, when peace settles like a warm blanket around the land, when the character of this story reaches over and turns out the lamp, knowing that all is well in this new place and that she shall live happily ever after with peace as her constant companion. Yes, Lord, when this journal is finished and closed, I pray that You are smiling as you lay down the pen. In the Name of Jesus I pray, Amen.

A Prayer of Marvel (2007)

The LORD is so Good, so Faithful. His Goodness encamps around us and His Favor is our shield. He blesses the Righteous with Good things. I'm so thankful that we have a Father Who always sees, always hears, always protects, always directs. A God full of wisdom Who rains down His Fullness into our lives. We are His Righteousness, blessed and highly favored. He kisses us with His character, and we walk in His Purpose. Thank You LORD, Thank You Lord. You are our Master, our Savior, our Protector, our Provider. You guide us with Your Word and our path is straight and full of light. Praise You, LORD, for You are a Masterpiece God. You are a Marvelous Maker. You are Perfection, Holy and Awesome in all Your Ways. You travel the journey with us by Your Holy Spirit, we are never alone. Rain down on us today, Lord God. We bless Your Name and declare You GOOD! We declare You LORD. We declare You God. We declare You to a lost and lonely world who needs the light, the love, the guidance, the protection, the strength that comes from You. Let our hands be Your hands, our feet be Your feet, our words be Your words. The Living Word that never returns void. Thank You LORD for the privilege of being Christ to others. We lift You up LORD JESUS and as we lift, we ask that YOU draw all men, women, and children to You. Call 'em in, Lord ... we Lift Your Name. Call 'em in.

A Battle Prayer

The devil is a liar. By the Power and Authority of the NAME ABOVE EVERY NAME, THE NAME OF JESUS, we curse his every attempt to stop you, hinder you, halt you, diminish you. We curse his every plan, his every scheme, his every deceitful tactic that would try to hurt you. We hold his lie to the TRUTH OF THE WORD and we watch his failing plan dissolve like smoke in the wind. The devil is a liar and a defeated foe. We walk in Resurrection Power, given by the Son of God, Jesus Christ. We remember The One Who stomped the enemy's head underneath His feet. Satan's torment time is OVER, DONE AND FINISHED… every demon in hell, take notice, LEAVE THE DAUGHTER OF GOD NOW … WE DEMAND YOU BACK TO THE PIT OF HELL WHERE YOU WILL BE LOCKED UP FOR ETERNITY.

Every chain, every bondage, every stronghold, every grip you have on her, BE LOOSED IN JESUS NAME. You've messed with her LONG ENOUGH AND WE DEMAND YOU LET GO AND BE GONE! We shoo you away, knowing who our FATHER is and knowing that we walk in RESURRECTION POWER. ALL AUTHORITY HAS BEEN GIVEN TO US, THROUGH THE SON OF GOD, JESUS CHRIST, THE ONE WHO DEFEATED YOU AT THE FOOT OF THE CROSS.

I am sick and tired of the enemy's thwarted plans to mess us up!! I am FED UP with his rantings and ravings, I DEMAND HE BE GONE FROM THIS DAY AND THE SPIRIT OF THE LORD BE USHERED IN, MULTIPLIED AND MAGNIFIED, IN OUR LIVES TODAY.

LET IT BE SO, IN THE MIGHTY NAME OF JESUS.

Today's Prayer

My prayer today is simple
Plain and prudent some might chide
Still these words I set before Thee
Hear me, Master, Savior, Guide

First, I thank You for the heavens
For the starry hosts, the skies
For the people and the purpose
That You've placed within our lives

For all that You've provided
Lord receive this grateful song
For all that You have seen me through
I'll praise You all day long

Now I beg You for forgiveness
For the constant wrongs I've done
Please wash me, cleanse me, clear me
Of the sinweb I have spun

Now comes the plea for MERCY
For my loved ones pinned by pains
Please answer best for each, O LORD
Dear God You know their names

I cry out now for healings
For me, my fam, my friends
This fallen earth has sickened us
I beg You LORD, STEP IN

Step in and smile with
Love and power
upon those who are ill
Then tell the violent storm once more
To STOP IT and BE STILL

I ask You God for Vision
I ask You for Release
Reveal to me Your Glory
Refill me LORD with Peace

I hope dear LORD
You'll use us
You'll choose us LORD
this day

To show someone who's hurting
The Truth, the Life, the Way

I pray dear God for courage
To share my patched-up heart
With those who stumble lifeless
Shuffling downward in the dark

I end my prayer with one more line
To ask You LORD for Grace
For strength to walk
For faith to talk
For hope to show Your Face

I know You can
I believe Your Word
I trust You still, You see
No matter LORD what comes my way
I trust You LORD with me

The needs are overwhelming
Too many for this pen
So let's meet again tomorrow LORD
Same time
Same place
Amen

Rejoice always.
Pray constantly.
Give thanks in everything.
For this is GOD's will for you
in CHRIST JESUS.
1 Thessalonians 5:16

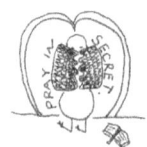

For The Mother Who Loves Her Son

There is great hope for your loved one. There is a great yearning in heaven for his heart, his head, his spirit to be SHALOM HEALED. The true meaning of Shalom is WHOLE. May Shalom come to your loved one today. May the Holy Spirit even now wrestle with him, may the Holy Spirit even now invade his thoughts, his day, his every turn, his every encounter. May the Holy Spirit have full sway in his emotions, leading him to the Rock that is higher than himself. May the Holy Spirit bring about THE KINGDOM in his life. Thank You, LORD for the Beginning as all of heaven leans his way, watching and waiting. Father, we ask that You complete what You started in this young man's life. We ask that You do the work by Your Sweet Strong Spirit. We ask that you take him to the end of himself and place a mirror there, so that he sees his true reflection … and that he is broken to the point where he has the courage to say, "I surrender it all." Father, we want new life for him; we want a fresh start. Lord, we want his new beginning to come today … put that same yearning inside him… we want all that your life has for him to be given to him … no more separation, no more hurt, no more past. We speak SHALOM over his life today, over his home today, over his family today. Strengthen us from the inside out, preserve and sustain us. Thank You LORD that the mother is willing to bear the brunt of the hurt on his behalf but LORD we are so thankful that You are the SHIELD that hides her and protects her from harm. Thank YOU, LORD GOD, that no weapon formed against her will ever prosper. Give her a double portion of wisdom and wise counsel, of discernment and knowledge. Give her moment-by-moment instruction. Let her see thru Heaven's Eyes. Hide her in the SAFE PLACE; use her for Your Glory. Let her love and her faith, her perseverance and holy grit be used to bring freedom for the captive. She is Your instrument, Lord Jesus. You are the melody.

Father God in Heaven, by Your Son Jesus we come into Your Presence, holding this broken son. We gently yet firmly lift him up to YOU … release him into YOUR swaddling arms and watch with great expectation … knowing that brokenness cannot remain shattered in Your Presence. Wholeness will be victorious. Let it be so, Lord Jesus. Let Shalom come.

A Deliverance Prayer (2009)

Our Father
Who Art in Heaven
Hallowed by Your HOLY AND RIGHTEOUS NAME
Hear Our Cry, O Lord
Hear Our Plea

We band together right now in this moment to pray for our sister, who needs Your Presence, Your peace, Your prevailing love. I ask Father God that you usher in angels to guard and protect right now, to watch over our friend; to encircle her and sing songs of victory. I ask Father God that you whisper Your Word into her spirit. I ask that You heal her, through and through. I ask Lord Jesus, knowing that You are the God Who Sees, the God Who Knows, the God Who can accomplish all things that pertain to her in this moment … and I ask that You do exceedingly abundantly more than she could ever ask or think. That You answer her prayer, that You make her complete, that You heal her, Lord, that You pour out Your Grace upon her like a cool and soothing stream. Father, I ask for Calm and Peace within and without; that Your Perfect Stillness banners over her. Lord, reveal Yourself to her in this moment, in this day. Turn the tables on the enemy who has threatened her. Catch him in his own noose. Bring about Your Justice and Your Liberty. We depend on You for manna, for life, for our very breath. We throw ourselves on the altar of mercy and ask that You run to her rescue, scooping her up into your Righteous Strong Arms and comfort her in Your Gentleness and Strength. We boldly approach Your Throne of Grace and ask that Your Mercy be extended to our friend who needs You now. And it is all because of JESUS our SAVIOR that we can voice this prayer and expect Your answer, Amen.

A Healing Prayer

Father, in the Name of Our Lord and Savior Jesus Christ and through the Authority of His Mighty Name; covered in the Precious Blood of the King of Kings and Lord of Lords, I stand in the authority of that Name and the power of that Blood and I speak to sickness and disease and tell it TO GO, IN JESUS' NAME. Illness, you are demanded back to the pit from whence you came. Sickness, you have no power in the Presence of the LORD. And the Presence of the LORD is here. I speak in faith and say to the household – Be whole from the top of your head to the soles of your feet. There is no sickness greater than His Name, and I speak that HEALING to your body and to the bodies of your husband and your children. Father, I ask for Peace and for Rest, both spiritually, emotionally and physically. I pray, Father God, for the Freedom and the Breakthrough and the Blessing to proceed as planned. I speak Healing and Health thru the Mighty Name of Jesus. I command every demon from the pit of hell to return empty handed, release your hold and be gone, your time is up! You have no power and you have no legal right. Be gone, IN JESUS' NAME! I command you back to the pit … we will not stand for this! Devil, we curse you in the Name of Our Father, Abba God, who has cursed you to the pit for eternity. I ask our Father in Heaven to release myriads of angels to cover, protect, minister and stand guard as God's Will for your life unfolds. I ask those angels to line the borders of your property and stand post at the doorways of your home. Father, let Healing reign and let Healing rain and let Healing rein into the family line … I curse every sick demon that would try and stop the Favor of the Lord. Spirit of Fear, be gone, in JESUS' NAME. Your time is up. Be gone like a vapor; there is a Mighty Rushing Wind of Healing and Blessing that will overtake this family, in JESUS' NAME. We will not stand for the devil's wiles any longer … I curse him in JESUS' NAME. Satan is under our feet, we remember his severed head, because of the Cross and the Resurrected Christ. We won't take no for an answer … the devil has to go. SO BE GONE! Father, release Your Favor, release Your Healing, release Your Power, release Your Plan … Let all that hath breath praise You … orchestrate our lives like a beautiful melody … purify us, cleanse us, mold us, make us. Let all the earth praise the LORD … You are our God and we are Your children … blessed and highly favored of the LORD. We depend on You for our very life and we bask in the Goodness of our Lord. Thank You for Your Healing. Thank You for Your Love. Thank You for Your Deliverance. Thank You for Miracles, Signs and Wonders. You are the Father of Heavenly Lights, Who gives good and perfect gifts, and You do not change like shifting shadows. You are Miraculous and Magnificent … we watch for Your Hand of Protection, Your Hand of Healing, Your Hand of Rescue. Praise You LORD. We serve a Mighty God. IN the NAME OF JESUS WE STAND, WE PRAY, IN HIM WE HAVE OUR VERY BEING, IT IS IN HIS NAME THAT WE REST AND WE WAIT. AMEN AND AMEN.

A Prayer of Blessing

I pray that Love, Grace, Hope and Mercy will find you today and sit with you awhile. I pray that the Lord of Love will shower blessing upon unspeakable blessing over you and your family, in this moment, today. I pray that every tangled knot in your life will be loosed by the oil of gladness; and that the pathway of praise will lead you to the beautiful meadow of peace. I pray that the dark corners of sadness will be spontaneously and spectacularly filled with His powerful beams of miraculous light. I pray that the Hem of His Linen Garment and the Train of His Royal Robe would be the bookends of your day, bringing His swaddled healing in the midst. May He do for you what He did for me. And then some.

Until we meet again, this is my prayer for you.

Luke 3 – "And while He prayed, the heaven opened ..."

A Vision Prayer

I want you to know I'm hurting with you, I feel your pain, I feel it ... I am praying earnestly for you, for the fullness of Time, for the Sovereignty of God, for the Shadow of His Wing. For the Safe Place. For the Relief. For the Release. There is nothing too hard for God and before we even ask Him, He already knows, it's already settled. It's already done. He will not let you faint away. He will renew, refresh and restore to you all that the locusts have eaten. There is a harvest from a field you can't measure. A ripe field needs empty baskets. I'm not sure what that means, but I see you, alone, on a hot summer morn in the Delta, sitting on the edge of a ripe field that goes to the horizon, with empty baskets. Quietly staring out over the plants that are loaded down with cotton (I don't know why it's a cotton field.) The only action you are taking is seeing. No sound, no movement, completely still. But you do see.
It's right there at your feet. You are one step away.

The sun and its heat have just about zapped all your energy and you are weak ...
But don't worry, the Son with His Strong Right Arm is going to show up and begin to fill the baskets.

Don't take your eyes off the field.

Overwhelmed (2009)

LORD, each of us are in jobs that overwhelm us, jobs that overtake us at times. During that, we each have family situations that need Your miraculous resolution. We deal daily with physical issues that need Your miraculous healing. Some of us wrestle internally with issues so private that no one is aware but You. In those secret places, Father, we plead for Your Mercy. It's a constant juggle, Lord; a steady struggle. It seems a continual uphill journey. Father, I ask today that you slow us down, allow us to breathe deep … to consider the lilies … that they neither toil nor spin, but that You care for them and clothe them with beauty. Help us Father to meditate on the sparrow and to know that if You care for it, as small and insignificant as it is, how much more LORD that You care for us, your children. Help us LORD to remember that when we ask for bread, You, the Good Father, would never give a stone. I ask LORD that you bless each of us with priority and excellence, wisdom and discernment; that you equip us for the day You've given us, that You continue to watch over our loved ones and guide them in The Way, and that you pour out Your Blessed Favor upon our many needs. Help us to be still and know that You are God. Help us to take refuge in the fact that nothing else matters, apart from Christ, The ONE Who loved us and laid down His life, just for us. We reflect on the Cross of Christ. We delight in the Love of our Lord. We know that resurrection is comin'. In Jesus' Name, Amen.

Hope (2004)

I am praying to the GOD OF HOPE on your behalf. You will make it, righteous one. You will look over your shoulder and see the providence of Jireh, the presence of Shammah, the calm of our Shalom. You will breathe in our Adonai and worship our Elyon. You will sense the security of our El Shaddai, our Rapha is aiding you even now. Our Roi is watching all that pertains to you. Our Deliverer is preparing the bridge that will walk you from the wasteland to Eden. Our Gardener will walk with you in the cool of the day. Do not despair, oh righteous one, the King of Righteousness has clothed you. Wrap yourself in the security of knowing that the LORD of Hosts is on your side. He is fighting for you. He is singing over you. He is standing behind you. He is shielding you. His arm comforts you. Who is this King of Glory? He is the God of Hope, and the righteous will live in measureless bounty of His Hope. Lift up your head, for the King of Glory is coming in. Do not despair. The enemy is a liar. The Truth is our Way and our Abundant Life. The Resurrector will raise up every dead thing from the tomb. Do not despair, oh righteous one, remember the ancient paths, this weeping may last for a night, but the Joy of the LORD will rise with the dawn. Hold on. Dawn is coming. You are so loved.

For the Fathers

Throughout my writing journey, I have known explicitly that what I write is intended for my sisterhood to read. I have never written anything intended for a male audience – other than my love poems to my love, Steven. That's a boundary I have set for myself and I have no desire to cross over. However, the LORD will use each of us, if we let Him, in ways we never intended. I realized after the following happened, that it wasn't a male audience I was speaking to. We were family and these were my brothers in Christ. It's funny that right now today it's Father's Day 2023 and I'm editing this compilation. Again, nothing is by coincidence. I don't know what year this happened, but I remember it clearly.

I was sitting in Sunday school one Father's day. The room was crowded with couples. In my heart, I suddenly heard words and was compelled to scribble them furiously into my journal. I knew in my heart that I was to gather the men to the front and pray this blessing over them. Was this a normal Sunday thing for me? Absolutely NOT. Was this something I had planned out the night before or even on my way up the stairs to the classroom that morning? Good gracious, absolutely not. I had not the faintest idea that the LORD would speak to me and through me to encourage my brothers in Christ. Did I know HE was telling me to do it? Yes, I did. Some would ask, "How did you know?" Girl, when HE talks, I promise you - you hear.

I do know that one of the enemy's greatest deceitful maneuvers is exchanging the roles of men and women, husband and wife. The LORD created all things in His perfect order. All things created have order. That includes marriage, which is the picture of Jesus and His church. There is a holy order for a husband and a wife to abide by and live under. The enemy has stealthily yet boldly switched the roles. Dear wife, please hear me. You are not the spiritual leader of your home. Dear wife, you are not the provider, you are not the lead. You are not the protector. You are not the stronger. Being louder doesn't make you so. Tantrums are not in the play book. If you see yourself as any of the above, please I beg you, search the scriptures for your God-ordered role then graciously give your husband his territory back. Empower him by allowing him back into the order that God originally gave him, but you somehow felt the need to step in and step over. With all love in my heart as I say this, Let go and let God. Many women see a need and feel it's their responsibility to fill it.

176

Sometimes it is; sometimes it's not. Find God's Order, the real G O, and use it as your M O. O K?

So, that Sunday morning, that Father's Day, I asked the teacher for permission to pray for the men in the room. He had seen me writing and graciously permitted the prayer to take place. The men came to the front, formed a circle, bowed their heads, then the LORD prayed this prayer over them. I pray it again today for the men in my tribe.

Father, may you give these men
The wisdom of Solomon
The eyes, ears, and mouth of Isaiah
The boldness of Daniel
The heart of David
The hands of Nehemiah, that they repair broken walls with a sword in one hand and a tool in the other. May you bless, multiply, and prosper the work of their hands
Give them the strength of Samson
The gentleness and compassion of the good Samaritan
The feet of Abraham, that they will walk where You tell them to, even if it leads to a place of sacrifice.
Allow that walk to lead them to the faith of Abraham.
May they proclaim with Joshua as they stand in their homes and say, 'Choose you this day whom you will serve, but as for me and my house, we will serve the Lord.
I bless them today in Jesus' Name. Amen.

We need our men back in Godly order. We need our brothers in Christ to take their place, in the strength and the power of the LORD. We need our men to take their stand in their homes and their families, in their workplaces, in their hobbies. We need our men to take back their rightful place, found in the order of the Lord's Word. And we need our wives to let them. Wives, you might need to let go of something, walk away from something, keep quiet about something so that the husbands can do what they were originally "order"ed to do.

I could go on, but I'm going to now quote Forrest Gump, "That's all I have to say about that."

2004

I pray I shall never be a clanging cymbal, ringing just to make noise. I pray to be the mouthpiece of the LORD, letting the trumpet of GOD resound! Let it be so, Lord Jesus. I am so faulty and so foolish and so ignorant of His Ways. I am an unschooled apprentice to the Master Carpenter, being taught how to mold and to make and to piece together a beautiful thing. Letting His Hands cover mine to guide me in every detail. For my good and For His Glory. Let it be so, Lord Jesus. I am in awe of this wonderful God who knows me through and through.

A Prayer of Intercession (2004)

Lord, I come to You in Jesus' Name, through His Name, covered in His Righteousness, weak in myself but strong in the power of His Might. I cast myself upon You, I lay at Your feet. I run to You, LORD. I intercede for my knitted friend, my sister in Christ, my gift from You. My friend. I ask even now as I pray that You are releasing angels of mercy to tend to her, to minister to her, Father, to wash her face and calm her struggle. Father, I know You remember Jesus in the desert being tempted by the tempter, the prince of this world, daring to tempt the Prince of Peace. Jesus, You were and are and will be Faithful and True. You are ENOUGH. You are all we NEED. I ask Oh Jesus that You will surround my friend with a shield of Favor. That the word of God will force the tempter to flee! I pray Oh Jesus that Your angels will tend to her, that Your comfort will ease her, that Your Joy will flood through her. You are her bread. You will not give her a stone. You are her drink, You will not give her a cup of dust. You are her abundance. Pull out the chair at Your table, Oh God, and let her sup with You even now. Set the table for her, God, in the heavenlies and let her feast upon the Goodness of our Lord. Hide her in the pavilion, Father. You see her obedience and Your Word says that You are delighted in Your child being obedient to Your Word. Be her manna today, Lord. Draw the bucket up from the well and give her a long, satisfying drink, a drink of Your completeness. Your sufficiency, Your eternal view. God, she presses into You and You will not forsake. Show Yourself strong on her behalf. Oh Father. Even now, Lord Jesus come. Your daughter is calling her Abba. Come, Lord Jesus. You are welcome here. You are needed here. You are here. Thank You, my Jesus. Let her cup run over, let her soul be unable to contain the measure of blessing You place within her, thank You Lord Jesus. We do not look back and long to return. We look forward fixing our eyes on Jesus the Author and Perfector of our faith. Perfect my friend even today. Lord, Your Word says that the daughters are like pillars being carved to adorn the palace. As she is carved today Father knowing the carving is painful, I know LORD that the outcome will be beautiful. For You are carving us into the image of Christ and You Oh LORD are lovely. A beautiful Savior. A trusted friend. A Warrior and a Shepherd. Our Bread and our Cup. With You, Oh Lord, we can do all things. We love You, LORD. We love You and we thank You. In Jesus we pray. Amen.

Obedience (December 21, 2004)

I sat down to do my quiet time. Loving the luxury of having the time to do it and stay in it as long as I want. I immediately began to think of how the galaxy(ies) all have their set courses. How the universe runs on complete, precise pattern in complete orchestration and rhythm. How if anything out there ... the earth, sun, solar system, anything were to move out of its pattern an inth of an inch one way or the other, then everything God set into motion in creation would be disturbed. Then I thought, but they can't move out of their pattern for the LORD JEHOVAH has created the pattern itself as well as the particular thing that runs the path. He set it in its place and therefore IT CANNOT BE MOVED. The sun, day after day, year after year, rises in the east and hastens to the west – because God told it to. Matthew tells us that at the end of time, the sun will go out and the SON WILL APPEAR. Praise God. Year after year, the earth orbits in the path God chose for it. Why? Because God set it in its path and it CANNOT BE MOVED. Think of the seas even ... they flow and ebb and tide from one body of water to the next, circling the earth with their currents ... continuously ... overwhelmingly ... unceasingly ... powerfully ... why? Because God told them to. He created them to. They have no choice.

Now, I return my out there thoughts to in here me. God created me, and He created a path for me to walk and a purpose for me to work out. Just as He threw the stars out there and knows each one by name, so He "threw me" to this earth and wrote my name on His Hand. He has an orbit for me, places for me to go, a pattern for me to walk, a chosen set of steps for me to "circle" this earth with. But unlike the sun and the stars and the sea ... He gave me a choice. Oh God, Why! Why did YOU choose to give us choice! How many, many, many times have I stepped out of the pattern; moved out of the orbit and gone off on my own created little spin ... which in the spiritual places have set things off course. How many? But God in His Grace gently firmly continuously nudges pushes shoves me back into my own personal circle so that I can complete the orbit He wants me to circle this earth with. I am overwhelmed at the thought that the planets without choice obey the voice of God; yet I in my foolishness, step out of His Will over and over and over.

Lord, my prayer today is urgent and earnest. Oh that I may live today in the path You set for me. Just as you threw the stars out and know each one by name and they stay their place in the heavens, God let me stay my place today. Keep me on track today. Just like the seas that flow from one body of water to another, let me be a sea of living water that can flow to another body today. Just like the rising of the sun to the setting of the same, let me be aglow afresh with the Word of God and hasten out into a dark place. Let me like the planets circle the earth in order and in perfect Will of God. Help me stay the course, Oh God. Keep my feet in place. I choose Your plan today. Help me to walk it out in order and in rhythm and in perfect unison with the other believers around me. Don't let me roller derby another from their course! Perfect rhythm, perfect rhyme. Perfect God whom I call mine!

A Prayer of Provision

Our Father
Which art in Heaven
Hallowed be THY NAME
THY KINGDOM come
THY WILL be done
On earth
Just as it is in heaven

We ascribe glory to YOUR NAME ONLY, KING JESUS
We lift empty hands to heaven and we BLESS YOUR NAME
Our eyes search for YOU in the lonely twists and turns. Our hearts hunger for YOUR TABLE.

For THE LORD IS GOOD, and HIS MERCY IS EVERLASTING
He is FOREVER FAITHFUL and FOREVER WATCHING HIS OWN
Thank you, KING JESUS, for holding us, protecting us, guiding us, saving us. All of our prayers are before YOU as incense. And LORD there have been many.

All of our tears have been stored in YOUR jar. And LORD YOU KNOW those jars are full.

Nothing is left undone, unheard, or unsaid. FATHER, YOU know it all. Oh GOD, the work YOU have done in our life is ETERNALLY GOOD and oh, how we THANK YOU for the works YOU HAVE DONE. YOU have answered prayer after prayer on our behalf and for that WE PRAISE YOU AND THANK YOU, LORD JESUS! Our prayer today is DEAR JESUS, DO

IT AGAIN! LORD! DO IT AGAIN! Heal us, LORD JESUS. Whole us, Father. Bring clarity, bring focus, bring understanding, bring wisdom ... make every crooked thing straight ... search out every nook and cranny of our situation, FILL IT, LORD, WITH YOUR BRIGHTNESS AND WHOLENESS, dear JESUS, with YOUR UNFAILING LIGHT and UNBEATABLE LOVE. Bring restoration and reconciliation. Love us, LORD, with comfort and peace. Give us understanding and wisdom as we walk with eyes fixed on YOU, THE AUTHOR AND FINISHER OF FAITH. Let us see what others cannot. Speak YOUR WORD to us IN THE SHADOWS OF YOUR WING.

YOUR LOVE is UNSINKABLE, UNSTAINABLE, UNWAVERING, LORD GOD. We plead for YOUR UNFAILING LOVE to do exceedingly, abundantly more than we can even think or imagine. We forever sing YOUR PRAISE and claim only YOU as KING JESUS. Let the REDEEMED OF THE LORD SAY SO. Amen.

2018

Our Father in Heaven, through the Mighty Name of Jesus, the Christ, and by the power of YOUR Holy Spirit, we ask that YOU hear our prayer.

We begin our prayer with praise for all YOU have done and for all that YOU are. We praise YOU for being our Redeemer God, our Provider God, our All Sufficient God. Words can never define or contain YOU. Words can never properly praise YOU. But we try. In our limited state, LORD GOD Almighty, we praise YOUR Beautiful, Eternal, Victorious Name.

We ask forgiveness for all sin we have committed, cleanse us so that we might be pure before YOU as we pray. We plead the BLOOD OF JESUS CHRIST to cleanse us now from all unrighteousness. Let us be white as snow before YOU, wearing the righteousness of Christ.

We believe YOUR Word, Lord. YOUR word says that if the righteous cry out, the LORD will hear, and YOU will deliver us from all our troubles. Lord Jesus, today, we cry out. YOU know our needs before we even ask, but YOU have commanded us to ask. Knowing this, LORD, we lay before YOU the issues at hand.

None of these issues are a surprise to YOU, oh LORD. YOU are Jehovah Roi, the GOD WHO SEES, and YOU see and know me, through and through. YOU know these struggles are strangling me. I cry out to YOU now for guidance and help, for answers and solutions, for a way of escape.

181

Oh LORD, YOU make a way where there seems to be no way. For the woman reading these words, we speak LIFE over and into her by the power of the Holy Spirit. We ask that YOU open eyes and ears to the way she should go. We ask LORD JESUS that she feel YOUR LOVE wrapping her like a blanket and she becomes secure in who she is IN YOU. YOU'VE promised her a future and a hope, plans to prosper her and not to harm her. We plead with YOU LORD to open the way for her now.

Answer quickly, O LORD, for my spirit fails. Do not hide YOUR face from me, Lord, or I will become like those who go down to the pit.

Let me hear YOUR lovingkindness in the morning. I trust in YOU. Teach me the way in which I should walk for to YOU I lift up my soul.

I believe that YOU, Oh God, are *my refuge, and underneath are YOUR everlasting arms.* YOU will never let me fall.

I believe that YOU, LORD, *are a shield around me, my glory, and the lifter of my head.*

YOUR Word promises that the LORD upholds all who fall and lifts up all who are bowed down. Lord Jesus, I am bowed down. Please lift me up.

I believe YOU will heal the brokenhearted and bind up their wounds. We wait for YOU, LORD, to do what only YOU can do.

The LORD is near to the brokenhearted and saves the crushed in spirit. Many are the afflictions of the righteous, but the LORD delivers her out of them all.

YOU are the WAY, the TRUTH, and the LIFE. I cry out to YOU now LORD to show my family the way, speak to us the truth, and fill us LORD with LIFE.

I will fear not, for YOU are with me. I will not be dismayed, for I AM is my God. YOU Oh LORD will strengthen me, will help me, will provide for me, will uphold me with YOUR righteous right hand.

I will wait patiently for the LORD; YOU will incline to me and hear my cry. YOU will draw me up from the pit of destruction, out of the miry bog, and set my feet upon the rock, making my steps secure. YOU will put a new song in my mouth, a song of praise to my GOD. Many will see this and hear this, and put their trust in the LORD.

YOU, LORD, are my lamp; the LORD turns my darkness into light. YOUR word says that those who hope in the LORD will renew their strength. LORD, my HOPE is IN

YOU. Let me soar on wings like eagles; let me run and not grow weary, let me walk and not be faint.

Jesus told us these things, so that in HIM I may have peace. In this world I do have trouble but I will take heart because CHRIST HAS OVERCOME THIS WORLD AND FOR THAT I PRAISE YOUR NAME. My eternity is secure because of the Blood of Jesus Christ.

I humble myself under God's mighty hand, that HE may lift me up in due time. I will cast all anxiety and depression on HIM because HE CARES FOR ME.

I will taste and see that the Lord is good; blessed is the woman who trusts in YOU! I will delight myself in the Lord, and YOU shall give me the desires of my heart.

YOUR word says that those who sow in tears shall reap in joy. YOUR word says that the joy of the Lord is our strength. In YOU, Oh LORD, I find JOY and STRENGTH.

Finally, LORD GOD, help me to think on whatever is true, whatever is noble, whatever is right, whatever is pure, whatever is lovely, whatever is admirable, all things excellent or praiseworthy. Let me think on these things and cast down any other thought that is not of YOU. Keep me LORD in perfect peace as I keep my mind stayed on YOU.

I know that YOU ARE JEHOVAH JIREH and will provide for YOUR lamb all that is needed. I kneel before YOU, bruised and battered, but wholly loved by the Savior, fully owned by YOU. I surrender these struggles to YOU, LORD. I ask and trust YOU to make a way where there seems to be no way, to open up the windows of heaven and let YOUR blessing flow forth. If there is action we are to take, then give us guidance and wisdom to know what to do. Let us hear only YOUR voice and give us courage to do what YOU say. This is our heart's cry this day, LORD JESUS. My friend and I pray these things in YOUR NAME. Amen.

Parables

The Meadow (2003)

Here I come, LORD. Finally. At long last. I know You've waited. I thank YOU for patience. I thank YOU for standing there. Waiting. Watching. I thank YOU for not giving up, for not turning Your back on me … as I did to YOU. Thank you for not giving my place at the table to someone else. I deserve a reprimand. I deserve to be humiliated. You deserve a reason. I don't have one. Yes, I do – it's the same one I've used before – you know it completely. I tell you once again that I chose to turn. I chose to look away. To walk away. I chose to separate the fruit from the vine, once again.

Here I come, LORD. I stumble toward you. What strength I had has vaporized. What vision I had has blurred. The voice I heard within me like thunder, now ominously silent. My heart has turned toward home yet my feet trip over the pebbles that seem like mountains. My hands fumble, uncomfortable with the weight of emptiness. My mind carries the guilt of my sin, my thoughts multiply with each fumbling step. In my darkest moment, a glimmer of LIGHT reminds me of home, reminds me of YOU. A spark of fire within me begins to kindle. The warmth of The Light invades my soul and revives my fight. My senses return and my feet stand up.

Here I come, LORD. I pick up my pace as my vision begins to focus. Glimpses of what we had together now fight the conviction of the sinner I've become. The road to remembrance strengthens my knees and feeds my soul. I remember, LORD. Do YOU? Yes, YOU do. I backtrack my steps. I remember The Way. I see the Light outside this dense thicket and I know I'm headed due east. I'm coming LORD. I'm coming. How quickly the Light returns.

Here I come, LORD. The trees are thinning, the meadow is just beyond. The path is littered with my belongings I carelessly dropped on my way in. On the way into this thicket of brambles, I dropped these possessions without thought. On my way out, I gather them, treasure them, one by one, as I retrieve them from the mud. They are now the trail that is leading me out. I never realized their value. I get on my knees to pick up worship. I run to gather up praise. I see the Word tossed aside. I pick it up, blow off the dirt, straighten the pages. Underneath it hidden in the mire is prayer. Under the brush nearby, shining like a jewel, is repentance. One by one, I gather them to my heart. One by one, they lead me out. I see you, Lord. Here I come.

Here I come LORD. I see You! Can I run on these feeble legs? Is there strength? Don't give up – it's me! I wave my white cloth – do you see me? My back is bent, my clothes are dirty, my wounds are bleeding, yet I run. I forget what I've done and remember IAM. I wave this surrender – do you see me? My vision blurred by sweat and tears ... can you see me clearly? I'm coming, LORD. I'm coming.

I run to YOU, LORD. I run to YOU. As fast as I can get me there, I run. I'm coming home, LORD JESUS. I remember. I remember this place. I remember Your face. I remember your love. I remember your grace. I remember. This is home. This is home. May I never turn away again. Thank You, LORD, for never forgetting me. May I never again live a day forgetting YOU. I run to YOU. But wait! I see You now – running – toward me.

Better is one day in your courts than a thousand elsewhere. Psalm 84:10

Her (2004)

She stood nervously at the back of the room. Afraid to go forward, too afraid to go back. Frozen in her place, her eyes fixed on the One who had given her life. She looked at the gathering, the voice inside screaming to her that she was not welcome; she was not accepted; she was of no account. She stood there, frozen. Her mind whirling with a thousand different strategies of what to do next. She held close the only object of worth to her, the hidden box held deep within her coat, the only thing that had not been opened for anyone else. She knew in her heart what she wanted to do, what she had to do, but she knew in her head that she couldn't do it. Then as she watched Him, He saw her. The twinkle in His eye, the tilt of His head, the posture of His body, the gentle motion of His arms told her that she was welcome. That in the midst of a great gathering, there were only two – her and He. That the plan in her heart was the right one. That the hidden thing within her would be safe with Him. She walked forward, nervous at first but determined to reach Him. No words were spoken but infinite things were said ... Oh, if she could just get to Him ... she pressed through the prejudice, she bolted through the fear, she sidestepped through the scorn, and lowered herself at His feet. She brought out the locked box, the precious hidden secret that she had saved. With fear and trembling she exposed the contents to an audience of One, and ever so gently poured it out at His feet.

The joy, the relief, the cleansing that all happened within her at that moment was too overwhelming to take in, her tears were a sign of her heart saying, "Finally it is done. Finally it is His." When the box was empty, He touched her head and blessed her life. Grateful for her willingness to be vulnerable enough to reveal the hidden thing. To let it go.

Oh frozen one, let it go. Pour your box out, friend. It is safe with Him.

The Gardener (2004)

My heart is so fertile right now. I'm not in a bearing fruit place; I'm in a plowing place. God is removing the boulders He has unearthed while plowing the heart of me. Can't you just see Him? Rising up early with the sun and the chickens, walking alone through this dirt field called me, opening the wire gate and getting straight to His work. He walks around the field, measuring it off, fencing it in. This is now His garden. NO TRESPASSERS ALLOWED He writes on the sign that He then hangs on the entry – an old, marred, weather-battered piece of wood that is used as the door into this field of mud. No gloves permitted, He's pulling stray weeds, burning sticker bushes, hauling off rocks and shooing away birds. Binning all trash, bagging broken glass, shoveling out clay, covering with hay. Straightening the zigzaggedly ruts into orderly rows as He plows the unknown underneath. Turning the unseen toward the Son to be aired out. The Gardener has much to do and wastes no time. He leans down low, grabs a handful of dirt – my dirt – clenches it in His fist, rolls it around in His palm, all the while smiling about the future planting. He knows full well the baskets of fruit that are sure to come. Yes, there is fruit to come. But first, the sweat, first the pain, first the plowing up and the hauling off. The time of pulling up and burning off. The rains, the droughts, the building of the wall to protect this square of earth from those who would steal, kill, or destroy. The Gardener's wisdom cannot be questioned. The dirt lies still as He carries on with His spade.

Then comes the day of rest. "Oh, blessed day," cries the sod. The Gardener laughs as He instructs the sod to rest. "Stay still until," He says, with love in His eyes. The dirt surrenders and does just that. The dry, brittle clods lay dormant for a time, a needed time … and over time, as the clods soften and transform, the garden is filled with the richest of soils, mixed to perfection, ready to take in whatever the Gardener desires. In His time, the dark, rich soil is now ready to cradle the seed. The seed will take root and rise upward. The vines will travel north and south, east and west. And one sweet day, sweet fruit will come. Knowing that end from the beginning, He continues to smile and continues His toil. Because this dirt is worth it.

"That's enough for today." The Gardener walks toward the gate, looks back lovingly at His handiwork, nods with pleasure, and heads toward home. "A good day's work," He thinks to Himself. He sits at the table and plans tomorrow, while outside a gentle Holy rain begins to fall. There is work yet to be done for this garden to thrive. His eye is ever on the harvest.

Trust the Gardener, Robin. He will not leave this field undone. He will not desert this plot of dirt. Let the pain produce rain. Let the hurts enrich the dirt. Let the Son shine on every seed. Watch for the sprouts to slowly burst through the sod's roof pushing courageously up to the warmth above.

Then, somebody, hurry! Pretty sure you're gonna' need some baskets. Fruits a'comin'.

Everyone ate and was satisfied. The disciples picked up 12 baskets of leftovers. Matthew 14

Katrina (2005)

To say that the past month has been tough would be a grandiose understatement. We watched with horror as Katrina forced her way into our life, deleting and destroying. Depleting and desolating everything in her path. On Monday, August 29, 2005, we were placed in a situation we didn't choose, sought safety where we could, and walked out on August 30 to a new world, a new way of life.

Our most important function was to find family. To make sure our loved ones were safe became our priority and focus. Thank GOD, all of mine were. I pray yours were too. Sadly, many were not. As the days clicked by, our routine became anew ... to help a neighbor move fallen trees, to find a store that had a bag of ice, to take some clothes down to the shelter, to find a station that had a gallon of gas. These were the daily assignments. Our lifestyle drastically changed and our priorities shuffled to new order.

Personally, I think the gas crisis scared me the most. I remember a panicked feeling, thinking that I would not be able to get gas and that somewhere sometime soon, I would ultimately be stranded. We rationed our travel to the bare necessity. When we heard rumor that a certain station had gas, we would get up early in the morning, go and sit in the line and wait. We would then pray that we'd make it to the pump for our turn before the gas was gone. Sometimes we did, sometimes we didn't. I know you know how this felt. Even now, with the gas crisis supposedly over, I am still leery of the gas gauge needle and think very differently before traveling to needless destinations.

While I reflected on all of this, the LORD gave me a spiritual lesson. Just like Him, don't you think? Nothing is unusable in His sovereign plan. Everything can be used to teach and to mature His children. To break us out of the old. To clothe us with the new. This is what He said to me:

Remember the crisis.
Consider the gas station as the Word of God.
Consider yourself as the car.
Consider your gas tank as your spirit.

"Now, Robin, what does your gauge read right now? F? E? Somewhere in between? Are you running on fumes or are you spilling over? Have you paid a price to be filled up? Are you looking daily for a place to fill up? Robin, do you sense the urgency to go and to sit and to wait on the Word? To "Line up" with the Word? To get up early in the morning, seeking only ME? Or do you wait for a crisis to make you understand the importance of it? Do you hope for it? Long for it? Are you relieved when you get it? Or are you making needless trips to destinations that are empty?

It's self-serve, you know. I decide when I need it and I get myself to it. When I roll up to the station and begin to fill my tank, the HOLY SPIRIT comes to my aid … making it FULL SERVICE. He goes right to the work HE loves … filling my tank (my cup runneth over) cleaning the windshield (Lord, give me insight), wiping away the bugs of the day (forgives my sins) so I can see clearly. He checks my oil (anoints my head) makes sure the tires are balanced and safe (gives me direction and protection) checks the map for me (I'll follow you, Lord) and sends me on my way. I drive away refreshed and relieved, knowing that I'll make it through yet another day, because my tank is full.

Oh, that my tank would ever be full! Oh, that I would not depend on a crisis to force me to His Word! Oh, that I would pay the price, sit and wait, and receive the fullness of Who He is. To navigate through each day with a full spirit, headed in the right direction, and equipped with a discipline to do the necessary things. Fill me up, LORD. I will wait for YOU.

As the deer panteth for the waterbrooks, so my soul pants after Thee, oh God.
Psalm 42: 1

When You said to me, "Seek My face,"
my heart said to You, 'Your face, O Lord, I shall seek." Psalm 27:8

100 Minus 1 Equals
The Littlest Ewe (2021)

For no known reason, she had always been unknown. She never knew why. Over time, she had somehow unjustly accepted that she was an Un. *Unknown. Unwanted. Unworthy. Unloved. Unneeded. Unseen,* that is. The weakest, smallest ewe. She had lived many years with the bleating voice in her head, *"No one could ever use a ewe like you."* These words had branded her, broken her, blamed her, shamed her. Over time, this collection of UNs had accomplished its bidding – it had sheared ewe's wooly heart into a shredded pile of slivers. Broken hearted. Littlest ewe.

Since birth, the world had used her and abused her. Shuffled from one owner to another, lost in the dust of an angry herd, she remained a nobody, an unknown. Sure, she had fleeting moments where she felt she had something to offer but frankly no one had taken the time. Like links in a chain, person after person after person had nudged her by. Judged by the jury without going to court, guilty was she. She felt gone. Lost in the fray. And here she stood, once again, like so many times before, at market, *unwanted.* The Un up for sale with no buyer in view. No reason to hope. No reason to be. Unwanted, Unwanted, Unwanted was she. That's what they said so that's what she believed. Eyes cast down, she stood there silent, sheepishly, shamefully shaking her head.

The banging of the hammer vibrated through the small stadium. The people in the stands came to attention. Let the bidding game begin. "Yeah, right." She thought. She stood there in the cold gray light, waiting. And just as she had guessed – there was silence. She awkwardly kicked the dirt, waiting for some sort of getaway plan as the routine rejection compounded her reality. Waiting for the gavel to hit the last time, an eternity of space in between the two loud bangs. Suddenly out of the shadowy corner a strong voice belted out, *"Finally! There she is! I want that one!"* Gasps were heard, heads were turned, eyes were squinting to see. Who is this unknown so and so buying this no good ewe eww ewe? Who is wasting His money on this matted mess? People talked in hushed voices behind their hands as the Farmer stepped forward into the light, paid the price, carted ewe up, and carried her home.

Home? Now that was a place this Un had never known. She'd never been in one spot long enough to call it home. But just as the truck came to a slow stop, a sliver of sun shot through the trailer window above her, warming her face with light. Somehow sending a fleck of hope. The back door of the trailer opened and she saw "home" before her, bursting forth in vivid color. The sun shone like a spotlight on the pasture and revealed a land like she truly didn't believe existed. Without wasting time, the Farmer gently unloaded her, placed an ID collar on her neck, picked the sticks from her coat, brushed her wool down smooth, nuzzled her ears and with a reassuring smile said, "There now. Go play, Little One. Dinner will be soon. Don't worry, I'll call you." Completely bumfuzzled, she watched as He then went from lamb to lamb, saying the same to each. Different sizes, different shapes, Different hues. All these ewes. One by one; One with one. One message to all. Enough kindness to go around. She thought to herself, "Who is this new Owner of mine? And did He just call me a One? Doesn't He know I'm an Un?"

Hemmed in by the safety of thick, wooden beams on every side, the littlest ewe trotted off into the expanse of the pasture. Is this real? Is that an ounce of joy I feel? Dare she allow herself to feel it? Oh, what a beautiful sunny, breezy day. She lifted her chin and breathed in deep, taking in the wholeness of the fresh farm air. Gone was the cold light of the market. All that she saw was lovely and lush in this little plot of land. She was free to romp through green grasses, lie down by still waters, soak in warm sun and breathe in fresh air. All. Day. Long. There were berries to nibble and cool spots to nap. Never before had she been in such a meadow. She was in the Farmer's pasture. She toyed with the tag on her new collar, thinking to herself. Had He really paid her price?

For a fleeting moment she allowed herself to feel the acceptance, the safety, the old "owned" feeling. But before she could release an age-old, held-back sigh of relief, her slivered mind remembered rejection. Here in this pasture of safety, her mind tumbled down the slippery slope of fear. She once again heard those familiar voices shouting, "*Unworthy. Unusable. Unowned. Unlovable. That's who ewe are.*" Little Ewe's mind flipped like a pancake as she once again believed the all too familiar Un's. She suddenly felt out of place. She felt she was in the wrong place. Her mind made her run. *Run, Un! Run!*

Well, NOW, she knew the Farmer had most assuredly made a mistake. She could NOW remember who she was – she furrowed her brow and clamped down her teeth. How did He not know? If He did, He most assuredly would never want her! He could only unlove an UN! She decided then and there that it was her responsibility to fix this mess that He had obviously created. But how? One thought came to mind. ESCAPE BACK INTO YOUR UN THAT'S KNOWN. Yeah, that's it. She looked along the horizon and saw the far-off fence line. A row of solid beams. And just like that, she knew she had to jump. That. fence. She had to escape. She had to get out of here before He found out her truth. With her eye on the distance, she trotted to the far side until she came to the fence line beam separating her from "the other side."

Backing up slowly so she could run forward fast, she mentally gauged the height she needed to fly to clear the beam. As she studied the fence with her eyes and planned her ascent and ultimate escape, she noticed a slat of wood nailed to the fence with three rusty nails, dangling precariously in the briars. She stared at the words. It named the field in which she stood. She read it slowly, "*PROPERTY OF Father's Love.*" "Hmm," she thought. "This pasture is called Father's Love?" Silence. Deep sheep thinking. Unable to accept the four written words, she blurted out, "Well, NOW I definitely know for shear that I'm in the wrong place! I do not belong here! He cannot include me in His Love! This pasture is for all those worthy ewes. Now, how does an UN get out?"

She looked for a gate. There was none to be found. She tried to crawl under the lowest rail, but, let's face it, she was too thick. Her last resort was to jump. She knew sheep had jumped fences in their dreams but never in reality. But she had to try. So she backed up slowly, counted to three, ran forward fatly, and with all her might, hurled herself over the fence. As she plopped down on the other side, catching her breath, she found herself sheepishly shaking her head. She looked at her new location, once again safe in her familiar UN known.

She turned her head from side to side, taking in the panoramic view. She saw that she was once again hemmed in by wooden beams. She stared while blinking. All she saw was lovely and lush. Green grasses, still waters, warm sun, fresh air, All. Day. Long.

"Wait." … insert puzzled sheep face here … "What? this field looks the same. But I'm on the outside now, back where I belong. What's going on?" She looked at the horizon. In the distance she saw yet another fence line, just like the one behind her. She bounced her way over to the wooden beams on the far away hillside and peered into the briars, breathlessly looking for a sign. Sure enough, dangling there was an old, slanted, slatted wood that read, "*PROPERTY OF Father's Love.*" Perplexed and confused she looked back at the fence over her shoulder (the one she just jumped) then glared back at the fence beside her and the expanse of land in between. "This cannot be!" She exclaimed. "Did I jump the wrong way? I didn't jump backwards, into the same pasture, did I? Wait a minute, wait a minute, let me get my bearings. Whatever, whatever, let me baaaa-ck up and just jump out again."

You had to give it to her. She wasn't a quitter when it came to judging herself. She was determined, you had to give her that. She was willing to do whatever it took to wear the label others had knitted on her. She backed up slowly, tediously planning her second escape. She hurled herself into the air, over the fence, and landed in a plop, thankfully padded by wool. "There!" she said to the wind. "Now, I'm for sure out of that pasture!" She got up, shook herself off and looked around. Once again hemmed in by wooden beams, all she saw was lovely and lush in this piece of land. She was free to wander through the green grasses, lie down by the still waters, soak in the sun and breathe in the air, All. Day. Long. She was in the pasture of the Master, A land called *Love*.

"NOW WAIT JUST A WOOLY-WONKING MINUTE! THIS MAKES NO SENSE! Am I … What tha … How did …" She looked behind her and sure enough, she saw the two fences in the distance that she had just cleared. She then looked forward and only saw lush green and sky blue. Sun and Shade. She forgot all about those good things and squinted her eyes for the fence. There it was, once again at the far horizon. Seeing it, she determinedly ran as fast as her skinny black legs would take her over to the beam on the hill. When she reached the fence, she hurriedly nudged her nose into the briars, found the wooden sign, flipped it to the sun and read with shock, "PROPERTY OF Father's Love." It was identical to the signs in the previous two pastures! Silence. Staring blankly with mind racing, at her own wit's end, she bleated into the heavens, "Stop it! Stop it, I say! I don't belong here! I must leave here! Right this minute! Stop tricking me with these signs!" So once again, she determinedly backed up, counted to three, ran for the third time toward the wood beam, hurled herself over and PLOP, just like that she was – for the third time – free from the fold. She caught her breath, shook her head, focused on her surroundings and saw ……. green pastures. Blue waters. Warm sun. Fresh air.

Oh, what a beautiful sunny, breezy day. All that she saw in this pasture was lovely and lush in this little plot of land. She was free to romp through the green grasses, lie down by the still waters, soak in the warm sun and breathe in the fresh air. All. Day. Long. Never before had she been in such a safe haven. She was in the pasture of the Farmer. He had placed her there with love. Littlest Ewe couldn't focus on the beauty; all she saw was bleak. All she thought was, "WHY?" Her mind couldn't, wouldn't shift. Her emotions wouldn't settle. Her broken heart refused to fuse. Exasperated and exhausted, she crumbled down into the grasses. There in her familiar aloneness, she started to cry. Eyes closed, quiet sobs, broken heart. Tears, remembering her name of Un.

As soon as the first tear drop eased down her nose, the Farmer was beside her, leaning on his staff, smiling. Before she could utter her rants, whines, whats and whys, He cut her off with his strong, country drawl. "Fancy meeting you here, Little One. Now, that you're somewhat still and I have your attention, I'm here to tell ewe something, Little One. Ewe can jump every fence 'til the cows come home, but you'll always land right back where I put you - right smack dab in the middle of *The Father's Love*. You can't outrun me or outwit me. That sign you keep finding, the one that hangs on the beam? Well, let me tell you … it's made from a very special tree … one that helped pay for you to be here. I saw you when no one else did, I bought you when no one else would, I placed you where I purposed you, and that's the full TRUTH, start to finish. Ewe've been believing the lie so long that it sounds like truth. Can you just believe truth in your heart and trust in your mind? I know you can. Little One, ewe've listened to false folks way too long. It's time to listen to truth. And that, by the way, would be Me. Aren't you tired of running? It's time ewe learned to dwell. Ewe, an UN? Well, that's unlikely. Let's let that go now. How about now you believe you're a ONE?" He stopped talking, giving her time to really hear what He had just said. As she slowly chose to choose this Truth, His Truth, He patted her head, nuzzled her ears and with a reassuring smile said, "There now. Go play, Little One. Dinner will be soon. Don't worry, I'll call you."

That was the beginning of her beginning. Since then she's been romping in green grasses, lying down by still cool waters. Breathing in the warm sun. Accepting the truth of who HE is, and who she is. Yes, the Farmer still goes to market. Yes, the pasture sign still dangles in the briars. Why, just today another trailer pulled up. Another little bewildered ewe was unloaded and led inside the fold. But this time, she was greeted by a wise old sheep, who spoke these words. "Well, hello, there, little one! Welcome to the Father's Love! This is the most wonderful place, hemmed in on every side. Don't waste your time jumping, hon. You can't escape from The Father's Love. I know, I know, you thought you were an UN. But THANKS BE TO GOD now you're a ONE. Welcome in, little One. Go play! And don't worry, He'll call you when dinner's ready."

> *What man among you, who has a hundred sheep and loses one of them,*
> *Does not leave the 99 in the open field and go after the lost one*
> *Until he finds it? And when he has found it,*
> *He joyfully puts it on his shoulders and takes it home.*
> *Luke 15*

The Hat Box

The Bible does say at the end of this life and the beginning of the next, that we each will give an account of our actions and reactions here on this earth. We'll have to re-visit the story of our lives and most likely have some 'splainin' to do. Do you think, once we get there, that He'll hand us "our time" and ask us to look at our days, one by one, and explain just what we were doing down here?

Picture yourself in heaven being handed a hatbox of your very own. You plop down on heaven's floor and open your box of days gone by. Taking them out one by one, like old worn love letters. You look at each day for the true worth it had. Holding the "good" days to your chest and smelling it, like a fresh towel just brought in from the line. Clutching it like a long-lost friend. And the LORD, being the Friend who sticks closely by, would kneel down beside us and point to a certain day and laugh, "Oh, that was a good day, wasn't it?" and we'd agree and we'd grin. Then He'd grab another, pat us on the back and say, "Oh, remember that one? That was such a good day!" Yes, LORD, I do. That was surely a very good day. And we'd bask in the goodness of the good gone days.

But then. Then all silence would break loose as "that" day and "that other day" and "Oh no, not that day" would shuffle to the top of the heap, and we'd hang our head in shame and embarrassment, because we remember "those" days very well. Those were the days we longed to forget. We'd clench those days to our chest – only for a different reason – and we'd cry out, "Why! Why did I do that! Why did I waste it! Why did I ruin it! Lord, forgive me; Lord forgive me."

The angels would stand still, frozen in their places, watching with care as the tears roll down our faces. They'd want to help us but they would not know how. Our Helper knows how, our Lord, our wonderful LORD, would take his Nail Scarred Hand, take the bad day out of our own and say, "I already have, child, I already have."

Ephesians 5 tells us to "make the most of our time." There are a lot of yesterdays I wish I could revisit. Remove. Redo. But praise GOD those days have a Crimson Stain upon them and I have been forgiven. It is that very forgiveness that motivates me to live today in a way that brings Him glory. I want my box stuffed full of those glory days. And I don't mean Bruce Springsteen. Don't you?

The Strainer

She brushed the wisp of graying hair away from her dimming eyes. Her wrinkled, translucent hands fumbled as she stood at the kitchen counter to prepare her evening meal. She went about her task slowly as she had hundreds of times before, as the window in her mind continually opened into the past. The house was empty except for her, a quiet humble cottage tucked on a side road, a plot of land with overrun peonies and old roses, rusty bikes and faded paint. A place where vibrant life had once lived. A place that once seemed far too cramped, chaotic and small, but now seemed vast and vacant. And way too quiet. She smiled to herself as her heart again reassured her, "You did good, Vera. You did real good. They're out there living their life, they're strong and happy and belong to Christ. You did good."

She pulled the dangling string in the pantry to shed some light into the shadows, she stared into the pantry at the items on the shelf; grabbed two small potatoes from the cupboard and headed to the sink. "Where does the time go?" her mind asked for the millionth time. She reached for the old plastic strainer and dumped the potatoes in. "Where did my life go?" Her mind continually asked as she thrust the water on. The water streamed out right on cue; she watched as the flakes of dirt strained through. The powerful clear fluid was steady and constant. She listened to its rushing hum. She took a small brush and gently but thoroughly scrubbed her to-be dinner. Small specks of dirt and grime began to disappear down the drain, until the potatoes were clean.

Her heart broke the silence. "That's what God has done for you." This thought startled her ... but she welcomed this conversation as she had so many times before with her Best Friend. "Well, good evenin', Lord ... and what did you just say? That's the first time You've ever called me a potato." "Well, good evening to you, Vera. Looks like a good dinner you're planning. Remember when you were young, newly married and you didn't know Me? But you met that Mrs. Eldridge - your neighbor - and she led you to Me? Remember?" "Yes, Lord, I remember. I loved her so." "Well, on that day - the day you met Me - You were just like those potatoes ... in need of a cleanin'. That very day - your new life day - I placed you in the strainer of Christ and turned on the stream of Grace. You've been there ever since."

Vera reached down and took her apron corner, raised it to her face and wiped. This thought was new to her, her old mind quickened and it caught her attention. "Why, Lord, I never thought about it quite like that ... please go on ..." She patted the potatoes dry and laid them on the counter. She cut the stove on and bent to get a pan.

"All that sin, Vera, the dirt of your life, the habits and patterns handed down to you from generations before - well, they had to be washed off. Some had to be scrubbed off (remember?). It took some quality time but slowly and surely it all drained through, right into the sea of forgetfulness. Leaving a beautiful, clean, useful Vera behind. Once you were in Christ, you were worthy, holy, and righteous. The old things had to go so that you could become new."

She sat down on the worn straight back chair as she took this revelation in. The creak of the chair exploded with sound as she eased her tiny frame down. The Lord was her constant companion, and she welcomed His company there in her kitchen. She'd spent many years talking to Him and His Presence always brought calm. She let this message sink deep in, remembering her past, remembering His Grace. She took one of the potatoes into her hand and rubbed its smooth, washed clean skin with the other; she circled it in her palm while she thought this through. The Lord went on ... "and then you met Cecil and you had the children and life came at you, hard and fast. Remember the fights, the sickness, the crises, the pain? Remember when nothing made sense and worry and fear and panic would come? Remember how at night, after all had gone to bed, you'd sit in that corner chair in the den and talk to Me about it all?

Vera snapped to from her thoughts and said, "Why, yes, Lord, I remember - and I'm so glad You do too. I had to pray about those things ... there wasn't anything else I could do. All I knew to do was pray ... that's one of the things Mrs. Eldridge taught me ... I loved her so. So much happened that I couldn't fix, but I knew You could. And You did. By the way, Thank You again for that." She smiled to herself and shook her head as a wellspring of thankfulness flowed into her heart. So very thankful for every answered prayer. All the while she peeled the potatoes and dropped them into the boiling water.

"All you did, Vera, was place it in the strainer. I took every one of those prayers, every whisper from your heart, every silent plea in the middle of the night, and I placed it in the strainer of holiness, of wisdom and counsel, of peace and provision. Of purpose. Everything selfish and prideful - every ounce of flesh - had to wash off those prayers. Every answer of Mine came from the washing of the Word. Some of those took some time - and surely some scrubbin' - but the Answer always came - right on time. "Do you see?"

This literally made Vera gasp -- she wasn't sure if it was from shock or sweet surprise, but the picture the Lord had just painted for her took her breath away as she began to understand. Every sick child made well, every bill paid, every mouth fed, every lost one found, every tear dried, every life found Christ ... all answered through the strainer of God. The thread of all those answers stitched the hem of her heart once again, around and around and around, making her once again strong. "Why, Yes, Lord, I see! I do see - I do!" An instant energy coursed through her from head to toe as this truth anchored her heart. Reassured her heart. The Lord had never left, had always heard, had always seen, had always cared, had always answered. Every prayer she had prayed had first been purified through Him. Even when she didn't know what or how to pray, He heard. Tears of thankfulness stung her eyes as she once again said, "I want to thank You, Lord. For .... for ... for everything. For all that washed down into that sea You talked about, and for all that remained in the clutch of Your Hand. Thank You, Lord."

She welcomed the silence that followed as her heart absorbed the moment. After a few minutes, she cut the stove off and left it there, she shuffled to the sink and picked up the strainer. She gently patted it dry and walked with it to the corner chair in the den. On the side table there by the lamp, was a worn leather bound bible, the flap curled up from the years, the ink of days gone by had smudged but still legible ... the names of children ... the dates of victories ... the underlined hope. Vera stared at this setting, this place where she had truly lived. This holy place. Then with confidence, she set the strainer down right there, in its new place, right beside the Holy Word. She smiled and turned to walk away. As she did, her heart spoke again ... "You did good, Vera. You did real good. They're out there living their life, they're strong and happy and belong to Christ. You did good."

Pearl (2003)

The oyster on the ocean floor, a creation of the Creator, floating mindlessly, silently, slowly along. The slit between two shells serving as a vacuum of sorts for all that floats beside. Sooner or later, a flake of dust glides mindlessly, silently, floatily between the two hard shells. While no one was watching or caring to notice, a small piece of sand, a sliver of dust, is greeted only by cramped darkness, sandwiched between two hard shells. Pressed. Trapped. Jailed. No exit. No sound. No joke. Trapped. Sand Surrender. Gone is the open ocean. Life for the flake quickly became small. Walled in. Suddenly and mysteriously, a friction out of nowhere wages war against the flake. Scrape, scrape, scrape, rub, rub, rub. The flake is ferociously massaged, over and over and over again. All the while the darkness envelopes, the pressure surmounts, the beating repeats. Continuous scrape, relentless rub. Tumble, tumble, toil and trouble. Scrape, scrape, scrape. Someone, give this flake a break! On and on and on, until just as quickly as it had started, the friction mysteriously stops. While no one was watching or caring to notice. The timing planned out by the

Creator Himself. The oyster is found, its double-wide home pried open, and there in the center, behold, a pearl.

It's a quite stunning miracle, don't you think? A flat flake of sand tumbled into a perfectly round pearl of great price. A thing of beauty. A jewel of worth.

In God's eyes, we are that flake. And life on this earth is quite the oyster. We, the dust of the earth, being tested and tried, tumbled and scraped, pressured and prodded, through GOD ONLY KNOWS WHAT (and by the way, He does know), over and over and over again … for what? For why? Life comes at us hard, relentless, darkness crouches at every corner, waiting to overtake us. Stresses suck us in, pressures pop their monster head into our face … For what? For why? Certainly not for darkness to win or for pressure to prevail … certainly not for naught. The ultimate and end result is God's passion – for our true beauty to be brought out. Yes, you heard me. I passionately pearly hope you heard me. Our Artist God desires that we, aka "the flake," become a pearl.

You. A jewel of great worth. A precious stone of great beauty. A one-of-a-kind magnificent pearl. Yes, this life is hard. Yes, problems are daily and steady. Yes, sometimes we feel trapped. But a much bigger yes is that as long as we stay under the brush of the Artist, our Creator God, as long as our eyes look beyond this darkness into His marvelous light and we hope in Him as the tumble rolls on, our hard life will result in our beauty. For you and you and you.

The scriptures tell us that there are twelve gates of pearl in the wall that surrounds the new Jerusalem - three pearl gates on each side of the square. What if those gates, what if those doorways, what if those pearls of heaven were created by the frictions endured by the saints while on earth? The miracle of the oyster with sand is not to be taken lightly (the flake doesn't take it lightly, that's for sure). It's not to be unseen. God changes us, molds us, beautifies us, perfects us through the trials we find ourselves trapped within. Could the gates of heaven be a symbol of the pressures on earth that taught us to trust in Him? As we are led through the entrance into the city, will we fully know that it's because we allowed the Creator Artist God to lead, purify, perfect our life? Will we be allowed entrance through the Gate of Pearl because we surrendered to His Will under His Mighty Hand as the world rubbed and scrubbed us to pieces, and yet we saw Him at the helm? Will we remember those pressures when we walk through the gate? Will we remember the tumbling or mumbling we made? Will the twelve gates eternally stand as a reminder of how He fashioned this flake into a pearl?

Asking for a friend. She's a flake too.

And the twelve gates were twelve pearls; each one of the gates was a single pearl. Revelation 21:21

Do not be afraid, for am I in God's place? As for you, you meant evil against me, but God meant it for good to bring about this present result. Genesis 50:19-20

Clean Plate (2021)

"Clean your plate, Robin. You're not getting up until you've cleaned your plate."

1971. I sat at the table, feet dangling above the floor, hands in lap, fork on table, scowl on face. Mad. Thoughts running crazy quick through my tousled head ... "How dare she make me eat this. I'll show her. She has no idea who she's messing with. I can outsit her at this standoff. I'll just wait it out. She'll see I'm set. Heels dug in. Don't wanna. Ain't gonna. Then she'll sigh. Yeah, then she'll cave. Then I'll have her right where I want her. Ha - She'll probably eat it herself then say I did. She'll ... she'll ..."

"Eat, Robin. Finish. We don't have all night."

My eyes dashed back and forth at the empty chairs around me. Brothers had finished - no problem (they'd eat anything obviously) and were back at play. I, the poor pitiful waif, (Oh the ache of the mistreated sole daughter), sat alone, staring at those piles of foods I did not want. I dared not eat. Seriously, how many green things can one person endure? Unbeknownst to me, she worked behind me continuously but her eye was ever on me. My thoughts continued its strategy ... "Ok, since that 'mad thing' obviously didn't work - when she makes eye contact with you, try the 'sad thing.' Force tears. Yeah, that's it. Lay your head on the table with tears in your eyes and beg. Plead. Moan. Cry with feeling. Force a fit. That'll show her JUST HOW MUCH you DO NOT want to eat THAT."

"Robin."

Just the way she said it made me know she meant it. Made me know I was losing time. Made me know I was one step closer to another something I did not want.

"It's good for you."

"Ahmmm I don't think so."

"It's full of things that help you grow. Make you strong."

"Ahmmm I am strong."

"So you think. But this - whether you believe it now or not - is what's needed to make you so. Robin Renee, THIS is GOOD FOR YOU."

She'd shifted to my middle name. Things were getting serious.

I heard the clock ticking its steady cadence. I stared at the piles of yuck on my plate. I was at an impasse. A crossroads. It was decision time. It was surrender time. Every tactic of mine had failed. Every thought of my own had lied. The mama standing behind me had her own plan and the plate in front of me was part of it. Surrender. White flag. I picked up the fork with caution, slow motion I stuck it into the heap. With weighted arms I lifted it with horror to my mouth. Eyes shut. Courage on. In it went.

"Clamp down, Robin. Clamp down. GOOD! Now start to chew ... hold your breath if you have to ... but chew, chew, CHEW! GREAT JOB! NOW SWALLOW! SWALLOW! KEEP IT DOWN! SEE!!! You did it! You survived it! You made it through the ... through the ... ok, it was just the first bite. But you did it! Ok ... now what you just did? Repeat. Repeat. Repeat until you see the plate."

Without realizing her presence behind me had tender eyes and smiling face, I slowly but steadily cleaned my plate. Then as was tradition (aka rule of the house) I said, "I enjoyed my dinner. May I be excused?" She quickly patted my shoulder with the damp dish rag and with the sound of accomplishment in her voice, she said, "Yes, you may."

I hurriedly scooted the chair back and ran out into the sun.

2019. I'm sitting at another table with a plate of life in front of me that I DON'T WANT TO EAT. In the stillness, I hear a Voice.

"Clean your plate, Robin. You're not moving forward until you've cleaned your plate."

I sit at this table, feet firm on the floor, hands in lap, fork on table, scowl on face. Mad. Thoughts running crazy quick through my tousled head ... "How dare HE make me eat this. I'll show HIM. HE has no idea who HE's messing with. I can outsit HIM at this standoff. I'll just wait it out. HE'll see I'm set. Heels dug in. Then HE'll sigh. Yeah, then HE'll cave. Then I'll have HIM right

202

where I want HIM. Ha - HE'll probably clean my plate for me. HE'll .... HE'll ... ..."

"Eat, Robin. Finish. We need to make it through this night."

My eyes dashed back and forth at the empty chairs around me. Others had finished and moved on ahead. I, the poor pitiful waif, (Oh the ache of the mistreated sole daughter), sat alone, staring at those piles of life I did not want. I dared not eat. Seriously, how many grief things can one person endure? Unbeknownst to me, HE worked behind me continuously, but HIS eye was ever on me. My thoughts continued its strategy ... "Ok, since the 'mad thing' didn't work - when HE makes eye contact with you, try the 'sad thing.' Force tears. Lay your head on Life's table with tears in your eyes and beg. Plead. Moan. Cry with feeling. Force a fit. That'll show HIM JUST HOW MUCH you DO NOT want to eat THAT."

"Robin."

Just the way HE said it made me know HE meant it. Made me know I was losing time. Made me know I was one step closer to another something I did not want.

"It's good for you."

"Ahmmm I don't think so."

"It's full of things that help you grow. Make you strong."

"Ahmmmm I am strong."

"So you think. But this - whether you believe it now or not - is what's needed to make you so. Robin Renee, THIS is GOOD FOR YOU."

Eek. My middle name.

I heard the clock of time ticking its steady cadence. I stared at the piles of yuck on my plate. Grief, loss, pain. I was at an impasse. A crossroads. It was decision time. It was surrender time. Every tactic of mine had failed. Every thought of my own had lied. The FATHER standing behind me had HIS own plan and the plate in front of me was part of it. Surrender. White flag. I picked up the fork with caution, slow motion I stuck it into the heap. With weighted arms I lifted it with horror to my mouth. Eyes shut. Courage on. In it went.

"Clamp down, Robin. Clamp down. GOOD! Now start to chew ... hold your breath if you need to ... but chew, chew, CHEW! GREAT JOB! NOW SWALLOW! SWALLOW! KEEP IT DOWN! SEE!!! You did it! You survived it! You made it through the ... through the ... ok, it was just the first bite. But you did it! Ok ... now what you just did? Repeat. Repeat. Repeat until you see the plate."

Without realizing HIS PRESENCE behind me, His arms open, His face smiling, I slowly but steadily cleaned my plate. I ate the yuck. I digested the grief. I swallowed the sorrow. Bite by bite. Then as was tradition (aka rule of the house) I said, "I INJOYed my dinner. May I be excused?" HE patted my shoulder with the nail-scarred Hand and with the Voice of completion said, "Yes, you may."

I hurriedly scooted the chair back and ran toward the Son.

"Weeping may stay overnight, but JOY will come in the morning." Psalm 30

"Father, if you are willing, take this cup from me. Nevertheless, not my will but Your Will be done." Luke 22.

"Your grace is sufficient for YOUR POWER is MADE PERFECT in my weakness." 2 Corinthians 12

"For I KNOW the plans I HAVE for you, says the LORD ... plans to prosper you, not to harm you ..." Jeremiah 29

"Even if HE kills me, I will hope in HIM." Job 13

"EVEN THERE YOUR HAND will lead me, YOUR RIGHT HAND will hold on to me." Psalm 139

"I will lift up my eyes to the HILLS, from whence cometh my help. My help comes from THE LORD, THE MAKER OF HEAVEN AND EARTH." Psalm 121

Tell Them To Sit Down (2007)

In the scriptures, in the gatherings on the hill, Jesus said to the disciples, "Tell them to sit down."

Rewind their day back to sunrise. Rewind each one of them back into their homes that morning. Going about their routine chores, checking schedules, preparing for another day.

One woman woke up to sickness. She had been dealing with it for a very long time, learning to live with the illness in her body, surrendered to its power over her. She got up that morning with that same sickness, that same infirmity, and she made a decision. She decided to leave the repetitive routine of her day behind and find this Jesus she had heard so much about. Who knows? There may be hope for her. She had heard He was a Healer. She made a decision that morning to find and follow Him for the day.

One woman woke up to sadness. Something had happened in her family, in her life that had left her with a hollow, deep grief. Perhaps it was the death of a child, a spouse, the death of a relationship, the death of a dream. She woke up in mourning, put on her black shawl, and sat down at her table. She thought about the routine hollow day ahead. Then she thought about the stories she'd heard of this Jesus. She had heard that Jesus could restore Life. She'd heard that He could turn her mourning into dancing; her sorrow into joy. So she made a decision at that table to get up and find Him, follow Him.

One woman woke up with secrets. Everyone in town outside her four walls thought her world within them was wonderful. They believed that she had all she could ever possibly want. She tirelessly worked to keep them believing that imaginary life, she held up that mask in the village square to prove to others she had it all. She alone knew the emptiness inside herself and the ache in her stomach. She knew the weight of keeping secrets hidden. She got up and began to prepare for the day. She began the process of beautifying herself in an effort to hide her real self. As she did, she thought about this Jesus she had heard so much about. How He could take away the burden. How He, who was Truth, could handle her truth. How He could break the chains of this façade of a life, the chains that she alone had forged. She was weary of the illusion. She made a quick decision that this was the day she would find Him, she would hear Him, she would follow Him. This was her day.

One woman woke up surrendered. She knew this Jesus, face to face, and she couldn't stop herself. She had believed Him when He said to her, "Your sins are forgiven." This day she would once again find Him, follow Him, believe Him.

Four women from different corners of life came together that one morning. Different circumstances had brought them to that rocky hillside but their need was on the same plain. They needed Jesus to level their life.

Now, I ask you to rewind YOUR day … what did you wake up with this morning? Perhaps you started your day today with sickness, or with sadness, or with secrets. Perhaps you have surrendered. But this morning at dawn, you made a decision. Who did you decide to follow?

Sing this with me –
I have decided to follow Jesus
I have decided to follow Jesus
I have decided to follow Jesus
No turning back, No turning back

Sitting on that hillside, listening to Him, the four women began to sense His authority, His power. They began to sense a Peace they couldn't comprehend. It was true, there was something different about this Rabbi. Someone real. For the first time in a long time, they felt a veil of hope enwrap them. They sensed light in their darkness. They felt healing in their heart. They looked around the crowd and realized that everyone seemed to be awakening to the same. There in the chaotic multitude, He had calmly found each and every one. It was true. He was true. Yes, there was something so very different about This Man.

Sing this with me –

Jesus, Jesus, Jesus
There's just something about that Name
Master, Savior, Jesus
Like the fragrance after the rain

Jesus, Jesus, Jesus,
Let all heaven and earth proclaim
Kings and kingdoms will all pass away
But there's something about that Name

He had taught all day. They were captivated by His message. As the setting sun cast shadows across the hillside, they had heard Him, they had experienced His Presence. The disciples wanted food provided for the crowd, some sort of physical food to quench their physical hunger … but the disciples didn't know that there was nothing they could ever possibly supply that could quench the hunger in their spirit. That manna was for the Lord only to provide. And on that hillside, that is exactly what He had done. Those folks on the hillside began to hum ….

He's all I need
He's all I need
Jesus is all I need
He's all I need
He's all I need
Jesus is all I need

I pray that is the hunger you are seeking to fill.

The Lord instructed the people to sit down. He wanted them still, He wanted them quiet, settled like sheep beside cool waters. He wanted their focus. No distractions. Once the crowd settled, the Lord Himself lifted the bread and blessed it, then broke it. Then smiled. He gave it to the multitude, one by one by one. Every hungry man, woman and child. The bread fed all who were there. Bellies full. The Bread of Life filled all who were there. Hearts full. Each returned home at sunset with peace, with hope, with healing, with life. Including those four women who now returned home different, knowing they'd never be the same. Each already making the plan to find Him again tomorrow.

I ask today that you see in your mind's eye, some three years later, the situation reversed. This Jesus, the Bread of Life, was lifted up by human hands not to be blessed, but to be cursed on a cross. No one was sitting, no one at peace. Mockings and insults hurled as they tried to break Him. This Bread, The Bread of heaven, Blessed of heaven, lifted up on a cross by human hands, cursed and refused by human lips. Scourged. Beaten. Bruised. Broken. Drained of blood and water until nothing was left. All He had was given.

Why? Because He knew we were hungry. Why were we hungry? Because we had sinned. Why did He care? Because He first loved us. Why did He die? Because He wanted us to live.

Bread of Heaven, broken for you. Why?
Bread of Heaven, poured out for you. Why?
Bread of Heaven, lifted up for you. By you. Why?
Bread of Heaven, died for you. Because of you. In place of you. Why?
Bread of Heaven, raised for you. Why?

Perhaps these are the questions you must take with you today as you find Him and follow Him. As you sit on a hillside and listen to Him. As you ask Him the why's of your life. The hungrier you are for answers, the happier He is to offer you the Bread.

Are you hungry? Receive The Bread of Life. Take this Body. Take this Blood. Follow this Jesus. He only is our God.

Jesus took bread, blessed it, broke it, gave it to the disciples and said,
"Take. Eat. This is My body." Matthew 26

Stalls (2005)

Have you ever wondered if there are stalls in heaven? Not the kind for people; but the kind for animals. And maybe not all animals – just certain animals – have you ever wondered? I kinda' likta' think that there are a few and that one day, I'll get to walk stall to stall to greet the four-legged servants or two-legged messengers who helped in their own way. For instance, do you think the first stall would hold the donkey that carried a very pregnant Mary to Bethlehem, the City of David, for census? I'm just thinking and can see them in my mind's eye … that little donkey's head popping over the half door peering next door to the stall holding the colt that carried our LORD into Jerusalem for the very last time. Do you think they've talked in their own language about carrying our Savior? If you were to look up into the rafters, would you see a nest with a dove settled down cooing peace, with an olive branch in her beak? As you walk along the corridor, would you find a fresh hay-filled spot for a lamb … the one caught on Mount Moriah on a very specific day … and Isaac was oh so glad to see him? Do you think? I'm just wondering through my fingers, and unfortunately you have to listen. I know animals don't have souls and can't be saved … but don't you think certain animals have a place there? One day we'll know for sure. My goodness, do you think Peter has a weekly heavenly visit to the patch of ground where the rooster lives, there at heaven's gate? It was the rooster's crow that brought Peter's return in order to strengthen the brothers. The rooster has a solid place in heaven's history so surely he has a patch of holy ground … do you think he's there? Don't you hope he's there?

I don't know the answer to any of these questions, but I love to think that every answer is YES AND AMEN. In my mind's eye, I see the stalls … tiny, little, shadowy sections holding furry creations that God used along the way to bring us back full circle to Eden. A very long line of very important stalls. And the best is last to come. For there at the end of that very long barn hall, with all the furry heads popping over their doorways and looking in unison down to the very end … for there, at the wall of it all is a magnificent white steed, a horse not yet ridden, but saddled and ready to go. His eyes like bronze and his legs like steel. His tail swishing like the four winds. He snorts into the air, anticipating. He paws into the dirt, exhilarating. He knows he'll carry the Master. One day. That horse has to be there – the Bible says it's so. And that day all eyes will see the reins in the reigning hands of the King of Kings and Lord of Lords. This horse, who comes from the line of two that floated in the ark, created with one purpose, is ready and raring to go. Yes, the last horse is ready.

Perhaps the stable angels are leading that steed to the entranceway of earth right now. Perhaps the Master is mounting his back. Right. Now. Can you see the LORD preparing to ride? Can you feel the click of His heels into the sides of the steed, while the trumpet blares His entrance?

Lift up your heads, all ye peoples, Redemption rideth nigh.

The Shepherd's Story (2009)

"You don't have to believe me, and I'll understand if you don't. I know you think I'm just an old, washed-up shepherd and I've spent one too many nights in the dark, eyeing sheep. Believe what you want, as you wish, that's your choice. But this is my story and I'll tell you - and anybody else who will listen - today, and again tomorrow, and every day after that what I say is true. I've been telling the same story for years. It's really my only story. It happened. I was there. I saw it, I heard it, I believed it. And I've never been the same.

My name is Joram, the son of Jehoshaphat. My family comes from a long line of shepherds. Some say we have the same skill as young David; but I'm not one to brag. I will say that my dad was one of the strongest men I've ever known, and I felt such honor being trained for my future by his wisdom. I felt chosen. He had the uncanny knack of knowing what the sheep were going to do long before they did. It was as if he understood how they thought and was able to keep one sheep – I mean step - ahead. Because of his herdsman skills, he was well known throughout the country as one who raised the largest, healthiest flock. Of course, that meant his sheep brought the best price at market. We spent all of our nights in the fields, taking care of those herds. Keeping them safe. As far back as I can remember, I was always watching out for sheep, while my father watched out for me. I was just a young boy on that one specific night, just celebrated my eighth year.

Of all my life's years … days and nights and nights and days … that one particular night stands out as if it were the only one I've lived. The only one that mattered. The beginning of everything. It was unusually quiet. The sheep bedded down early, huddled together on patches of green a few miles east on the hills outside Bethlehem. There were about ten of us awake, another five or so taking a turn to rest. To be honest, I was supposed to be among those resting, but for some reason, I just couldn't sleep. But I didn't let father know. I laid there and listened to the sheeps' lulling, rhythmic snoring noises mixed with the loud snores of the shepherds lying on their mats. Seems they like sheep could sleep anytime, anywhere. I listened to the others talking. I listened to the silence of the night. And as usual, I listened to Asa sing. Not that I was given a choice. That's a story in itself. Asa loved to sing. He knew most of the songs of David and would sing them over and over and over. Nobody had the heart to tell him he couldn't carry a tune in a bucket. He was old and slow and wasn't able to do much with the sheep anymore; so his only contribution (dare I say unwanted offering) was to sing. My father told the others that was all he had left, and a man needed something to give. So although it was a little off key and a whole lot off pitch, Asa would belt out the words from the songs of the great shepherd … "The LORD of Hosts is with us! The God of Jacob our stronghold."

I was overcome by the darkness. It was so thick. It was an intensely thick and quiet blackness. Eerie darkness. Normally we had a sky full of stars to glow over our camp; tonight though, for some strange reason, I couldn't see my hand in front of my face. It made me a bit uneasy but I knew for sure that my father was awake and that he was watching. Knowing that, I reassured myself that I was safe and seen. All of the sudden out of absolutely nowhere - well, what I mean is - one second it was black pitch dark and the next second there was this intense golden light, this indescribable brilliance - right there in the middle of camp. Those who were awake, scrambled back; those who were asleep, jolted clumsily forward. It was quite funny, now that I think back on it. The frenzy of it all … anyway. By this time we were all huddled together - just like the sheep - pressing in to each other corded about in our own fear. I pushed my way through the legs to find my abba. When I did, I grabbed hold of his legs so tight, so afraid I was in that sea of kneecaps. Abba reached down with his strong arm, lifted me to his chest, held me just as tight. That's when we realized there was something, someone, a being, right there, in front of us, an angel …

Okay, this is the point where people start to doubt and walk away. But I promise, an angel, standing right there in front of us. Standing in silent power, eyes full of authority, watching us, waiting. There was a peace I can't explain that gradually wrapped us, enveloped us, canopied over us. It cut the cord of fear that bound us. As we gradually grew quiet the angel spoke. And guess what his first words were? DON'T BE AFRAID! That's what he said ... don't be afraid! The angel went on to say that he was bringing news ... great news to the people ... not just us raggedy shepherds ... but to everyone ... news that would bring us great joy. He said that a child had been born that very night ... well, not just a child ... I should say THE CHILD ... the one Israel had been waiting on ... He had been born that night in Bethlehem! When the angel said Bethlehem, we all turned and looked at the walled city, there in the distance, still in their sleep, unaware of anything different. Unaware of Anyone new.

The angel told us that the Child is our Savior, our Christ the LORD. The one that David (and yeah, Asa too) sang of, the one our fathers had told us would come, the one the prophets of old had promised. The Messiah. Israel's Redemption. The King of the Jews.

Now, the angel didn't tell us exactly where He had been born, but he did give us hints on how to find Him. He said there would be a newborn lying in an animal's food trough, swaddled in cloths. The second he gave us this clue, immediately a dazzling, shining white myriad of angels illumined the dark night's sky ... as quick as a snap of the fingers or a twinkle of the eye ... one second there was one; the next second, there were millions ... from horizon to horizon ... and guess what they did! They sang! That made Asa happy, for sure. They sang a new song though. A song we'd never heard. A song we'd never forget. It went something like this:

"Glory to God in the Highest ... and on earth ... PEACE ... good will toward men."

As soon as the song was over, they were gone. The whole band of them, just gone, vamoosh, vanished as quickly as they had come. We stood there in the returned darkness, in shock, in awe, in every emotion you can roller coaster through, we experienced them all in a constant, continuous stream. No one spoke. No one could. Everyone just dealt with it in their own way, trying to absorb what had just happened. Finally abba broke the silence and said, "Well, what are we waiting for? Let's go find Him!" Everyone, still dazed and in shock, immediately agreed and headed out. Funny thing is, we didn't even think about the sheep; we just left 'em. We left our rods, our mats, our food, our senses, our everything ... we left it all ... we didn't care ... all we knew was that we had been visited by Heaven and the race was on to find Him!

We ran the whole way. I could keep the pace at first (it was mostly downhill), but it didn't take long before I started to lag behind. Let's face it, my legs nor my lungs could match theirs. My father must have known because he slowed his gait and waited, just for me. At some point, he swooped down and lifted me up. He ran the rest of the way with me bouncing on his back. What a strong abba.

When we entered the city gates, we stopped to catch our breath, then started the search. We were on mission and were oh so close. We knew from the angel that He had to be wherever animals were, so we went from stall to stall, disturbing donkeys and cows and goats and chickens all along the way. Nothing. No one. Refusing to give up, we circled up and strategized. Just as we agreed on the way we should go, we immediately saw in the distance, by the very back wall of the city gate, the glow of a small fire within a shelter, one Light in the dark. We could feel its warmth drawing us in. Pulling us toward. Could this be the Place? Our own plans thwarted with a resurgence of warm hope, we sprinted to the door then skidded to a stop in our very own tracks. Sure enough, just as the angel said, there was a family, amid the glow of the fire and the stench of the stall, there in the manger laid the newborn Babe, swaddled in cloths, asleep in the hay. The new mom and dad were startled when we converged on them. Just picture a band of ragged shepherds busting into the delivery room from nowhere. We told them to not be afraid (which seemed a bit ironic since it was the same phrase the angel had said to us just a few hours prior). We all tried to talk at once, making no sense at all, then my father raised his hands for silence. Abba looked at the man and the woman with compassion and purpose, and then began to speak. He introduced the group to the couple, he told them of the angel's visit and the angels' song. He told them that we had left our camp to find the Child. Everyone grunted in agreement, falling on their knees in a circle around the manger, grappling with the Way, the Truth, and the Life of that moment. Joseph thanked us and invited us to stay awhile. Mary was quiet, resting peacefully on straw beside the Infant, exhausted from His entrance, toying with His fingers, watching His sleeping face. Everyone quiet in this Sanctuary of Silence, Peace, Joy. Ahmmm, and guess what happened? Asa slowly stood up, lifted his face to the heavens, and began to sing ... and no one stopped him ... he sang the words of David that went something like this ... "But You O LORD Abide Forever! And Your Name to all generations! You Will Arise and Have Compassion on Zion; for it is time to be gracious to her, for the appointed time has come." Way off pitch, but that night – perfectly on point.

That happened some 70 years ago but, in my mind, it was yesterday. Most of my memories are fuzzy and blurred, but that angel memory is crystal clear. That Child grew up, began to teach, began to heal, performed miracle after miracle, He taught of the New Covenant, He explained our salvation through stories we could grasp, He had compassion and mercy. Why, He even brought back the dead! I followed Him, I listened to Him, I believed in Him. Whenever anyone would listen to me, I'd tell them about the angels I'd seen descend on the dark to tell us about The Light so many dark nights before.

Some years ago, they killed Him. I was in that crowd too, that Passover festival. I was on the streets of Jerusalem, with my own son on my shoulders, filled with grief and anger at the torture of the Son of Man, the Son of God. That Babe I'd seen some 33 years before. I watched Him suffer, I watched Him die. I was there at His earthly Alpha, I was there at His earthly Omega. When He drew His last breath, that darkness returned from every direction and surrounded us, swallowed us, that same darkness from that night in the field. I waited for the angel. Surely he would return. He didn't. But the veil in the temple tore and the earth quaked while people scrambled for their life.

I hurried away in mourning, through the chaotic crowds, back to the sheep, shaking my head in hopeless grief. In disbelief. I wrestled with the memories. I knew that He was true. I'd been a part of the joy of His birth and the agony of His death. I sat with the sheep in silence, staring into creation.

Until.

The first day of the week: the GRAVE – HIS GRAVE - WAS EMPTY! Yes! He filled the manger but then He emptied the grave! The grave couldn't hold The KING! Yes, He died but Yes, He lived! No, wait, let me rephrase - He Lives! I know it doesn't make much sense, but believe me, with the faith the size of a mustard seed, you too can believe HIM! He rose out of death, walked out of the grave, returned to heaven, and sat down at the right hand of His Father, His Abba. Now He waits to receive those who believe. The Messiah. The Redemption of Israel. The King of the Jews. The Alpha. The Omega.

Like I told you at the start, it's your choice to believe. The story I tell is Truth and He will bring you Life and show you the Way. It's your choice. I believe, even tho I'm just a washed-up old shepherd. Too old to tend sheep anymore but I still hang around the camp, just like an old shepherd before me. And sometimes, in the midst of dark nights, I can't help myself. I slowly stand, lift my face to the heavens, and start to sing."

Poems

These leftover bits and bobs didn't seem to fit in any of the other categories, so I gathered them up together as their own little family and have inserted them here. A bit random, yes, I would agree. But randoms need a nest too.

The Speed of Life

Life is laced with love and loss
With lessons learned and letting go
With highs and lows, with belts and bows
With some yesses, lots of no's,
This is the sting of life

With straight aheads and turn arounds
Exits off and hammers down
Winning laps, trophies, crowns
This is the speed of life

With strollers, diapers, little spoons
Dolls and thumbs and messy rooms
Bikes and slides, and tire swing rides
This is the best of life

With growing up and moving on
With hoping for tomorrow's dawn
With praying through the hanging on
This is the key to life

With graying heads
made-up beds
Quiet rooms
stillness looms
Best of friends
till the end
This husband and this wife

This is the speed of life

The Straight Back Chair (2010)

For my back yard friend who moved away.

I never knew just what would send me
Through the door and down the way
Perhaps a troubled mess would lead me
Perhaps just the joy of a bright, breezy day

Perhaps the need for quiet presence
Perhaps the need for counsel wise
Perhaps the sound of her fun laughter
Perhaps the spark in her mischievous eyes

What ere' the reason, it seemed not to matter
She never knew what drew me there
But time would come that I'd go walking
And soon sit down in a straight back chair

There in the kitchen at the calming wood table
Two friends would talk, and think, and share
Days of the past would be remembered
Days like today would be bathed in great prayer

She'd sit and listen to all of my stories
She never rushed or hurried my stay
We'd sit and we'd share and we'd give God the Glory
Two friends, two cups, on quiet Fall days

With yarn in a basket and cats in the sun
And a big yellow dog laying lazily down
Problems were hashed out and chaos was cast out
Sometimes without even making a sound

Time has moved on and so has my neighbor
My friend in whom I would sit and confide
Gone are the days of two friends at the table
Gone are the gifts of that time set aside

Oh how I wish I could go back to the pathway
There's nothing on earth that could start to compare
To the path that would lead me to my friend's back door way
To my friend who offered me a
Straight back chair.

A friend loves at all times. Proverbs 17:17

Friends

I hope you have many. More than that, I truly hope you have few. The few that run to you when you signal, encircle you when you're scared, link arms with you when you're weak, get in your face when you're wrong, embrace you when you're grieved, carry your purse when you're bold, wave pom poms when you succeed. Sometimes even wear compression socks with sandals, just to see if you're truly their friend in return. ☺ Those few. Proverbs 17:17 says, "A friend loves at all times." Love is a noun. Love is a verb. A palpable, tangible cord of three strands. I have my few. I pray you do too.

Written for a birthday -

Lucy had Ethel
Mary had Rhoda
Ginger had Mary Ann

Bobbie Joe, Billie Joe
Cagney, Lacey
Marsha and sister Jan

Thelma, Louise
(Road trip, please)
Laverne and Shirley too
Mary and Martha
Naomi and Ruth
Just to name a few

Down through time
The friends you find
Are the pillars of your life

They hold you up
They drag you through
They make you laugh
At strife

They make you think
Won't let you sink
They pray you from the mire

They cheer you on
They stand steel strong
When you are in the fire

To have a friend is to be a friend
The saying goes, I've heard
I know 'tis true
Because of you
The friend to this tall bird

So add our names to the list above
Voted "Best Friends on the Planet"
You are to me - and forever will be
My bestie friend named Janet.

My Friend and Me (2013)

We met when we weren't looking
We sensed a friend to be
In God's own perfect timing
He knit my friend to me

She gets my corny humor
She loves a Hebrew word
She's walked me through my troubles
She's held a hummingbird

She treasures things I treasure
She hurts when I'm in pain
She loves a quiet sunset
She sees God in the rain

She calls to stay connected
She's drawn to graveyard walks
She prays for all her loved ones
She loves to sit and talk

Her heart is full of laughter
Her marrow full of praise
Her muscle is her mercy
She's kind in all her ways

We met when we weren't looking
We sensed a friend to be
In God's own perfect timing
He knit my friend to me

I wrote the following poem entitled, "WHEN" in the months after Roger's death. When he died, I think it was a natural reaction to spend time reflecting on the life we had as a family, where we'd been and what we'd done. Together. The memories, too many to share, form the story that defines me, just as yours define you. It's one of a kind, a marvelous collection of memories, gone in the WHEN, way too soon. And I wouldn't trade a minute of it. Right now today is the fourth anniversary of his death. I'm filled with thoughts of when. I'm filled with thoughts of him. Oh, how I miss him.

When (November 2019)

When I was five
I stayed outside
With brothers, running wild
Dogs and cats and sibling spats
Were friends of this waif child

Sandy was our pony
And Ribbon was our hound
Days were long and simple
With no one else around

Mama saved her Green Stamps
She'd stick them in a book
Then drive me to the Green Stamp store
So I could wish and look

I'd climb the plum tree in the back
The bark would scratch my knees
I'd eat the plums while singing songs
I'd watch the falling leaves

When I was ten
I made the friends
I have still yet today
Horses, bikes, and
cotton field fights
were constant, daily play

Annie-Over, Tennis Court,
Kick the Can beneath street light
Trampolines and old tree swings
We played hard, day and night

Mom sewed for me from patterns
She worked with focused zest
Perhaps a cape for Easter
Or a fringed faux leather vest

She made me take piano
So I could learn to play
I quickly learned that music
Could wash the world away

I turned fifteen
I learned to drive
I learned that boys are mean
I spent my time with church friends
(The *Arlington Acteens*)

My mama made us garden
Every summer we would sweat
Hoeing weeds, "Mama, please, can we
Go in?" "*No, not yet.*"

High School ended, class of '80
We moved to Jackson town
I met the man God made for me
We married, settled down

When I was in my twenties
We built our home with love
On Ridgecrest Drive in Ridgeland
Two daughters from above

My girls and all the neighbor kids
Became the best of friends
I'd watch them play both night and day
And I'd remember when

Then came my years of thirty
Teaching 4s in Sunday school
Leading Girl Scouts to their campsite
Spending summers at the pool

The forties came,
the forties went
My life on routine spin
With dogs and cats and sibling spats
With family and friends

THEN FIFTY? Are you kidding me?
I'm how old did you say?
But wasn't it just yesterday
I ran outside to play?

Wasn't it just days ago
I rode horses with my friend?
Wasn't it just hours ago
I biked for hours on end?
Wasn't it just minutes since
I shopped the Green Stamp store
Or stood so still while mama pinned
The hem dragging the floor?

The truth renders me speechless
To know all that is gone
It feels the once wide curtains
Are slowly being drawn

If I could pass one truth to you
It's this I would declare
**GIVE EVERY MOMENT <u>ALL</u> YOU'VE GOT
MAKE <u>THAT</u> YOUR DAILY PRAYER.**

For there will come a day, my friend
When you will also say
Where did they go? I'd like to know
Who took my yesterday?

Psalm 103 – As for man, his days are like grass – he blooms like a flower of the field,
when the wind passes over it, it vanishes, and its place is remembered no more.
But from eternity to eternity the Lord's faithful love is toward those who fear Him, and
His righteousness toward the grandchildren of those who keep His covenant,
who remember to observe His precepts.

The Old Me (2022)

My thermostat is stuck on HOT
My hair's gone M I A
My eyes are weak
My body leaks
My ears – WHAT DID YOU SAY?

My skin once firm and tanny beige
Now loose and downy white
My airway once wide open
Just closes down - gag tight

My tummy once could take it-
All the sauces, all the spice
My menu now is tasteless
Just to keep my tummy nice

I never had a belly!
I could always see my feet!
I never had a bedtime!
Now at dusk I go to sleep!

My weight is on the upswing
No ice cream now at night
(If loving ice cream is so wrong
I don't want to be right)

My cursive once so curly
Now shaky writing skills
My drawer once full of make-up
Now filled with bottled pills

My hips – I never worried
About walking to and fro
But sometimes now while walking
My left hip screams out, "**NO!**"

My knees – what now!
The middle leg,
that thing that bends in two

Well, let's just say
The knee I had
Has left by forceful coup

The clothes I wear once cute and chic
Now look like belted sheet
The shoes I wear – they're flat and soft
To calm two painful feet

The changes I have seen in me
The losses and the gains
The time that's metamorphosed me
The pleasures and the pains

I'm still the same down deep within
This body made of dust
I asked me, "Do you have to age?"
My body said, "I must."

So, young me's gone
She's left the stage
She's flown like thistles fly

She left behind the broken bits

The old me heaves a sigh

I'll keep on keepin' on with this
This hip, this heart, this hair
Till Jesus takes me home for good
To meet the new me there

One of my greatest fears is that one day my picture will be framed and hung on the wall of Cracker Barrel.

Written For A Friend

I love you friend
Through thick and thin
We walk this road
With eyes on Him
We worry not
We trust His Word
We know our prayers
Are always heard

We walk the road
Through day, thru night
We pray till Faith
Turns into Sight

*Ask, and it shall be given. Seek, and you shall find. Knock, and the Door Will Be
Opened. Matthew 7:7-8*

1 Thessalonians 3:11-13
*Now may our God and Father Himself, and our Lord Jesus Christ
Direct our way to you. May the LORD cause you to increase and overflow
With love for one another and for everyone, just as we do for you.
May He make your hearts blameless in holiness before our God and Father
At the coming of our Lord Jesus with all His saints. Amen.*

I must preface the following writing with a short explanation. It's of a different genre than all other pieces that have been read thus far.

When our niece, Brooke, was attending Ole Miss and marching in the Pride of the South marching band, I wanted one chance to see her in action on the field. My kind brother Randy, her father, gave Steve and me his tickets for one Saturday's home game. We were so excited. We had never been – what a fun adventure and what thrill to see her in step with hundreds of uniforms, doing what bands do. So, off we headed to Oxford.

Needless to say, once was enough. We haven't been back.

Now you can read the following. I think that's enough prep.

How To Survive A Day Of S E C

Having completed my first on-campus SEC adventure, I feel compelled to share my personal lessons learned, my come-away thoughts, and my future strategies of survival so that the naive, those wet behind the ears, those eager yet foolish coming behind me can prepare for their future first. Please mull over and through the following truths so that you can survive your first step onto the college campus arena of your choice for a day - yes, a full and complete day - of football. (Editor's note: it is assumed and preferred that anyone planning to attend a college campus for a football game has a notarized Last Will and Testament already in place.)

1. You will need to practice walking long before you arrive on school grounds. For six months prior to your first SEC game, all Mississippians should walk from Laurel to Byram twice a day, about 75 miles or so one way, preferably along I-55 during rush hour traffic. This will help you acquire the ability to dodge oncoming traffic while maintaining a suitable rate of speed forward in order to reach the destination on schedule as well as keep you from getting trampled from behind. (It is quite possible to be run over without notice by a caravan of small wagons.)

2. You will need a compass and a star chart. Once you arrive in the parking lot in the early morning, check your compass for coordinates and your star chart for the constellation that will be directly overhead. Believe me when I say, the area in daylight looks much different after sundown. Having these two items in your survival kit will increase the possibility of finding your vehicle after the game.

3. Study the campus map prior to arrival. Perhaps take a night class or join an online discussion where the layout of all important structures is memorized. Find someone to mentor you, perhaps meeting at the local public library over coffee and friendly campus quizzes. Once you finish the class, you should be able to stand on any foot hill on campus, face any direction, and name at least three significant structures you can reach quickly to ask for assistance.

4. Prepare for the seat. In order to endure stadium seating, spend 3 hours a day sitting on a 2x4, suspended between two kitchen chairs. This allows your underside to prepare for the indention that will inevitably appear on game day as well as familiarize yourself with the allotted width of space you have before infringing on your soon-to-be-plank partner's allotted space. Your space ends where your sweaty neighbor's begins.

5. Prepare for the heat. Another important - dare I say critical - feature of SEC football in the South is the need to survive the heat level. Do not let the names of Fall months fool you. "October" means nothing this side of the equator. Let's face it, it never gets cool here. And the stadium is basically a pre-lit grill. So, in order to prepare for this, during the full month prior to your ticketed date, turn your oven on BROIL and stick your head in it every day, 3-5 minutes at first, building up your stamina to the length of a football quarter - 15 minutes - or in my vocabulary - eternity.

6. Check your calendar for national as well as little-known "new" holidays of significance. You want to ensure you are in the right attire in order to fit in with the thong – I mean throng. You can only achieve this by knowing calendared facts. Perhaps it's Valentine's Day - then wear pink or red. Perhaps it's Thanksgiving - then wear pilgrim shoes and a cute black tie collar. Little did I know that yesterday was "Wear a hankie for a dress" combined with "Just Say No to Undergarments" day. I was not aware and completely totally overdressed. I stood out like a clothed sore thumb.

7. Keep up with the ball. This is the hardest part of the entire process. When watching SEC on tv, the cameras do this job for me. I'm always aware of where the ball is in the play, thanks to the zoomed-in lens of the sidelines cameraman. He/She obviously does not get enough credit. Thank you, camera persons of America. In the stands it's not that easy to keep up with the ball - unless you first prepare. So, for two weeks prior to the game, ask your best friend to accompany you to an

open field where you take turns throwing small rocks at each other. This will train your eye to zero in on the rock (a k a ball) once you're seated. (Refer to #4 above)

8. Learn to say, "I need water," "I need a restroom," "What's that smell?" and "Where is Lot E" in at least five different languages. Rosetta Stone has many language apps available to download on your phone.

9. Be sure your phone is protected from flowing sweat from your face, arms, chest and hands. There are many cases available for purchase that are sweat proof.

This completes my help list for now. There are so many more I could add but I know you're tired of reading and are ready to get back to scrolling. And I need to go spray some Biofreeze on my everything.

Covid (2020)

Father God, bless every healthcare professional that courageously showed up day in and day out during the world shutdown. Thank you for every hospital that stayed open, every doctor that never went home, every nurse that never stopped, every aide that never quit. The things they experienced will stay with them the rest of their days. The lives they revived, the hands they held as lives slipped away. The following was written for them.

His hands are red from scrubbing
Yet he scrubs them hard and clean
His eyes won't blink from staring
At the oxygen machine

Her ears are tired from hearing
Yet another buzzer call
Her legs are sore from running
To the room way down the hall

His mask has made impressions
On his face that seem like dents
But he wears it as he sees to
All his patients hooked to vents

Her lunch was never eaten
The time she spent instead

Holding hands with one, life fading,
Humming hymns beside their bed

He's speechless yet speaks comfort
To the scared one, all alone
He tells them that "they're in good hands--
They'll soon enough go home."

She's weary yet she's ready
Once again she dons her scrubs
Another day of wires and tubes
And IVs filled with drugs

He reads the history record
He updates the daily chart
He runs to fill the needed 'scrip
He tracks their slowing heart

The paperwork relentless
Long hours through the night
The duties overwhelming
More sick with morning light

Their breaks last only minutes
In a room that's dimly lit
Trying to doze and energize
Before the changing shift

They work in Mississippi
Healing us is their prime skill
He and She are heroes
Caring for our ill

Thank you, Healthcare Hero
For your day in, day out fight
Caring for our loved ones
With your heart, your soul, your might

You daily face the madness
You daily feel the grind
You daily do what's needed
With others' health in mind

We may never get to meet you
Or thank you to your face
Please know you're loved and prayed for
By the whole Magnolia state

*One of my long-ago friends had a baby girl who was born sick. I wrote the following poem
for her. I believe the year to be 1990 or '91.*

Sweet Megan Leigh

Nine months of excitement
Were ended one morn
When sweet Megan Leigh Wallace
Was finally born

The mom and dad cried
And thanked God above
For giving them a brand new
Angel to love

Soon after her entrance
Into her new world
A problem was found
And then she was hurled

Into a world of round-the-clock nurses
And x-rays to make
And tubes and temperatures
And pressures to take

Raggedy Ann sat in the corner
Of the bassinet she was in
In that world full of noises
She came to depend

On the visits from mama and
Daddy each day
And she'd listen so closely
To hear each of them say

That they loved her and wanted her
To get well real soon
They wanted to take her home
To the bed in her room

They whispered sweet words
Into her ears
They cuddled her gently
While they fought back their tears

But the problem grew worse
And sweet Megan tried
To recover from surgery

But then
She died

And at that moment
When life she released
Her world changed again
From pain to sweet peace

The angels smiled sweetly
And welcomed her home
They led her to Jesus
And she sat at His throne

She now lives in Heaven
Where one day we'll be
When we enter the gate
We'll meet Megan Leigh

Moving (2016)

Empty cabinets
Empty drawers
Packing boxes
Cleaning floors

Spackling walls and
Spraying fumes
Bursts of Glade now
Fill each room

Through it all
I've come to see
That all my life
Is packed in me

These things I think
I need to store?
Are merely things
And nothing more

My heart is packed
With hoards of love
For family, friends
For HIM above

So with this love
That's packed within
Then life will be
What life has been

Life behind me
Life ahead
In between is
Where I tread

So I'll keep on
A'moppin floors
Until the day I
Close this door

Then travel down
The road to see
A brand new door
Open just for me

And there I'll dwell
With my sweet man
Same love, Same joy
But a few less pans

Come, Father (2020)

The following poem prayer, "*Come, Father*" comes from a place of grief, shock and heaviness. In Joshua 5, Joshua asks, "Are you on our side or our enemy's side?" And the Commander of the Armies basically said, "Neither. I didn't come to take sides. I've come to take over." Oh, how we need Him to come.

Billy Graham was once asked, "*What do you believe is the world's greatest social problem?*" Billy quickly responded, "*Racism. Racial or ethnic prejudice is a sin in the eyes of God. No Christian should allow his or her heart to be filled with the sin of prejudice.*" That discussion took place decades ago. And just look how far we've come.

A young boy died today
At the hands of a man
Cruising the 'hood
A boy out on foot
And because of his shirt
Shot dead in the dirt
He shot the young boy
Dead (#Trayvon)

Come, Father

Another man died today
At the hands of two men
A vibrant young man
Just out for a run
His face felt the sun
His life full ahead
Then father and son
Aim, pull, then dead

Death for hire
Think after fire
Shot dead by two
All because of skin hue
Dead (#Ahmaud)

Hurry, Father

Another man killed today
He squeezed the life from a man
Hiding behind a job
A one-man lynch mob
Hearing him beg for air
Lifting knee when lifeless stare
Was all that was left
Death by theft
Daring to say, "Justice?" (#George)

Oh God. Come, Father

Another boy died today
Sleeping in his bed
Dreaming of meadows
Then bullets - his head –
He never knew why
Shot dead
In his bed (#Rory)

Come, Father
Another young man died today
By the barrel of another young man
Bullets flying, young man dying
Daily, Deliberately,
Dead in the sand (#everycity)

What could he have been?
Isn't murder a sin?
The Original Top Ten?
Why oh GOD
Did man kill again?

Why are men killing men?

Oh God
Our men
Separated in two
Divided by hue
Broadcasting a breach
Is LET THEM LIVE within reach?

Broken men breaking men
Sin after sin
Being shot for his skin

A great divide
Deep and Wide
Declaring choice
Two lethal lines
of angry voice

Which side are YOU on?
How many men gone?

Oh God Oh Father
It's just too much
To think of such
Evil in hearts
Anger in hands
Mindless kill
Men lie still
Death begets death

We do not understand
All this blood in the sand

Let sides now be DONE
Let men stand as ONE
Let LIFE be our CRY
LET NO MORE MEN DIE

Oh God, Come, Father

Our sorrow is screaming
Our grief sees no end
We beg You Oh Father,
Please come for our men.

Joshua 5: 13 Now when Joshua was near Jericho, he looked up and saw a man standing in front of him with a drawn sword in his hand. Joshua went up to him and asked, "Are you for us or for our enemies?" 14 "Neither," he replied, "but as Commander of the Army of the LORD I have now come."

Do not harbor hatred against your brother.
Rebuke your neighbor directly and you will not incur guilt because of him.
Do not take revenge or bear a grudge against members of your community,
But Love your neighbor as yourself;
I AM the LORD. Leviticus 19:18

How good and how pleasant it is when
brothers live together
In harmony. Psalm 133

Precious

The following writings are included for the sake of my family. I love you all but if we are not blood related, you may choose to skip this precious chapter of my life. And I am A O K with that decision. Family has and always will be the fabric of this earthly life and I love each member of mine with all of my heart. The following pieces were written to honor them. Perhaps you may choose to get some paper and write your own rather than reading mine. And I am A O K with that decision too. Might even prefer it.

Maw Maw was a P31

My precious mother-n-love. She accepted me into the family in 1982 and began the gift of pouring into me her thinking, loving, living. Her humor, wisdom, energy, focus. Her service. Her excellence. Her biscuits recipe. ☺ Her support. The gift of her. I was completely unaware of the indelible mark she would leave on my life. Another stick pin on my life's map. My energetic, busy, constantly giving mother-n-love got sick in early 2016. We watched the energy slowly ebb away. That September she slipped silently from that wrinkled bed, that dark quiet room, straight into the glorious, live and in color presence of Christ. I can't wait to see her again. Perhaps she's made biscuits for the Bread of Life.

She is clothed with strength and splendor
She looks to the future cheerfully
Her mouth is full of wisdom
Her tongue with kind teaching
She oversees the activities of her household
And never eats the bread of idleness
Her children declare her happy
Her husband praises her
Many women have done well
But you surpass them all
Extol her for the fruit of her hand
And let her works praise her in the gates

Maw Maw's Eulogy (2016)

Jimmie Mangrum, our beloved mom and maw maw, the matriarch of our family, the plumb line for the Powells, was a woman of great beauty, of quiet strength, of fire-proof wisdom. A true artisan. A Proverbs 31 woman. The cornerstone of her family. Her hands were never idle; she never wasted time. Her heart was never selfish; she did all things with love.

Jimmie Loraine Reed was born March 8, 1928, to Tom and Lizzie Reed. She lived in downtown Jackson on West Silas Brown with her brothers and sisters. Her father owned a thriving barber shop downtown. Her mom stayed home and ran the household. She attended George Elementary and then Central High School, where she graduated 70 years ago on May 31, 1946. She married Bobby Ray Powell just three months before her senior year in high school was complete and soon started their family on King Drive in Pearl. Over time, Leonard, Ricky, Steve, and Debra were born. One of her greatest heartbreaks was losing Ricky as a baby, when he passed away. Just weeks ago she cried as she once again told the story of watching him wave "bye bye" to her. No mama should ever have to endure losing a child. But life continued and so did she. Her life with Bobby was soon pressured with trouble. Jimmie withstood even more heartbreak in her relationship with him but she stood strong in the face of adversity. It wasn't easy. After Bobby's untimely death, she began the task of raising her children on her own, making sure their needs were met. These were hard, lean years. Jimmie never wavered. She never lost hope. She never quit. She set her face like flint and put her hands to the task of making a life for her kids. She balanced work and family and made ends meet. And then her prince - a big ole' country farmer from Kosciusko with a great smile and an infectious laugh rode in and swept her off her feet. Bill Mangrum taught her to fish and ride in a boat (once and only once!), how to garden, play bingo, and dominos. He took her to the American Legion to dance every Friday night. And he occasionally brought home a hot loaf of Hardin's bread. He adored her. He called her "Hon." They married in June 1970, bought a big orange recliner for the living room, and began their journey together.

Everything about my mother-n-love is beautiful, that is certain. The Word says that the two greatest commandments are to Love God and to love others. Jimmie Mangrum did both with grace. The words that follow will meekly try to define for you the love in her heart by describing to you the works of her hands.

Her hands were never idle. She was a hard worker. She raised her kids, kept her house, cared for her aging parents, worked full time. She set her hand to the tasks and her shoulder to the wheel of life. She refused to waver and she never complained. When things got tense, a quick game of solitaire at the kitchen table always seemed to calm her down. She loved her family through thick and thin and she showed them daily by doing. She had to go to work, so she chose the career of drafting when the oil business was booming in Jackson. She sat at a drafting board day after day and taught herself the trade -- slowly, meticulously, perfectly drawing maps by hand for oil exploration. Then for extra money, she'd take maps home to color at night.

Her hands were never idle. She was driven to create. This truly was her life's passion. Her home is filled with her treasures. Creating brought her real joy. She was a true artisan. I don't remember a time in the 34 years I've been in the family that she wasn't "mid project" in something. She would be the first to laughingly tell you that she hated to read - that her mind would just wander off when she picked up a book, but that she loved to work with her hands. She loved to see a project to completion. Once it was finished, she'd neatly and orderly stack it on the dining room table, then head back to her chair, pick up more thread or mix up more porcelain, and start something new. Creating was her passion -- whether it was crocheted doilies, baby blankets, baby shoes, bedspreads, table cloths, Christmas stockings, quilts, afghans, lapghans, house shoes, scarves, porcelain dolls, porcelain Christmas ornaments, knitted bags, pot holders, glass coozies, dish rags, etched glass, beaded jewelry, plastic canvas kleenex boxes, or cross stitch - just to name a few. The list goes on and on. If she ever saw something that she wanted to make but had no pattern - no problem! She'd just figure it out on her own. Every Fall when the fair would come to town, she'd load her creations in plastic tubs and drive them down to the Trade Mart for the annual craft show. Two weeks later she'd return to retrieve them along with all the blue ribbons she had won. Her hands were always busy, always working - up until just a few weeks ago as she made tiny crocheted penny purses in her blue living room Mama Bear chair, with her sweet shihtzu Bear wedged in the space right beside her. Creating completed her. It made her happy.

Could we talk for just a minute about the Christmas yards? She and Bill would start at Thanksgiving and end near Christmas Eve creating the most wonderful, playful, child-loving Christmas display, complete with driveway lights made from pvc pipe and tuna fish cans and a porch Christmas scene - full of porcelain toddlers, a granny and grandpa, the carolers, the Christmas tree, and the centerpiece - her porcelain nativity. Night after night, the procession of lookers would slowly pass by in their cars, taking it all in. This made her smile. 3203 King Drive's yard won the BEST CHRISTMAS YARD sign for the city of Pearl, year after year.

Her hands were never idle. She had the most beautiful penmanship. It was important to her to write things down. It was important to her to remember. Her calendar was always filled with copious notes of birthdays and anniversaries ... even the annual "I stopped smoking" note was written on her calendar. All written in perfect penmanship with her beautiful hand. The only thing she didn't write were her recipes. So one day Debra followed behind her in the kitchen, measuring the scoops of flour and the cups of buttermilk, scribbling it on paper, just so we could make her biscuits and cornbread.

So, let's talk about her food! What a cook our maw maw was! She was one of the best cooks I've ever known. Her hands just knew how, that is for sure. No recipe required - she just cooked. Macaroni and cheese for her grandgirls, biscuits in the cast iron skillet for her Bill, roast in the electric skillet, hamburger steaks and gravy, best cornbread muffins in the state, chicken 'n dumplins for Jess; chocolate pie with homemade crust for Steve, banana pudding for Leonard, sweet potato pie for Deb, fresh peas and butterbeans, let's not forget her potato salad and deviled eggs! And we all know the story of the clown birthday cake she made for her grandson, Jeremy. When Jeremy was a baby, maw maw decided to learn to decorate cakes. Then for his birthday, she made him the most adorable and colorful clown cake. Jeremy was so excited. He stood in the kitchen chair, hovering over his best cake ever ... then he told his mom to go in the other room so he could show his grandmother the wedge of cake he wanted (and received I might add!). Jeremy now has three beautiful girls of his own; Jimmie's great grands whom she loved with great passion. And who can forget the time we were all seated in the dining room at a family dinner ready to partake of all Jimmie's wonderful concoctions, when all of the sudden the entire floor dropped down about an inch! In a panic everyone jumped up and started grabbing the food first AND THEN the children ... what a memory! Oh, and if you showed up unannounced and were hungry, no worries! She'd just throw on a pot of the best spaghetti in town. (She said that Worcestershire sauce was the secret ingredient, but we're still trying to duplicate it without success.) Never a recipe, her hands just cooked. No matter what she made, it was always finger-licking good and we always ate till we couldn't. And somehow, after every meal, the bowls were still full! So she'd gather up cool whip containers and send everyone home with leftovers. That was her. The giver. Her hands at work, showing her family her love.

One of my most poignant memories of her is when Jess was born. We were headed home from the hospital – Steve and I were excited while at the same time terrified about bringing this seven pound brand new human home with no owner's manual. We were exhausted but running on adrenalin ... we turned the corner to our house on Pecan Park Circle, and there, sitting on the cement porch stoop, was Maw Maw, surrounded by cookware. She had risen early that morning and had been cooking all day, just for us. She knew we'd need to eat and oh, how she met that need. Just another example of her loving us through the work of her hands.

Her hands were never idle. Whether it be crafts or cooking, or helping at the senior citizen center, or leading the American Legion Auxiliary, or teaching a craft class at the library, or making easter baskets to take to the nursing home, or sending cards to her Sunday school members, or taking plates of food across the street to the Jacobs, her hands showed her love. When Bill was sick with cancer and his back would hurt, I remember him saying that he would only let Jimmie rub his back because she somehow knew how to gently ease the pain away. Yes and Amen - her hands were a gift. Her hands were a picture of her heart.

You see, her heart was made of kindness. Never selfish or self-serving, never jealous, never mean spirited, never bitter. Always joyful. Always hopeful. Always cheerful. She always seemed to find the bright side of things, no matter the situation. And if for a brief moment she didn't, a quick game of Phase 10 with her grandgirls would help. My mother-n-love's goal in life was to love her family, her friends, her neighbors, and even complete strangers, each and every day of her life. She never put herself first, she never ignored a need, she touched each one of us deeply to our core by loving us individually, for who we were. Always believing the best in us and for us. We've all given her many reasons to fuss, that's for sure. But she never did. She just loved. Her heart was for her family and she demonstrated her heart by loving us through her hands.

And now her hands on earth are still. She is now with Jesus and with loved ones who have gone before. No more pain. No more tears. Brand New Body, Brand New Life. I like to imagine the LORD hugging her real tight, then showing her to her house on the real KING Drive. He would open the treasure chest of crochet thread stored up for her there and with a twinkle in HIS eye, give her a golden crochet needle with JM inscribed on its stem. I won't know if that truly happened until I get there but I do like to imagine it for now. I do however know for certain that until I see her again, I pledge to take up the baton that she has now passed. I believe I speak for all of us when I say - I want a heart like hers. Her legacy will live on through us as we try to imitate her selfless, kind ways. Love is a verb, an action. Something that we do. Maw Maw understood that. Her life was the truest example of that. She showed love daily in tangible ways. She loved GOD and she loved people. The two greatest commandments. And she did it well. Every time I hang a porcelain Christmas ornament, or stir up chicken and dressing, or attempt to conquer the chocolate pie recipe or pat the top of a doughy biscuit, or lay underneath a colorful afghan - I want to see her. I want to see her working or creating, serving or cooking ... and I want that vision to spur me on to do the same. To love like she did. To never be idle. To never give up. To always see best. To love through my hands.

Yes and amen, I want hands like hers.

For Maw Maw,

Death, you're still a loser (September 17, 2016)

I've learned that death is quiet
Stealthy vapor, cunning wind
Unaware, it cloaks our loved one
And slowly soaks her in

It never asks permission

It slips in through the door
And when no one is watching
It starts its tug of war

It fades away her twinkle
It slowly drains her might
It zaps her zest for talking
It zeroes out her fight

It steals her hands
It robs her legs
It blankets her with still
It quietly
but forcefully
Withdraws even her will

It waits for her to come to it
To take her final breath
It longs for her to
quietly
Give in to quiet death

It smiles and readies for the game
It snared within its lair
It thinks it's taking home this one
That's lost her taste for air

BUT JUST BEFORE
IN THROUGH THE DOOR
STRIDES JESUS IN HIS LOVE
HE LEANS DOWN CLOSE
AND SAYS, "DON'T FEAR!
IT'S TIME TO RISE ABOVE"

HE WHO OWNS
this still one's heart
Now stands beside her bed
HE joyfully transfuses life
What death had stamped as "dead"

HE looks at her
Then eyes dark death
And boldly says "GET OUT.
THIS ONE'S MINE.
YOU HAVE NO RIGHT.
SHE CHOSE SALVATION'S ROUTE

YOU THOUGHT YOU HAD ANOTHER ONE
TO ADD TO YOUR DARK TEAM
BUT ONCE AGAIN,
YOU WERE WRONG
I'VE TRUMPED YOUR QUIET SCHEME

RETURN NOW TO YOUR PIT OF DARK
YOU HAVE NO LEGAL RIGHT
I NOW REMOVE HER FROM YOUR GRIP
AND TAKE HER HOME TO LIGHT

IN HEAVEN SHE WILL
FEEL NO PAIN
SHE'LL WEAR MY CLOAK, MY RING
SHE'LL WALK AND TALK AND LEAP WITH JOY
OH, DEATH, WHERE IS YOUR STING?"

And then her SHEPHERD takes HIS lamb
to her home beyond the skies
Where death can never cloak her
With his quiet cunning lies

And just as it was ordered
Death slumps back through the door
Without its prize it wanted
Empty handed as before

I've learned that death's a loser
A weak, defeated foe
It tried to steal our maw maw
But THE LIFE told it to "GO."

I will ransom them from the power of Sheol
I will redeem them from death
Death, where are your barbs?
Sheol, where is your sting? Hosea 13:14

For Paw Paw. Gone Way Too Soon.

Bill Mangrum, Hardin's bread truck driver, country boy from Kosciusko who served in Korea, loved to garden and grow arched roses, loved to fish. Had a big orange corduroy recliner with an ash tray on the side table. Used grease to comb his gray hair back, Dick Tracy style. Had to have two shirt pockets – one to keep his black eye glass case and the other for a pack of smokes. Always smiling. Always laughing. Loved eating. Loved his Hon. Every Christmas you'd find him in the yard stringing lights right where she wanted them. Loved his grandchildren. Wore black dress shoes with white gym socks every day of his life. Played Bingo at the American Legion. Sat out on the front porch in a bear-sized rocker and watched the neighbors and the traffic. Maker of schnitzel. Hands like paws. Heart of a lion. Smile a mile wide. Our favorite.

Oh – The one thing he refused to eat: celery. "A pig won't even eat celery," he'd say at the table, while enjoying Hon's handiwork after a long day on the road.

We love you, Paw Paw. We miss you. Grow us a watermelon when we get there, okay?

Mother's Day (2020)

"On the count of three, say ICE CREAM."

1981. Mama and I had been in Jackson for less than a year, fearfully forging a way. In the midst of all the new things we had to face, we joined a new church … one that just happened to be taking pics for their new directory. Mama scheduled us a sitting. Ugh. Of course she did.

Sitting there on the piano bench, side by side, in the darkened room with fake books all around, feeling completely out of place and awkward, the photographer said, *"On the count of three, say ICE CREAM."* And just like that, time stood still. The whole world stopped. It's one of those moments in my life that I will never, ever forget. The minute he said it, mama and I lost it. You know that level of laugh where you can't stop … and even if you try you just laugh harder? Ahmm, yeah, that. We were trying so hard to be proper but our charade quickly fell apart at the seams. We laughed for a solid five minutes. Trying not to make eye contact because that just made us laugh harder. The photographer, perplexed and a bit frustrated, waited somewhat (im)patiently

245

for us to get it together … then the minute we struck our pose, we lost it again. And again. And again.

The final pic was the result of about 27 tries. And there are tears in our eyes.

What the photographer didn't know was that some months before in another town, another life, mama and I were at the Dairy Queen drive through. I had given mama my order and she was ready to talk to the bullhorn when it came our turn. She drove closely to the microphone so our order wouldn't be misinterpreted, and she waited to be acknowledged through the speaker. Suddenly and oh so ear bursting blaringly, some obvious giant from within the DQ screamed at her with friendly passion, wanting to know what he could serve her that day. I'm pretty sure her hair flew back from the sound waves. Ahmm, Dear DQ, please turn the volume down. Well, that did it. We started laughing. And we laughed till we couldn't. She couldn't get the order out and that made it even funnier. The DQ giant just told us to drive forward and get ourselves together or we weren't getting any ice cream that day.

I think the LORD knew my mama's sadness as she sat on that piano bench these so many months later, so I think He made that photographer say, "ice cream." It was a gift He knew we would get. The photographer – not a clue. Mama and I took the gift and squeezed all the joy out of it in the moment.

Mama. My mama. Our trail of life has taken us so many places, some have not been so funny. It's gone by way too fast. This is just one of those frozen (pun intended) memories that will stay with me forever. Yes, we've had tears in our eyes for many reasons, but I choose to remember the tear times like this. Her and me, side by side, tears in our eyes, unable to say *ICE CREAM*.

> *Weeping lasts for a night, but joy comes at Dairy Queen …*
> *I mean in the morning.*
> *Psalm 30*

Tree Climber (November 5, 2012)

Mama's birthday was one day after mine so every year we had to arm wrestle over who was going to be celebrated. Let's be honest, neither of us wanted to be. Some years I won and she received the party; other years, to my chagrin, she won and I got the cake. For 2012, I asked (okay, I commanded) that my brothers gift her with some sort of angel ... I wanted an angel themed party for her because she truly was our very own angel in residence. I bought her an angel painting and wrote a feely card about how she angeled all of us, each and every day. Roger – I think a card and cash was his gift. Following is Randy's gift to mama. See how well they do what I tell them? But truer words have never been written. Who knew angels wore steel toed boots?

Written by my brother Randy for our mama's 77th birthday.

Momma,
Robin told me to write something about angels for your birthday...She is always telling us what to do. I do like angels, Momma, I have nothing against them. They are divine beings who act as messengers of God...Who wouldn't like that? And truth be told, I could probably sit here and write an eight page, single spaced manifesto on the mystical, magical wonders of angels, and all who read it would weep great tears of joy and declare the splendors of my work. But just to spite Robin, I am not going to write about angels. I am going to write about something else. I am going to write about something Robin would tell me not to write about. I'm going to write about climbing trees.

Have you ever noticed how life is a lot like climbing a tree? I have. You always climb a tree on your own, no one is there to push or pull you. No one can help you climb a tree. You have to decide where to grab and how to hang on. These decisions are yours. No one is there to move your hand into a firm grip or guide your arm around a branch. You have to find the right perch, a limb strong enough, sturdy enough, to support your weight. Sure someone can offer advice from the ground, but ultimately you have to decide. If you make the wrong choice, if you make a mistake, you wind up again at the base of the tree and the climb begins again. In a way, I think we've all been down here on earth climbing a tree.

Momma, over the course of time, you have climbed a very tall tree. And you have managed, it seems, to always take the right holds and grab the right places. Your tree has not always been a perfect, vertical, solid oak. There have been weak branches to bypass and dead limbs to avoid. But you never stopped your climb. You worked your way around the obstacles and continued your ascent. You never gave up and you are still going.

247

I don't think you've reached the top of your timber, Momma. There's still a ways to go. Roger, Robin and I have watched your progress and we're trying to climb your same route. You've been a very good tree climber and an excellent life example. I hope we can climb as high as you.
Happy Birthday Momma!
Randy

Memory, For Mama (2017)

Dear mom, I'll be your memory
The one who knows your past
My memory, like a vice grip
Your memory, fading fast

Dear mom, I'll be the teller
When you no longer say
The words you know you knew before
Before they went away

Dear mom, I'll be your mouthpiece
Just tell me when to start
I'll tell the things you know you knew
For I know them all by heart

I'll tell of Oklahoma
And a family, last name WHITE
I'll tell of land, of wind, of pain
I'll tell the story right

I'll tell of how you sweated
Hoeing peanuts in the field
I'll tell of sinks of taters
Where you washed and scraped and peeled

I'll tell about the driveway and
The train across the road
I'll tell about the dresses that
You taught yourself to sew

I'll tell about the windmill
And the big ole' black iron pot
I'll tell about the smokehouse

And the sleeping on a cot

I'll tell about the running
Waving sticks and chasing bees
I'll tell about the laughter and
The always scratched up knees

I'll tell of wearing bonnets
Of making quilts and such
I'll tell about your mama
Never loving on you much

I'll tell about your daddy
A hard one, my grandpa
I'll tell about his cowboy hat,
the toothpick in his jaw

I'll tell of how you walked each week
A mile or more to church
To hear the gospel, walk the aisle
And learn a bible verse

I'll tell of how you gave your life
To Jesus, God's own Son
And started down your journey
With you and GOD as one

The castor oil
I won't forget
A tablespoon for all
You seven kids would gag and spew
That horrible black draught

I'll tell about your wedding
Wearing satin baby blue
Standing in the kitchen
Is where you said I DO

And DO you did
For 25 years
Raising four kids, house to house
Moving with the preacher man
Poor as one church mouse

I'll tell about the laughter
All the tricks you played on us
The gardens that you planted
While listening to us fuss

The sad parts I will weave within
The story, sad but true
Our Butch who died, I saw you cry
Standing in his room

Or when you packed the truck to leave
Selling furniture to pay the bills
And moved yourself to Jackson
The memory gives me chills

You set up house
You set us first
You held your head up high
You started over, started new
You weren't afraid to try

Your banking jobs
Your servant heart
Your work in prison rooms

Your Sunday School
Your love of shoes
Your fragrant yellow blooms

Dear mom, I'll be your memory
I'll tell the story true
I'll never lose the memory
Of how much I love you.

One Year Later. For Mama (May 3, 2022)

She never searched for fortune
She never craved for fame
A pedestal she never climbed
No bullhorn blared her name

She hungered not for fancy
She turned away from shine
She loved the meek, the simple
The plain, the unrefined

She lived life in the Shadow
Humbly walking through her day
Making sure she shared the Savior
He was her Truth, her Life, her Way

She shared Him through her errands
She shared Him through her words
She shared Him through her laughter
She shared Him as she served

She shared Him through her presence
She shared Him through her time
She shared Him through her pocketbook
Her dollars, nickels, dimes

She held hands with the weary
She sat with those who mourned
She forgave those who had hurt her
She mended what was torn

One year ago the Lord saw fit
To take her home on high
And every day I've lived since then
I've tried to say goodbye

Her absence left an absence
A void no one can fill
This ache I'll carry onward
Day by day by day until

I find myself in Glory
Headed straight toward Gates of Pearl
And there she'll be, face beaming
Waiting for her brown eyed girl

I'll hug her for a thousand years
Then hold her hand two more
We'll laugh and live there side by side
Just like we did before

For the LORD Himself will descend with a shout, with the archangel's voice
And with the trumpet of God, and the dead in Christ will rise first.
Then we who are still alive, who are left, will be caught up together
With them in the clouds to meet the LORD in the air,
And so we will always be with the LORD.
Therefore encourage each other with these words.
1 Thessalonians 4: 16-17

Rose June's Eulogy (May 10, 2021)

Good morning,

Thank you, Regina, for playing the piano for us today. Regina and her family are longtime friends of our family. Thank you, Valissa, for opening our service with Grace. Valissa is one of the healthcare professionals that has cared for mama and other residents at Willow Creek in Byram. I would go in on a Sunday morn and she'd have them all circled up in the day room, and she'd be singing to them. Thank you for being here with us today and honoring mama in such a beautiful way.

In 1973, our oldest brother, Butch died. In 1997, our father died. In 2019 our youngest brother, Roger, died. And here we are. 2021. Knowing this, I have one thing to say to my brother, Randy – WE HAVE GOT TO STOP MEETING LIKE THIS. ☺ Randy and I do plan to have an arm wrestle competition after today's service to see who gets to do the next funeral. I think I can take him.

Seriously, Randy and I thank all of you for loving mama and for being here today.

I want to thank our family watching online in Oklahoma, Arizona, and Texas. We love you all and know you are here in spirit and prayers. And Zoom. Ha

Yesterday mama's sister, Zelma, aka Auntie Z, called to tell me that she and her daughter, our cousin, Janet, were driving over from Texas. We are so blessed to have them here with us today.

Randy gave Roger's eulogy in 2019. After it was done, I said since he did such a stellar job on Roger's that he might as well go ahead and get mama's eulogy drafted up. He looked at me and said, 'Well, I think you get the next one.' So here I am with the overwhelming challenge to share with you a few thoughts that would honor her. As the one and only daughter, mama and I had a oneness to us that I can't explain. As I've written my thoughts, I have known through and through that this – to be standing here talking to you today – is my final opportunity to honor her. And that is my desire – to honor her through this. To relay to you tidbits of my mama's life that hopefully will strengthen you somehow, or perhaps lighten you somehow … maybe challenge you somehow … it's an honor and I, with calm but massive anxiety, accept the challenge. For her.

I feel a little like that 4 year old boy brimming over with excitement who has you cornered at a family get together … you know the one, he smells like puppies and his clothes are all disheveled and his hair is slicked back and he's talking non-stop to you about all things of his day and he won't finish a sentence, he just keeps connecting thoughts with and and and and … and you alone are his captive audience … that's a little how I feel. There's so much I want to share. So many things have come to mind over this past week and I want to blurt the memories out to anyone who will listen. But I pray that I have focused my thoughts in such a way that the following makes sense, is brief, and is a blessing. And I promise I won't corner you. ☺

I could stand here and talk to you about her love for the LORD. If you read her obituary or if you knew her for five minutes, you know she loved the LORD. I don't have to convince you of that.

I could review her life of giving … for she was a cheerful, constant giver. But then again, if you knew her – you know that is truth. She was happiest when she was giving. Whatever she had or whatever you needed … she freely and joyfully gave.

Oh I could share with you about her incredible sense of humor … Randy and I have come to understand that our humor came straight from her. A cheerful heart is such good med. She loved a good prank or practical joke or surprise … anything that would bring a laugh … she had such a quick wit … anyone remember the old man mask she would put on then answer the door? Or have Randy and I told you about the time she got us kids so excited about ROASTING SNOWBALLS on a coat hanger over an open flame? Yeah, she thought that was hilarious. What about when I opened my honeymoon luggage and all my personals were sewn together? Or when I was sunbathing at a crowded pool and she snuck into my room and changed the music from the coolest radio station ever (WZZQ) to her 8 track tape of THE CHUCKWAGON GANG? And I could see her silhouette in the window, doubled over laughing … Or what about on our trip to Wyoming years ago as a family, we kept seeing these fields of wild flowers that were just gorgeous … one day, when it was just me and mama, she decided it would be great fun if

253

she were to lie down in one of the wild flower fields and pose … you know what I mean … lay down on her stomach and prop her head or her chin up (the way Olan Mills used to make us do) and I took pictures while we both were just literally breathless from laughing. Yes, mama loved a grand laugh and she loved to pull a good prank. Goodness, she got through some tough stuff in her life with her humor.

I could tell you about her short term mission trips, her banking jobs, her love for any kind of exercise equipment or her ever growing collection of kitchen gadgets. I could tell you about the time we were shopping and we both went to the counter, unbeknownst to us, with the exact same dress. I could remind you of her love for cute shoes in every color. I could tell you about her dabbling in the crafts with her macrame lion or her crocheted afghans. I could share her recipes (although you really don't want it) for every chilled green gelatin with cottage cheese and pineapple dessert known to man. But after some thought and quiet reflection, I have decided to spend this time speaking to you of June's prunes. And no, I don't mean dried plums that keep you regular. Even though she would find that hilarious. I mean the type of pruning that brings forth blooming. Because my mama was a perpetual bouquet.

Years ago a little book came out called THE SECRETS OF THE VINE. It was a small pocket sized book that was written from the text of John 15. In this scripture, It was the night after the Passover meal and Jesus, as He was leading them to Gethsemane, was telling his disciples the following,

"I am the True Vine and my Father is the Gardener.
Every branch in Me that does not produce fruit He removes

AND He prunes every branch that produces fruit
So that it will produce more.

You are already clean because of the Word I have told you.
Remain in Me, and I in you.
Just as a branch is unable to produce fruit by itself unless it remains on the vine
Neither can you unless you remain in me.
I am the vine, you are the branches
The one who remains in Me and I in him produces much fruit
Because you can do nothing without Me.

Blessed be the living words of Christ Jesus.

Pruning. Right here in this scripture Jesus tells his followers, "I prune every branch that produces fruit … why? … so that it will produce more fruit."

What is pruning? Webster put it like this, "To cut off or cut back parts for better shape or more fruitful growth."

In other words, to bloom, you must first accept the prune.

My mama, Rose June White Ammons, surrendered to the prune. She allowed the prune. She accepted the prune.

I see her life separated into three volumes of time ... her childhood and young adult life in Marlow, Oklahoma. Her young married to family mama to senior divorced life in Mississippi, and the third volume - her six year nosedive into the disease of dementia.

The LORD used his pruning shears regularly and often severely in each season of her life.

Her childhood life growing up on the farm I believe is where she received her first pruning from the hand of God. She came from parents who had survived the depression and because of that, they were very unemotional people who were extremely hard workers. Life was about work to survive and that was their MO. This generation of people weren't ones to demonstratively show their love for others, so mama came away from her childhood with an empty love tank. With a feeling of being unloved because (and she confessed this to me many years later) that she never truly felt love from her own mama. Prune. Prune. Snip. Snip.

She married my father shortly after high school. She was working with my Aunt Joyce at the phone company; He was in the military at the time, worked in some oil fields, and ultimately surrendered to ministry. Four children came quickly and mama's life of hard living continued as the family of six scraped by on meager incomes in rural settings. She always worked to help pay the bills but every summer she'd quit her job to be home with us. Interesting note – she worked at Sperry Clocks on the assembly line. She was responsible for putting the hands on the face of the clock. If you are of the younger generation, just google the word "clock" for an explanation of that. ☺ But no matter her employer, every summer she would quit that job for us - Most likely to keep my three brothers from killing me but that's a whole other talk for another time. She never had much because she always made sure our needs were supplied. She told me about one time she wore a new pair of shoes to church and everyone commented on them ... because she'd been wearing the same shoes for so long it was so obvious that she had new ones ... this embarrassed her so ... she also told me that in that same church, when the tithe check she wrote bounced, one of the church deacons pinned it on the bulletin board, making her feel belittled and small. Not enough. Ashamed. Prune, prune, snip, snip.

In 1973 when Butch was killed in a car wreck at the age of 14, mama had to take years to forgive herself for that. She told me years later that she felt tremendous guilt over that because she almost told him to stay home that morning, she felt this urge to let him sit home with grandma … but she ignored that feeling and let him go … she understood later that was the Holy Spirit speaking to her … it took years for her to work through forgiving herself for that decision the morning of November 1, 1973. prune, prune, snip, snip

In 1980 my father made critical errors and the end result of those decisions blew our family apart. She and I moved to Jackson two weeks after my high school graduation; my brothers soon followed. We were in an apartment with folding chairs for furniture. She got a job with what was then Deposit Guaranty and a second job checking groceries at the Warehouse on I-55. And still the power was cut off a time or two because money was TIGHT. She felt overwhelmed, exhausted, scared, alone. Prune, prune, snip, snip.

She ended up remarrying dad, moved to Oklahoma where he was at the time, but quickly re-divorced him and moved back to home to MS. She kicked herself for that decision and felt stupid for having made that choice. Prune, prune, snip, snip.

There were many other snips that cut her back over her lifetime up to that point. These are just a few I remember at the time of this writing. What I'm here to proclaim to you today is that these were PRUNINGS. Instigated by the MASTER GARDENER. She had a choice with each cutting and each time she chose to ACCEPT THE PRUNING, SURRENDER TO THE PRUNING, from DAY 1. She never wallowed, she never raged, she never ignored, she never zoned out, she never froze, she never complained, she never ever gave in to self pity. She never cornered you and began some dissertation of disasters in her life. No. She didn't become bitter. She became BETTER Because SHE ALLOWED THE PRUNING.

And with every single cut, something unseen was happening way down deep in the dark. The Gardener was at work. And mama in her weakness was being made strong, through her dependence and faith in Christ Jesus.

What was the LORD doing? He was preparing her to bloom. Remember, in order to bloom, you first must be pruned.

So here she was, new start. Clean slate. She joined Broadmoor. (bloom) At the time it was on Northside Drive. She joined a Sunday school class. (bloom) She met a circle of devoted friends. (bloom) (some of that circle are here today) She got involved in various ministries. (bloom, bloom, bloom) She met a woman named Aileen, found out she was the leader of the prison ministry at the women's prison in Flowood. Mama became a co-leader in that ministry (bloom, bloom, bloom) and for many years mama loved on a myriad of women who were hurting and starting over … women who didn't feel loved … women who had been betrayed … women who felt ashamed … women who had to forgive themselves and couldn't see a way to go on … sound familiar? … Enter Junie Bug stage left. Mama knew all about that. (bloom, bloom, bloom)

She went on a number of mission trips – Washington, Montana, Canada, The MS coast during Katrina (bloom, bloom, bloom, bloom, bloom) She regularly took food to the UMMC waiting room with her Sunday School class. She witnessed to pretty much everyone she met. She was always reading, studying the Word. She loved me / dragged me / pulled me through some pretty horrific life prunes too. Randy has the same drag marks. IF Roger were here, he'd be shaking his head up and down because she drug him too.
Bloom, bloom, bloom, bloom.

With every PRUNE the LORD found her surrendered, found her faithful, found her joyful. Mama was not one to rant "Woe is me!" She was always one to say, "Faithful is He." She herself over many years of life was cut back time and time again … sometimes to a point of asking the question, "Is there anything left to cut?" "Can anything grow from this?" But the LORD in His Master Gardener wisdom at just the precise moment began to grow buds of beauty that popped into the most magnificent blooms all over our Mee Maw's life. And everyone around her breathed in the sweetest perfume.

Let's talk about this third volume of her life. The past six years have been the hardest most severe pruning to date. The disease of dementia ravaged her, inch by inch, day by day, skill by skill. This pruning was most severe. Our family and you, her friends, have prayed for her, cared for her, helped and supported in all ways possible … with the most demanding question on our tongues, "Why June!" Why!! "How could anything bud from this???"

 I know that mama surrendered to this pruning, but did we? Did I? Did you? Let me be so bold as to say that It's quite possible this wasn't just the Master Gardener pruning my mama in isolation …. John 15 calls us "branches." Could it be that The Master Gardener was shearing multiple branches … to produce multiplied beauty … through this one six-year severe cutting back of my mom? Let me ask you, have you been pruned thru this unwelcomed guest called Alzheimer's? I know I have, I know our family has. Now here is the million dollar question - Have we allowed it? Have we surrendered to it? Have we accepted it? If we have, then we in our cut back state, need to watch for the bud to appear. If we haven't, then we have some work to do in our quiet time, don't we? Because we don't want to squander a good pruning.

Perhaps, just perhaps, this latest pruning … this volume three pruning in Junie Bug's life … was not just on her and not just for her but … for us … perhaps this pruning done over the past six years will surprisingly create the largest crop of blossoms yet … blooms from me … blooms from you … and you … and you … and you … Perhaps the LORD in His Wisdom honored my mama with such a severe pruning … so there would be rampant multiplied glorious blooming … in me and in you and you and you … Can we accept that today? Can we allow the LORD to use this six-year pruning through His servant June in our lives so that we can now produce blooms? In memory of June? And have the most fragrant of perfumes fill the air for others to enjoy?

Mama had an exquisite yellow rose bush at the front door of her home at 311 Peach Orchard. Mama loved that rose bush and her favorite color was yellow. She took pristine care of it. Every day she was out there, pruning, plucking, cleaning, spraying, whittling, watering … whatever it needed, June was there. It got to the point where she would use it as a directional landmark on the street so people could find her home … "Just park in front of the yellow rose bush. You can't miss it" You couldn't miss it – it was neon yellow and always covered in blooms. Today when you think of mama, I want you to remember that June's Prunes led to June's Blooms. That yellow rose bush outside her front door? Turns out it was a spiritual picture of her.

When you leave the sanctuary today, you'll see a basket of yellow stemmed roses. These are for you. Please take one in memory of mama. And in the coming weeks, let this lesson in pruning lead to some blooming. It has to - John 15 guarantees it.

Please. I beg of you. Whatever you are facing, whatever your challenge –
Accept the Prune.
Then Bloom like June.

Falling For Steven

"Come on, Go with me, PLLLEEEEAAAAASSSSEEEEE!" my friend begged. She needed a buddy to walk with her nonchalantly by the door to the drafting department at just the right moment, hoping – praying – to run into the him who had his eye on her. And she had loved this particular him from afar so the feeling was mutual! It was so exciting! This covert mission! Her course was set and she needed her side-kick for she couldn't go it alone. Enter me, the bestie, the hall buddy. I was happy to help as I'm known to do so we wasted no time. We headed down the long stretch to the back hall where all the drafters lived. It was the Fall of 1981; we were in between typing and shorthand classes and had charted out this empty 15 minutes with purpose. Not one second to spare.

We made it to the doorway, took a deep breath, gathered our courage, eased inside, tried to appear cool. Immediately almost, she disappeared and I was on my awkward own. Wasn't expecting that. Abandoned by my partner. I felt embarrassed and tall; I tried to appear as though this brown headed secretarial science major belonged there in the world of engineering wannabees. At some point in that eternal split second, my mind raced with strategies to flee. "Retreat! Retreat!" I heard in my head. In my panic, I made eye contact with one red headed, red bearded man, seated comfortably at his drafting board. He seemed friendly enough; he had kind eyes that settled me. I ambled his way and found my voice.

He was seated at his drafting board with pen in hand, looking as though he could change the world with one simple stroke of ink. Little did I know he was about to change mine. He was wearing a starched, pink button-down cotton dress shirt with jeans and cowboy boots. I took notice. We talked – I have no idea what about. We laughed. At that point, my friend was on her own. I had found my own dream.

Let The Fall Begin.

This red-headed boy and I planned to meet accidentally on purpose from that day forward. We'd wave through a window. We'd smile across the hall. There were little notes stuck in lockers and Ziggy cards left on windshields. A bottle of Chloe perfume. A Ziggy paperweight. On most days, I'd be sitting in class, minding my own business, when suddenly, I would "hear" him looking at me. I'd glance up at the door and see him staring, waiting patiently for me to "hear" the sound of his stare. He'd grin that little grin and walk away. Mission Accomplished. Bullseye Hit. Heart to the mat ... *I Fell Hard.*

The last day before Christmas break he asked for my number. (the number to the phone in our apartment – there were no cell phones) He said his birthday was coming up and he needed a birthday date. I said yes. He picked me up in a little yellow maverick -- "Old Yeller" we so affectionately dubbed her. We ate a meal, saw a scary movie, went roller skating, had our first kiss. I felt the earth move as I felt the *Fall*.

Four months later, I got the flu -- and the ring. Another five months down the road, on the 4th day of September 1982, I got his last name. It was official. The end of our beginning.

At this point, I could tell you about the first apartment, the first house, the first cat. I could tell you about the late-night drives, holding hands in the dark, holding life by the horns, holding on through the hurts. I could try to explain our talks without words, our walks without reasons, our life with our love. I could try and take you back to the birth of our babies, the joys in the blessings coupled with the storms in their seasons. Try as I may, I would fail, for I don't know how to pen for you a look from across a crowded room. I can't express on paper laughing hysterically with my best friend. Words can't detail *home* or the physics of how when one is weak, the other is made impeccably strong. There's no way to explain this Covenant forged by God -- this unbreakable, indestructible, undeniable Covenant. All I can say is this: there's a very private place where true love lives. Unbeknownst to this crazy, chaotic, crowded planet earth, there is a secret, mysterious land of *ONE* where few people enter and dwell. It's a land where One and two become *SEWN WITH NO SEAM*. Where two splintered halves are molded by The One to make a whole from three. Thee, he, and me. Where couples walk in sync and talk through looks. It's where a brown headed secretarial science girl and a red headed drafting boy gladly moved in and made home.

Come to think of it, it all started with a walk down a hall, and ended with the Fall of my life.

For My Steven (2011)

We move in perfect rhythm
Like waves upon the shore
Like geese in silent motion
Like dance steps 'cross the floor

Like stars in straight alignment
Like raindrops falling down
Like flowers in a garden
Like wind that has no sound

Like bees in flight
Like colts that run
In night, a lighted torch
Like strings that play
Like swings that sway
Like rockers on a porch

We move in perfect rhythm
Like words in perfect rhyme
Like clouds upon the mountains
My Precious Valentine

I love you, Steven.

The Man Who Lives With Me

A stronger man
I've never known
Than the man who lives with me

Stronger than the
Chains of iron
That steady ships at sea

A Kinder man
There's never been
Than the man with whom I live

He's soft to speak
And swift to serve
And quickly does forgive

A Gentler man
There's never been
Nor ever will there be

None could match
The Tender Heart
Of him Who Lives With me

A wiser man?
There's never been
Before or since his birth!

His wisdom, deep
His knowledge, sound
The marrow of his mirth

I live my life
Each day his wife
So thankful for his place

Please rest assured
This little bird
Tastes daily of God's Grace

I've seen him fight
I've seen him fall
I've seen him rise again

But through it all
A mighty wall
This man above all men

Through strong and wise
Through gentle, kind
My warrior prince is he

I thank You, God,
Yet once again,
For the man who lives with me.

I Do

On a bright September morning
Back in 1982

A red-haired boy and brown eyed girl
feebly said, "I DO"

Little did they know back then
What those words truly meant
But now these two can tell you
That those words were heaven sent

Two syllables was all it took
To bind this marriage chord
Two words the three of us would vow
(That's him, me, and THE LORD)

Standing at the altar
Holding hands and eye to eye
Repeating from the pastor
These words we're living by

I DO to hard
I DO to pain
I DO to laughs galore
I DO to joy
I DO to strain
I DO to stressful chore
I DO to grief
I DO to hugs
I DO to choices made
I DO to bills
I DO to babes
I DO to nights afraid

I DO to better
I DO to worse
I DO to build
I DO to nurse

I DO to have
I DO to hold
From that day until now

I DO to love
My red haired boy
This is my solemn vow

37 years ... and just getting started ... Love, robin

Forty (2022)

The days of the flood, of fasting, of Moses on the mountain top. The years of the wandering. The years of the waiting. Biblical connections of numbers. Quite fascinating really.

FORTY. Yeah, that's about right.

Today Steven and I have been married forty years. A blink ago we both wore white, oblivious to the path we were pledging to plod. Choosing each other from that day forward, through all that our feeble minds could fathom would come. So smitten in love with each other that we naively believed that all other things were already somehow magically conquered. In our youth we believed this lovely wedding door we were walking through would lead us to a marriage of all things good, all things perfect, all things ease. Every click of the camera on that Saturday afternoon, over punch and mints, memorized the mushy mushroom cloud of what our life would surely contain. Smile after smile after smile.

Completely committed. Completely clueless.

The world has walked through

Reagan, Bush, Clinton, Bush, Obama, Trump, Biden.

We saw the Wall fall. We saw the Towers fall. We saw the blasts of Oklahoma City, Sandy Hook, Pearl High School, The Pentagon, Columbine, Las Vegas, Boston, Florida. Just to name a few. We journeyed alongside Desert Storm, The war in Iraq, the war in our streets. The trials. The riots. The raids. The blackouts. The knockouts.

And we have walked
Through cancer. Chaos.
Through beacons. Betrayals.
Through promotions and promises.
Through lay-offs and lies.
Through lessons. Through loss.
So. many. losses.

And over it all, the LORD was working.

Dementia and demons.
Deceit and delay.
Doctors.
Death.
Failures.
Finishes.
Feuds.
Miscarriage.
Mistakes.
Misunderstandings.
Misgivings.
So. Many. Misses.

And over it all, the LORD was working.

Judgments.
Jealousies.
Pains.
Pennies.
Pressures.
Pranks.
Secrets.
Self serving.
Sacrifice.
Sickness.
Sin.
Trials.
Tricks.
Troubles.
Trauma.

FORTY. Yeah, that's about right.

Ah, but so is this.

Laughter.
Love.
Late night talks.
Living in rhythm.
Knowing his thoughts.
Catching his eye.
Watching him smile.
Hearing him laugh.
Holding hands while we sleep,
Holding newborns in the night,
Holding hope in the dark.
Our bodies aging
Our features changing
But yet I see you, and you see me
Supporting.
Suppressing.
Supplying.
Surrender.
Praying.
Pleasing.
Pruning.
Prying.
Peace.
Protector.
Refusing to let go.
Refusing to go back.
Acceptance.
Accessible.
Attentive.
Assured.
Never quitting.
Never sitting.
Pressing onward.
Step by step.
Forbearing.
Forgiving.
Forgetting.
Remembering.
Forever.
We do.

Forty years ago our future seemed so fairy tale. And there have been short chapters of those, for sure. But for the most part, nope. Girl, it's been hard.

But it was also perfectly written in advance by an Author Who loved us so much that He allowed us to learn through things that tried to kill us. He allowed us to surrender through things that tried to suffocate us. And He allowed us to grip Him so tight so that we could hold onto each other all the tighter. We got a lot of things wrong but Praise GOD we got that right.

A wedding is one thing. A marriage – quite another.
And it took FORTY years.
Yeah, that's about right.
I love you, Terry Steven.

Home

I watch my children from the window. They don't see me but I watch their every move. It's a warm day; they run from one corner of their world – our humble yard – to the other, laughing hysterically, excited about life and focusing on fun. They have no fears, no inhibitions, no cares. Not today. Today is filled with swings and sand and friends.

I sip my coffee and think. To be honest, sometimes I think too much. It's almost overwhelming to me that my mind doesn't know when to stop. I think of how things were, I think of how things are, and I think of how I want things to be. And my children tie each thought together. Because that's what my life is – the lives of my children.

Before these two were born, I was very much like they are today. No fears, no inhibitions, well, maybe a few cares. But on a different level. I worried about the clothes I wore, the car I drove, the money I made. Those things have lost their luster. I don't think about those things anymore.

And now I watch my kids. Two glorious miracles from heaven, rented to me for such a short while. I now think about their lives, their safety, their minds, their souls. How much can I control? How do my actions affect their memories?

It's funny how much a house can be part of those answers. I guess what we have to understand is that the house is a member of the family too. It has its own personality, and it helps make the memories.

I remember my grandparents' home. I never thought of it as my mama's home, I thought of it as my grandparents' haven. It's hard to believe now that people actually lived that way. Houses were miles apart, separated only by landscapes. No stop lights, no Exxon station on the corner. No Dollar General anywhere. We knew we were there when we saw the white fence row. We would turn up the long-fenced drive and listen to the gravel being crunched beneath the wheels. By the time the car came to a stop, grandma and grandpa were outside waiting to be hugged. They'd been watching for us and now we were here. They were going to get hugged, if they wanted to be or not.

The house, in my mind, was huge and white, a perfect Norman Rockwell painting. There were cows in the front, stickers in the back, barns and tractors and mounds of hay. There was a garden with long rows. And a strong dirt smell. There was a windmill, a smoke house, and a huge black cast-iron pot. There were a trillion places to hide, giant fields to roam, and a train track across the road. I can still hear that distant whistle blow, then running down the long gravel driveway to the mailbox to watch the train pass by. There was always a game of Chinese checkers right before bed and there was always pie in the ice box. I remember the smell. That sweet, moth ball smell.

There were cousins.

There was a basement. A basement full of old trunks and jellies. A closet full of bonnets and aprons, jars of buttons and pins, and one cowboy hat.

I pour more coffee and butter a piece of toast. My girls are gathering the sweet onion weeds in the yard. I'm sure a bouquet will be presented soon.

My home as a child changed every four or five years. My father was a country Baptist preacher, so we didn't stay in one spot too long. Just long enough to make it feel like home; then we were whisked away to a new adventure. Our home was always small and generic, very pastoral, the house itself owned by the church. Many had lived there before. However, when we did, it was always full of friends and noise. My mother loved the country gospel quartets, so we would have to endure her music most days. Funny thing is, now that I'm a mama, I'm kinda' partial to those quartets. And my kids think I'm strange.

On the outside, it always appeared as though my father, the revered pastor and blessed leader of the country community, was the head of our household. He never was. It was my mama that kept our home together. I think we all knew it but we hated to hurt daddy's feelings. Mama knew what her family needed – a warm, loving home where each felt at home and where anyone could talk to anyone else about anything. She knew how to be right where her children needed her at the time they needed her the most. And she taught us to laugh. To laugh hard.

I remember her flowers. Marigolds and elephant ears planted in bunches along the front porch. That was her signature statement to each home where this gypsy family lodged.

And now, I'm making a home for my children. What will they remember? Will their most prominent memories be of daycares? Microwaves? Malls? Will they remember with love these modest four walls with a roof? Will days like today be forever locked in their heart and will they try to recreate this moment, this here and now, for their families down the road?

I want their memories to be of days like today. Sunshine, tire swings, sweet onion bouquets. I want our home to be a warmth in their heart that they can retreat to when the outside world casts them out. I wouldn't mind a few stickers in the yard, a few jars of buttons in the closet or a pie in the ice box. I wouldn't mind a stereo blaring a southern gospel quartet. Vestel is always welcome under my roof. I want a home filled with the noise of laughter. And of course, there will always be marigolds and elephant ears blooming at our front door.

Heaven's Garden (1993)

I found them in her lunchbox
Frail fronds of fragile flowers
The colors quickly fading
Limp from darkened hours

I suppose she saw them anxiously
And gathered them in a bunch
Held them tightly and inspected them
Then placed them with her lunch

Intending to give her treasure
To someone that she loved
Each fragrance, stem, and petal
A creation from above

She felt anticipation
As she thought about her gift
She knew she'd make one happy
Someone's spirits these would lift

269

But as time passed by
And she went about her day
She forgot about her secret
In her lunchbox tucked away

And now it lays before me
This token of her love
And I realize the precious gift
God sent me from above

For He went to heaven's garden
On a clear September day
And picked a beaming daisy
Perfect in every way

He sent that daisy downward
Into this mother's arms
She grew into a loving child
Sweet, freckled, girlish charm

So when I find dried flowers
Tucked away in some strange place
I'm reminded of the love so pure
That lives in my child's face.

Aisles (2005)

She'll walk the aisle on Monday. I'll be seated next to my husband in the audience, nervously, anxiously, emotionally awaiting her entrance. She'll be dressed in blue cap and gown, with tassle hanging down. I can see her in my mind's eye even now, searching for and finding me in the crowd, making eye contact, and we both grin. Through our eyes we will talk and say things no one else can hear. "This is it … keep going … I'm so proud of you … you look beautiful … don't fall!" I know the ceremony will go off without a hitch and be a blur as I watch her walk across the stage and be handed a diploma. In a twinkling moment of time, one life will end and another will begin.

This isn't the first aisle she's walked. I distinctly remember a Sunday morning in January sitting on the second pew, listening to a sermon from the book of Mark. The bible story was of the little 12 year old girl who had died. Jesus came into the house, took her by the hand, and told her to, "Get up." And she did.

At the end of the service, my 12 year old girl tugged on my arm and told me she wanted to "Get up" and make her decision for Christ. I was taken aback but thoroughly pleased as I watched my firstborn sheepishly walk the aisle and gain life. Abundant life. In a twinkling moment of time, one life ended and another began.

And I know it won't be the last. I know that one day I'll be seated in an audience, nervously, anxiously, emotionally awaiting her entrance. Then the guitarist will start, the doors will swing open, and there she will stand, all dressed in white, holding onto her daddy. Leaning into him for courage. And he gladly gives it. I know we'll find each other in the crowd, make eye contact, and both of us will grin. Through our eyes we will talk and say things no one else can hear. "This is it ... keep going ... I'm so proud of you ... you look beautiful ... don't fall!" I know the ceremony will go off without a hitch and be a blur as I watch her walk to the front and covenant to the man of her dreams. In a twinkling moment of time, one life will end and another will begin.

She'll walk the aisle on Monday. Life is full of them isn't it? Aisles, passageways, corridors, tunnels ... something that connects two places ... some more important than others, but aisles just the same. Sometimes an audience will watch you walk it; sometimes you do it alone with only the Lord as your partner, with you leaning into Him for courage. Some aisles are places of horror, some unfortunately are places of shame. The life we live determines our steps as we walk. Some are easy and priceless; some are tough and painful. Sometimes it takes all of the strength we can muster to complete the walk, only to find out that the whole purpose was to strengthen our walk.

She'll walk the aisle on Monday. As she moves the tassel from one side to the other, I will know that the baby girl with the goofy grin who I taught how to walk is now preparing to walk away. I will know that her life, in a twinkling of a moment in time, will begin anew. And I'll be in the audience, trying to figure out how I will muster the courage to let her.

My Memories of You

(December 2015 – for Jess)

I walked into our attic
Stepping sure so not to fall
My eyes drank in the boxes
Dusting neatly on the wall

Each box stuffed with our slice of life
Sweet Memories, now contained
Stored neatly in the attic
And with marker, each is named

In quiet peace I reached for each --
"Wasn't that just yesterday?"
My heart surveyed the life we lived
Then I wiped a tear away

And suddenly a musty screen
Slowly began to fall
And just as slow our movie there
Projected on the wall

It was hard to see the image
So I leaned for closer view
The title crackled on the screen
"My Memories of You."

I felt the night God sent you here -
A sterile room of white
Smart nurses working fast to bring
My baby to the light

When doctor said, "Hey, It's a GIRL!"
I sang out **"PRAISE THE LORD!"**
Then every nurse (as if rehearsed!)
Joined in to praise HIM more

I saw the epic tears of joy
That streamed your daddy's face
I saw the dress you slept within -
A Feltman's cotton lace

I felt the pain we didn't want
When colic came to dwell
The no-sleep-pacing-back-and-forth
(It was a living hell)

I stroked the flannelled footies
That my baby toddled in
I smelled the squash and green beans
That smeared across your chin

I heard you squeal at Paw Paw
Climbing up and down his back
I saw him push you scary-high
On a swing made from a sack

I saw you through the daycare's glass
Up on an elephant slide
So you could watch me as I left
(I drove away and cried)

I saw your daddy hug you close
And nuzzle *"I love you"*
You'd place your hands upon his cheeks
And with love say ***"me too"***

I saw you market lemonade
On the edge of our small grass
Poor neighbors never stood a chance
You made them buy a glass

I saw you as a girl scout
Selling cookies door to door
And I'd say, *"Ok, that's enough"*
And you'd say, *"One house more!"*

The day you picked out Buddy cat
Was now displayed to see
Telling him in his lonely cage
"You now belong to me."

And belong he did. *(He loved you so.)*
He'd wait each night in bed
For you to lay and suck your thumb
Then he'd circle near your head

He would purr, you would drift
And I would stand and sing
A song still true- *"HE Never Sleeps"*
Ever watching as you dreamed

I saw the crowded room again
The crown upon your brow
The sash they placed upon your waist
MOST BEAUTIFUL
Then and now

The movie jolted forward
To the year we now are in
I see your finger glistening
With a diamond from your Ben

I see the epic tears of joy
That stream your daddy's face
I see you dressed in snowy white
Your jeweled veil of grace

I hear the chords a guitar plays
I turn from front-seat view
I see your dad in checkered shirt
In awe, he stares at you

But who could help
But stare at you
This vision that you are?
Then daddy takes your hand on cue
The almost Mrs. Carr

The groom, he waits with smile on face
Plum dashing in his gray
You slowly walk the aisle to him
Look in his eyes and say,

"I've waited all my life for you.
For this. For us. For now.
I'll love you 'till the end of time.
This is my solemn vow."

He says the same, kisses you long
The pastor then adjourns
Then cake and fruit and laughter
Then I slow-motion turn

I search to find my own true love
Amidst this crowded room
I slide my hand into his grasp
My own plum-dashing groom

"It's over now, our story ends,
These two are finally one"
He grins that grin that makes me safe
"Oh hon', it's just begun."

"This is the hour we've prayed for her
Our prayers have come to pass
This vision, tho' it tarried,
*Has come for her, at last."**

We hold hands as they make their way
Midst pompoms in the air

We pray their attic full one day,
Stuffed boxes lined with care

With that the movie
Fades to black
It's quiet as before
I touch the boxes one last time
Then inch back toward the door

Before I leave I turn again
To see them, just once more
And as I step into the light
I sing out, **"PRAISE THE LORD."**

> *... Our daughters, like corner pillars, that are carved in the palace style.*
> *Psalm 144:17*

275

A Week From Today

(July 2015 – for Mantha Rose)

A week from today
we'll give her away
to the man of her dreams
with ivory and creams
midst candlelight gleam

and I'll watch from my chair
with spray in my hair
and hold back the tears
while all of the years
implode in my heart
then quickly appear

I'll watch as her dad
escorts her in lace
but I'll see her pig tails
with freckledy face
holding the tire swing rope
in her hands
as I push her higher midst her demands
"The higher the better"
she'd say with a grin and I'd whisper a
prayer and end with Amen

I'll watch as she smiles
at her prince in gray hues
but I'll see her toddling
in baby bop shoes
holding a ball with her fat little fist
"A pwize for you, daddy" and give him a kiss

I'll hear as she vows
to love him through all
but the echo of show tunes
being sung down the hall
will ring in my ears as she tells
him through tears that her love will
grow stronger
year after year

I'll try to focus and stay in the now
as he takes her hand and solemnly vows
to love her forever and provide for her needs
While I see a little girl scampering up trees
with old cowgirl boots that she wore every day
and I'd have to go to the backdoor and say
"Be careful up there and don't go too high!"
and she'd laugh and go higher while helplessly I
would watch from the doorway and whisper a prayer
that the LORD would anchor her even up there

and I'll snap to attention
to the exchange of rings
the circles of gold
that covenant means
"I am yours;
you are mine"
but somewhere between
I'll see a baby, drifting to dream
with paci and duck, a lamp's dim sheen
a rocking recliner
while I'd softly sing
and hold her tightly,
caressing her head
then tiptoe silent
and lay her in bed

But now in a blink I wake to the sound
of a prayer then a kiss then applause all around

and I'll watch from a distance
as the dances take place
I'll watch Mrs. Klein
look up into his face
and gleam with such joy
that she brightens the place

and I'll whisper a prayer
thanking GOD for that gleam
and for every memory
I've stuck in between
the years of her life
so beautifully seamed
in my heart

like a quilt
folded and clean

Then all too soon
their life will begin
with rose petals thrown
in the air by their friends

A limousine driver
will speed them away
midst ivories and creams
and colors of gray

Then quiet
I know it
deep quiet
will fall

and swallow me whole

then I'll hear Steven call

I'll turn and head home
and whisper a prayer
midst ivories and creams
and spray in my hair

… Our daughters, like corner pillars, that are carved in the palace style.
Psalm 144:17

To Jessica Renee and Samantha Rose,

I was the dirt
you are the bloom
I was the clatter
you are the tune
I was the messy
you are the clean
you are the kindness
I was the mean
I was the tacky
you are great style
I was the inch
you are the mile
I was the cornbread
you are the roll
you are the diamonds
I was the coal

The LORD is great
And is highly praised;
HIS greatness is unsearchable.
One generation will declare YOUR works to the next
And will proclaim YOUR mighty acts.
Psalm 145:3-4

To My Beauties

Good morning, my lovely daughters ... I feel the need to tell you how proud I am of you ... that I am so blessed by the young women each of you are each becoming; you are exceptional strength ... yet feminine and grace ... mature and confident ... and funny! Thank GOD for your humor!! I'm so thankful to be your mom ... yes, we laugh and cut-up and yes we fight and disagree ... but at the end of the day, I go to bed and THANK GOD ALMIGHTY for the two treasures HE's entrusted to me, for just a little while ... it's hard for me to understand how fast time has skipped by ... it's hard for me to release and let go ... but I know GOD is going to protect you, guide you, help you, aid you, use you ... and I must let HIM.

How can HE take the wheel if my fingers are pried around it? Believe me, I'm trying, I'm unprying ... but just know, as you move forward into the life HE has designed for you, that I'm always here, always able, always willing ... I'm your biggest fan and loudest cheerleader ... I have many weaknesses and faults and way too few strengths, but always remember -- somebody messes with my youngins, they'll have to answer to me. I'll conquer hell and high water to clear a pathway for you ... you can bank on that.

Give GOD priority today.

I love you. Mama

In EVERYTHING, give THANKS ... 1 Thess. 5:18

Wings (2012)

My singer's back in Starkville
My firstborn's on her own
I'm wondering 'round this empty house
All too soon they're grown

I sit here in the quiet
With the dogs beneath my feet
I thank GOD for the memories
But today they're bittersweet

My assignment was to rear them
And let them stretch their wings
Problem is that no one told me
Of the pain that wings can bring

Again I say, "In EVERYTHING, give THANKS ... 1 Thess. 5:18"

Mav and Me

My grandjoy. This poem was written during his knitting in the womb, while I paced back and forth on earth, awaiting his arrival. In July of 2019, a tightly bound bundle in a blanket was gently handed to me, a little soft as dew face waking up to the world, trying to focus, searching for a face. Paw Paw and Grammie began a new adventure with this tightly bound bundle of energy, silliness, adventurous, curious, studious, inquisitive, cautious little joy. He came into the world 3 weeks after my brother left it. The Lord turned my sorrow into dancing … slowly ever so slowly, I inched out of the mire and learned to dance.

We'll play in the dirt
Catch bugs with bare hands
We'll pick all the flowers
We'll dig in the sand

We'll stomp in deep puddles
We'll climb up tall trees
We'll crawl through the ditches
Getting mud on our knees

We'll holler for echoes
We'll snuggle for naps
We'll swing till we're dizzy
We'll set big bear traps

We'll jump like a kanga
We'll fish with a pole
We'll make lots of diamonds
With old lumps of coal

We'll 'tend that we're cowboys
And romp on a horse
We'll search pirate's treasure
Then take it by force

We'll sing like an Indian
We'll make a teepee
We'll spy on his Paw Paw
Sly Maverick and me

We'll dance to the oldies
We'll build us a fort
We'll pretend we're invisible
I'll teach him to snort

We'll read by the lamplight
We'll gaze at the stars
We'll watch clouds from blankets
We'll rocket to Mars

We'll lasso a dinosaur
We'll trap us a bear
We'll sweat till we're stinky
We'll breathe the night air

We'll catch us some fireflies
In awe watch them glow
I'll clap as he puts on
His great magic show

We'll share all our cookies
We'll scream in the dark
We'll practice our pop flies
We'll play at the park

We'll run like a cheetah
From mud we'll make pie
Adventure's awaiting
Please hurry, July.

Love, Grammie

I lift my eyes toward the mountains. Where will my help come from?
My help comes from the LORD, The Maker of heaven and earth.

He will not allow your foot to slip; Your Protector will not slumber,
The Protector of Israel does not slumber or sleep

The LORD protects you,
The LORD is a shelter right by your side
The sun will not strike you by day Or the moon by night

The LORD will protect you from all harm
He will protect your life
The LORD will protect your coming and going
Both now and forevermore.
Psalm 121

The remainder of this section is reserved for any future grandchildren that may come our way. And there's plenty of room, so ….

Peak

The End of the Beginning

Well, this is it. The last entry. In the beginning of this venture on page one, my internal question was "How does one start?" I will end this collection with its bookend question, "How does one stop?" By stopping, I guess. It's been a journey back through my journaled time, and I appreciate you riding shotgun, mile after bumpy mile.

Oh, and by the way, the scribble art I've included is from my journal as well. There was a time in my past when I felt impressed to draw my journal entries, so I bought the book and the crayons and gave it my best shot. I allowed myself to not be good at it. Over time, I moved to colored pencils, then pens, then watercolors. I pray they've encouraged you … and I encourage you to buy the book and crayons.

Ultimately, you should know that each year I choose a word that I contemplate for 12 months. My 2023 word is "talents." Not as in "I have more than one" but as in the parable of the talents taught in Matthew 25. I chose talents as my word after I was convicted that perhaps these written words had been buried in me – by me – and it was the year for me to courageously dig them up. To humbly harvest them into a basket then meekly offer them, first Up, then out. Will it be multiplied? That's up to the Master. That's in His hands. All I know is that I've dug. Then I piled. Then I tipped the basket over and given out all I had except this one last thing … a prayer for you and me.

My prayer is that the Lord Himself has been revealed to you somehow, someway, through this meager attempt to bring Him Glory. I pray that mixed into the mumbles I've made, the Spirit has spoken articulately into your very heart, into your spirit, and that you have heard The Christ through these ramblings of a robin. I leave you with a prayer from my 2009 journal. A prayer from my heart. May it be our prayer. May the LORD answer His daughters.

Teach me Your Word, Lord
Show me Your Way
Counsel with Wisdom
Teach me to pray

Guide me in Truth, Lord
Reprove me in Love
Protect me with Armor
Send Strength from Above

Mold me like clay, Lord
Remake every part
Refresh my spirit
Create my new heart

Pour out Your Anointing
Lord, Release it on me
Send Power and Boldness
In Humility

Teach me Your Word, Lord
Show me Your Way
Make me like Jesus
Day after Day

Amen

www.ingramcontent.com/pod-product-compliance
Lightning Source LLC
Chambersburg PA
CBHW070912120626
46546CB00001B/226